Geopolitics of the Pakistan–Afghanistan Borderland

To understand the historical complexity of the Pakistan–Afghanistan borderland, this book brings together some of the foremost thinkers of this borderland and seeks to approach its various problematic dimensions.

This book presents an overview of the geopolitics of the Pakistan–Afghanistan borderland and approaches the topic from different methods and perspectives. It focuses on some of the least debated dimensions of this borderland, for instance, the status of women in the tribal-border culture, the legal status of aliens in the making of the border, material and immaterial manifestations of the border, political aesthetics of the border, and the identity crisis on the border. Given the fact that its authors come from diverse backgrounds, academic and geographic, they make an enriching contribution. Employing their expertise in different theories and methods, they focus on local memories, literature, and wisdom to understand the border. This book seeks to give voice to the plight of local tribal people, their culture, and land on an advanced academic level and makes it legible for the international audience.

The chapters in this book were originally published as a special issue of the journal *Geopolitics.*

Syed Sami Raza is Assistant Professor of Political Science at the University of Peshawar, Pakistan. His research focuses on topics of geopolitics, critical IR, and critical legal theory. He is the author of *The Security State in Pakistan: Legal Foundations* (Routledge 2018).

Michael J. Shapiro is Professor of Political Science at the University of Hawai'I at Manoa, Honolulu, USA. Among his recent publications are *Punctuations: How the Arts Think the Political* (Duke UP, 2019) and *The Cinematic Political: Film Composition as Political Theory* (Routledge, 2020).

Geopolitics of the Pakistan–Afghanistan Borderland

Edited by
Syed Sami Raza and Michael J. Shapiro

Routledge
Taylor & Francis Group
LONDON AND NEW YORK

First published 2021
by Routledge
2 Park Square, Milton Park, Abingdon, Oxon, OX14 4RN

and by Routledge
52 Vanderbilt Avenue, New York, NY 10017

Routledge is an imprint of the Taylor & Francis Group, an informa business

British Library Cataloguing-in-Publication Data
A catalogue record for this book is available from the British Library

ISBN13: 978-0-367-64769-8

Typeset in Minion Pro
by codeMantra

Publisher's Note
The publisher accepts responsibility for any inconsistencies that may have arisen during the conversion of this book from journal articles to book chapters, namely the inclusion of journal terminology.

FSC www.fsc.org MIX Paper from responsible sources FSC™ C013985

Printed in the United Kingdom
by Henry Ling Limited

Contents

Citation Information

The following chapters were originally published in the *Geopolitics*, volume 24, issue 2 (April 2019). When citing this material, please use the original page numbering for each article, as follows:

Chapter 1
Geopolitics on the Pakistan–Afghanistan Borderland: An Overview of Different Historical Phases
Rasul Bakhsh Rais
Geopolitics, volume 24, issue 2 (April 2019) pp. 284–307

Chapter 2
Of Pious Missions and Challenging the Elders: A Genealogy of Radical Egalitarianism in the Pashtun Borderscape
Jan-Peter Hartung
Geopolitics, volume 24, issue 2 (April 2019) pp. 308–343

Chapter 3
Legal Sovereignty on the Border: Aliens, Identity and Violence on the Northwestern Frontier of Pakistan
Syed Sami Raza
Geopolitics, volume 24, issue 2 (April 2019) pp. 344–365

Chapter 4
Security is a 'Mental Game': The Psychology of Bordering Checkposts in Pakistan
Maximilian Lohnert
Geopolitics, volume 24, issue 2 (April 2019) pp. 366–390

Chapter 5
Performing the Afghanistan–Pakistan Border Through Refugee ID Cards
Sanaa Alimia
Geopolitics, volume 24, issue 2 (April 2019) pp. 391–425

Chapter 6
Tribal Women, Property and Border: An Auto-Ethnographic Critique of the Riwaj *(Tradition) on the Pakistan–Afghanistan Borderland*
Noreen Naseer
Geopolitics, volume 24, issue 2 (April 2019) pp. 426–443

Chapter 7

Pashto Border Literature as Geopolitical Knowledge
James Caron
Geopolitics, volume 24, issue 2 (April 2019) pp. 444–461

Chapter 8

Writing Stars in the Sky or Decentring the Glocal Discourse of the 'War(S) on Terror' through Narratives of Those Displaced
Andrea Fleschenberg and Tariq Saeed Yousufzai
Geopolitics, volume 24, issue 2 (April 2019) pp. 462–486

Chapter 9

The Moving Border of the China-Pakistan Economic Corridor
Alvin Cheng-Hin Lim
Geopolitics, volume 24, issue 2 (April 2019) pp. 487–502

Contributors

Sanaa Alimia Leibniz-Zentrum Moderner Orient, Berlin, Germany.

James Caron South Asian Languages and Cultures, SOAS University of London, UK.

Andrea Fleschenberg Humboldt-Universität zu Berlin, Institute of Asian and African Studies, Germany.

Jan-Peter Hartung Institute of Social and Cultural Anthropology, University of Göettingen, Germany.

Alvin Cheng-Hin Lim Research Department, International Public Policy Pte. Ltd., Singapore.

Maximilian Lohnert School of Health in Social Science, University of Edinburgh, Scotland.

Noreen Naseer Department of Political Science, University of Peshawar, Pakistan.

Rasul Bakhsh Rais Department of Humanities and Social Sciences, Lahore University of Management Sciences, Pakistan.

Syed Sami Raza Department of Political Science, University of Peshawar, Pakistan.

Michael J. Shapiro Political Science, University of Hawai'i at Manoa, Honolulu, USA.

Tariq Saeed Yousufzai MPhil Scholar, Quaid-i-Azam University, Islamabad, Pakistan.

Introduction: Politics on Border—Critical Reflections on the Pakistan–Afghanistan Borderland

Syed Sami Raza and Michael J. Shapiro

The set of articles in this collection return in different ways to the common theme of "politics on border," which distils several ways that the Pakistan–Afghanistan border achieves legibility. The diverse interdisciplinary forays in the collection address a host of political concepts and predicates—tribe and the state, security and ontology, identity and human rights, subjectivity and discourse, and religiosity and egalitarianism. As they engage those concepts and predicates, the various chapters comprise a wide variety of methods, drawn from a broad range of disciplinary fields. What they all share is critical rather than merely descriptive (or representational) approaches. They all seek to unsettle traditional understandings of border politics in the region.

With the phrase "politics on border" we refer to two different dimensions of the politics of the Pakistan–Afghanistan borderland—geopolitical and critical. With the former we seek to highlight the global ramifications of the local politics and vice versa. With the latter we seek to engage critical IR theory and focus on the state of exception in the border politics. For instance, if we put the history of this borderland in the long view then we see its culture and politics growing under the dark shadow of wars. Throughout history we notice different regional powers indulging in an opportunistic geopolitics of difference, conflict, and war. It is this opportunistic indulgence that explains the phrase politics on border. In other words, it is a (border) politics in the sense that it takes place on the border of war. As Etienne Balibar puts it, the border is "no longer the shores of politics" but is instead "the space of the political itself" (1998, 220). Hence, literally and/or conceptually, the politics of Pakistan–Afghanistan borderland *is* a politics on border.

Our analyses are aimed at negotiating the complexity of relationship between border and territory. While this complexity is generally noticeable in other border venues as well, the case of the Pakistan–Afghanistan border is distinct because of its peculiar topology, the mountainous terrain. Although much of our focus is on this distinct border-territory relationship, we also wish to go beyond the peculiar territorial aspect of this border in order to avoid the pitfall of, what Yosef Lapid calls, the "territorial epistemology" (2001). We therefore strive to think of a broader framing within which we think of border as not only a periphery but also as a way of life, i.e., an ontology of embodied (body-border) experience. More specifically, we want to ask how border conditions the tribal ways of being in the face of state practices/authority and how this border culture—or rather a culture on border—comes to build and un-build its political relationship with the state. We raise these questions in order to transcend the way this borderland has been treated as a mere periphery even as it has been the center of various international and regional wars and geopolitical strategies.

Borders and other geo-territorial modes of separation (e.g., frontiers) have been the aftereffects of changing national sovereignty structures. For example, the border issues that roiled local relationships in the former Yugoslavia displaced what were once complicated culturally shared versions of life with narrowed versions, generated by a "reductive vocabulary" that allocated differential value to the bodies that lived across borders and frontiers (Alcalay 1998, xv). Frontier and border control apparatuses are one part of an ever-expanding, life-narrowing security *dispositif*. As the War on Terror, which embodies such a narrow security mentality, continues we argue that it is time to revisit the Pakistan–Afghanistan borderland to reflect on the changing geostrategic realities, state discourses, and border-making practices. We need to reflect on the ethical and normative aspects of the border control regimes and in that reflection to focus on the practices of commuting, crossing, and transgressing the physical, cultural, and normative border. In addition, we need to heed the subjects involved in border conflicts by focusing on the phenomenology of the border encounters through which the border is made and/or unmade.

Here are brief synopses of the papers included in this edited volume:

Rasul Baksh Rais presents a panoramic overview of the state's geostrategic intervention in the tribal borderland for over two centuries. Specifically, he explains how the states of British India and Pakistan intervened in the tribal borderland for promoting their geostrategic interests, and thereby adversely affecting the long-standing political autonomy of the mountainous borderland and its egalitarian tribal culture. He touches upon three major wars—the Great Game, the Afghan War, and the War on Terror—to argue that the state employed the policy of isolation and separation of the tribal borderland, rather than politically integrating it. This policy, Rais further argues, was the result of the geo-strategist approach adopted toward the borderland, which alienated the tribal people as well as resulted in the creation of several religio-political movements and organizations.

Jan-Peter Hartung writes that in order to make sense of the Taliban movement one needs to understand the deeper layers of radical egalitarianism on the Pakistan–Afghanistan border. Taking a genealogical course Hartung digs up the deepest layer that he thinks is the Rawshaniyyah movement of the sixteenth century, which was a subaltern voice, a regional expression of egalitarianism, and based on self-defined moral superiority. This movement struggled against the Mughal empire, which it thought to had deviated from the true religious path. Apart from this religious movement against the Mughals, Hartung underscores an ethnic movement led by Khushal Khan Khattak against them that was instrumental in making of a self-conscious ethnic identity of Pashtun. Hartung then points to a third layer of the Deoband religious movement of 19th century, which spread on the frontier and impacted the well-established local socio-political and economic authorities. However, these religious movements did not adopt a violent course of action like the one adopted by the Taliban. But it is also worth noticing that the Taliban sprang from the Deobandi movement. Hartung points out that the Taliban were the movement of young men who rode on "a wave of accelerated discourse over 'egalitarianism'" and challenged almost all contemporary cultural and religious institutions.

Syed Sami Raza takes up two incidents of coldblooded violence at the hands of security agencies in Pakistan—one against a group of aliens near the Pakistan–Afghanistan border and the other against a Pakistani citizen in Karachi. He juxtaposes these two incidents to highlight the tendency of discrimination against the aliens in the criminal justice system of Pakistan, which he argues rests on the political condition of personal identity rather than on the ethical and empathic conditions of human rights law. He further argues that the striking neglect on the part of superior courts to address such cases has resulted in the creation of structural violence in the criminal justice system.

Maximillian Lohnert studies check-posts in urban areas of Pakistan as extension and manifestation of the border in the wake of the War on Terror. He focuses on security check-posts in the cities of Peshawar, Islamabad, and Lahore, and interviews a host of local people to find out their ontological experience of (in-)security with check-posts. He concludes that while these check-posts might have been created for the purpose of beefing up security they in fact cause feeling of further insecurity among the local people. He emphasizes that everyday the people feel further alienated, their loyalty challenged, and insecure for their lives while crossing check-posts.

Like Lohnert, **Sana Alimia** also studies the extension of the border in the mainland Pakistan. She projects that "[t]he border is not simply located at the territorial frontier but is in process and comes into being through documents, the control over the mobility of citizen and non-citizen populations, and by enacting everyday forms of social exclusion." She focuses on how the Pakistani state's security policy sees Afghan refugees to embody the border and therefore creates structures of exclusion for them. Employing an ethnographic method, she studies the peculiar Identity Cards (ID) issued to Afghan refugees in Pakistan and argues that the refugee ID cards are specially designed to enhance the control of surveillance system on them and to restrict their mobility, rather than to include and/or facilitate them into the civil and political life of the society.

Noreen Naseer employs autho-ethnographic method to tell the stories of Pakhtun women from their own experiences. She focuses on six tribal customs that in one way or another discriminate against women. Her main emphasis in reading these customs is to demonstrate how women are treated as property of their male kin. Moreover, she debates how her very ontological existence is connected to family's honor, which she has to protect at the cost of her life. Naseer makes the point that the long-standing discriminatory customs got institutionalized as the colonial border was given a legal and administrative form.

James Caron reads a selection of Pashto literatures against the grain of world history, as critical thought about geopolitics. Drawing on Michael Shapiro's concept of aesthetic subjects, as well as on border theory, he argues that the authors, the content, and the literary networks of these Pashto works all critically comment on global relations of power, ranging from the local bordering effects of geopolitics to systems of knowledge embedded in the spatiality and temporality of empire. He argues that the fragmentations brought by past and current imperial processes have led to fragmenting effects in Afghan society, and literature both reflects and analyzes this. More than that, though, he argues—using the lives of authors as well as their reflections in their work—that literary activity in Pashto has actively negotiated such processes throughout all its recent history, and offers strategies for different notions of global connectivity. The decentralized and multiperspective images of life in these sources sit in counterpoint not only to the systems-oriented views that drive military and other policy in Afghanistan during the ongoing US moment, but also to the universalist perspectives upon which many disciplines, including world history and geopolitics, have traditionally relied. Pashto literature itself, as much as its contents, is alternate knowledge about the contemporary world.

Andrea Fleschenberg *et al.* focus on the issue of internal displacement and a host of other related problems connected to it. They carry out extensive fieldwork on and around the border to study impacts of the conflict-induced displacement in the form of everyday experiences and negotiations on the part of those displaced from the tribal border. They "trace and map how people experience and negotiate political violence, (protracted) conflict-induced displacement and the paucity of governance service provisions in a wider context of contested nation-building and transnational high-intensity conflict." They spend considerable time and energy on conceptualizing and responding to the challenges of belonging, resilience, and livelihood for the internally displaced people of the border.

Alvin C. Lim focuses on the China-Pakistan Economic Corridor (CPEC). He makes a case for the CPEC as a moving border-making event. According to him the CPEC represents the intrusion of globalization and capitalism led by the Chinese state in Pakistan's political and economic landscape. Employing Arjun Appadurai's model of globalization Lim throws critical light on five major dimensions of the CPEC. These dimensions include finance, technology, ethnicity, media, and ideologies. Lim argues that, on the one hand, the CPEC creates economic opportunity for both countries in these five dimensions, but, on the other, it also "inscribes difference" within Pakistan's ethnic and national politics. Lim says that this difference is inscribed as the CPEC draws a new border between the national and the global. The CPEC, he further says, has the "potential to recode the meanings of things which had originally been overcoded by local communities."

We mentioned at the beginning that the edited volume engages in not merely descriptive, illustrative, and/or ethnographic analyses, but that it makes conceptual advances as well. Let us briefly highlight some of these conceptual advances: Rais' essay is evidently a descriptive account of the long history of geopolitical engagement of various states at this border. However, when seen closely he presents his account to conceptualize the state-tribe relationship over this long period of time. He thinks that the colonial British state in India and the post-colonial state of Pakistan saw the tribal frontier as naturally autonomous border region because in that way it best served the geostrategic interests of these states. He alludes to the matter of fact that when state and tribe are related to each other on the basis of geo-strategy then this relationship leads to freezing of political development of the latter. Hartung studies the various religious movements that erupted on this borderland over the course of last two centuries. However, he also does so by aiming to make advances toward conceptualizing and expanding the horizon of the relatively new concept of "radical egalitarianism." This concept is based on another anthropological concept of "egalitarianism" in the context of border cultures. By reading a long history of religious movements Peter tries to conceptualize the relationship between religiosity, egalitarianism, and border.

Another conceptual thread in this edited volume deals with the relationship of state security with border. It indirectly conceptualizes the Pakistani state as security state. This thread weaves through three articles that of Raza, Alimia, and Lohnert. This thread highlights the border as a potent source of initiation and enforcement of identity-difference distinctions. This dynamic of the border that shows its inclusionary and exclusionary power with respect to populations is conceptualized as performativity of the border. The border is thought to create an ontological crisis of identity in the everyday life of both citizens and aliens, and it is carried forward and practiced at check-posts that are treated as material manifestations of the border in the mainland. Alimia also points to refugee ID cards as another material manifestation of the extension of the border.

Caron and Noreen further our understanding of two relatively new concepts of aesthetic subjects and auto-ethnography, respectively. Focusing on literary genres of short stories and autobiographies they conceptualize how local people level critique of geopolitics of the border. On the other hand, Lim for the first time presents a novel view of the CPEC project as a bordering event. While the project has mostly been debated from its economic prospects, he thinks that it carries certain critical characteristics of the border, especially those of causing and inscribing division and difference. Accordingly, he argues that the CPEC allows the border to enter through mainland Pakistan and create the conditions of difference in local communities.

In this edited volume the geopolitics of Pakistan–Afghanistan borderland is presented from multiple methodological approaches and critical perspectives. It focuses on certain hitherto untouched or least debated dimensions of this border, for instance, the status of women in the border-culture, the concept of alienage in the making of border, extensions and manifestations of the border, political aesthetics of the border, and so forth. Given the fact that its authors come from both local borderland and foreign well-known institutions they have expert understanding of local literature and primary data, which they engage with critical IR theories to present conceptually advanced analyses. In short, this collection seeks to give voice to the plight of local tribal people and their borderland on an advanced level and to bring them in conversation with an international audience seeking to understand them.

References

Alcalay, Ammiel. 1998. "Translator's Introduction." In *Sarajevo Blues*, by Smezdin Mehmedinovic, ix–xvii. San Francisco, CA: City Lights Books.

Balibar, Etienne. 1998. "The borders of Europe." In *Cosmopolitics: Thinking and Feeling beyond the Nation*, edited by P. Cheah and B. Robbins, 216–233, trans. J. Swenson. Minneapolis, MN: University of Minnesota Press.

Lapid, Yosef. 2001. "Identities, Borders, Orders: Nudging International Relations Theory in a New Direction." In *Identities, Borders, Orders: Rethinking International Relations Theory*, edited by Mathias Albert, David Jacobson, and Yosef Lapid, First edition, 1–20. Minneapolis, MN: University of Minnesota Press.

Geopolitics on the Pakistan–Afghanistan Borderland: An Overview of Different Historical Phases

Rasul Bakhsh Rais

ABSTRACT

This research focuses on the relationship between the tribe and the state in Pakistan's Western borderlands and how this relationship has been continuously affected by the security needs of the state. I argue that there is a dialectical relationship between the tribe and the state. Both of them represent an authority structure, institutions, leadership and rules and procedures to govern populations. While the logic of the state and the modern notions of national sovereignty and territorial control would require assimilation of the tribe into the larger national community, the tribe and its chieftain would strive to maintain their autonomy, traditions and time-tested political arrangements that have served their purpose. The ethos and structural needs of the two to survive and develop – for the state to expand and the tribe to resist and maintain its relative autonomy – clash.

The research explores the historical trajectories the colonial Britain and post-colonial Pakistan have pursued toward assimilation, integration or mere control of tribal regions. The central question I explore is how the geopolitical needs of the state and policy of intervention toward Afghanistan have changed this region from a neglected periphery to the centre of conflict. In answering this question, the article examines the role of dominant structures of world power and their effect on shaping the interests, strategies and alliances among local, regional and global actors. The focus is on how the three international systems – British colonial, Cold War, and American hegemonic – have defined and redefined dynamics and interactive process between tribes in the borderlands and the Pakistani state.

Introduction

The relationship of tribes and the state, at least in the context of Pakistan, has remained harmonious for the most part until the Afghan War began. For the Pakistani statesmen, the recent challenge has been how to go about assimilation or integration of tribal areas in the settled territory without affecting the local tribal culture. This is a classical conflict between the state and the tribe, but this represents a more complicated relationship between the Pakistan state and the borderlands because of their geopolitical situation as a periphery and proximity to the Afghan war zone.

Has the Pakistani state pursued a well-designed, elaborate and consistent policy of bringing about social change through modernisation processes in the Northwestern borderland or has it relied on the colonial framework of 'separation' and indirect control? This is a critical question that I wish to posit to carry out historical inquiry rather than to level a political critique of the Pakistani state for not doing enough about extending its writ or sovereignty into its frontier regions. Pakistan's dilemma on its Northwestern borderland cannot be explained or understood without an extensive look at the colonial legacy and the great geopolitical transformations that took place in the second half of the nineteenth century in and around Afghanistan and the vast Central Asia beyond it. The second most important factor is a long cycle of forty-year war in Afghanistan that began with the Soviet intervention in 1980 to the present US engagement in Afghanistan for well over fifteen years. These two developments have had enduring effects on the geopolitics of the borderlands around Afghanistan, most remarkably the region between Afghanistan and Pakistan.

Pakistan couldn't escape the fallout of the Afghan wars on its border and national security because of its intensive involvement with great power interventions across the borders. The greatest effect has been on the Northwestern mountainous border region of Pakistan, also known as Tribal Areas and administered by the centre, which have seen frequent outbursts of militancy, conflict and violence for about a decade.[1] A number of the militant groups that sprang from time to time over the past decade somehow have related themselves to the Tehreek Taliban Pakistan (TTP) – a religio-political movement which is at best a mix of Wahhabi and Deobandi denominations of Islam. The TTP has ideological similarities with the Afghan Taliban and shares their goal of establishing an Islamic state, enforcing Islamic law and pursuing *jihad.* This carefully crafted slogan has also been the centrepiece of global radical Islam in the modern time.[2] One of the threads in my essay also explains the impact of this slogan and the spread of global radical Islam, but in the context of the Northwestern borderland of colonial India and Pakistan. I observe that the linkages between the borderland and the global radical Islam go back to the Afghan War (1980–88) and other conflicts in the region and the Middle East, which have continuously redefined and restructured this relationship. Conflicts among tribes, ethnic groups, state and empire builders and rival powerholders in Afghanistan have been common throughout modern history.[3] However, the dynamics of internal conflicts and their interaction with the world powers and neighbouring states dramatically changed with the proxy Cold War conflict during the Soviet-Afghan war.[4] Since then, the border regions of Pakistan have remained connected with the conflicts in Afghanistan, causing a spillover of social, security and ideological effects across the Durand Line.[5] This has left a great impact on the old power relationships within the region and also with the state of Pakistan.[6]

Therefore, the main proposition of this essay is that the autonomy of the tribes, who have practiced their own customary law of governance for centuries and organised themselves in a hierarchical egalitarian social structure, has been affected by the interplay of power politics of three sets of actors – great powers, regional states and the local and transnational militant groups. These actors formed a complex web of relationships, often intersecting, conflicting and shifting over the past four decades. The conflicts in the recent past have affected the social and political society on the borderland as well as its relationship with the Pakistani state.

Theorising Tribe and State Relationship in the Borderlands

The Western model of nation state and state building that leaders and policy makers in the developing world uncritically pursue looks at the relationship of the tribe with the state as a conflictive relationship.[7] This perspective suggests that while the modern notion of national sovereignty and territorial control would require assimilation of the tribe into the larger national community, the tribe and its chieftains would strive to maintain their autonomy, traditions and political arrangements. Apparently, the ethos and structural needs of the two to survive, and for the state to expand, come into conflict. The states integrate tribesmen as citizens through a process of development, modernisation, and by structuring appropriate political institutions. It is not so simple however. The issue is of deeper historical nature because the tribes in this part of the post-colonial world and elsewhere found themselves as subjects or 'citizens' of new states and 'in many cases against their choice or will'.[8] The end of empires and dynasties, regional or European has left the tribes bounded by one or another state. In the case of borderlands, the same tribes are distributed among Iran, Afghanistan and Pakistan. This is a remarkable change in the role of the tribes from being on the 'highway of conquest' and playing a critical role in determining the fortunes of dynasties and empires to having been reduced to a periphery.

While prior to the establishment and expansion of the British Indian Empire in the Northwest, the 'tribe and the state formed a single system',[9] in the post-British era, the state acquiring territorial, centralised and sovereign character took the shape and features of European nation-state model. This left the tribes in the borderlands somewhat autonomous, but at the other hand on the margins of the state, and more as a problem of security and social order.

What I have argued in this essay is that colonial rulers and the Pakistan state have approached the tribal borderlands through the prism of security and social order of the areas beyond the tribal domain. Integration and assimilation of the tribes into the mainstream were never a policy; quite the opposite – separation and isolation were the policy. This policy has been rationalised on the ground of unique ecology of the region, character of the Pashtun tribes and the historical circumstances of Pakistan's birth, which recognised autonomy of the tribes. The policy effectively created two-political systems – one for the nation, and the other for the tribes.

This brings us to the need for understanding the character of the Pashtun tribes and the issue of the tribal periphery. Unlike tribes in the Middle East that have played a central role in making the post-Ottoman sates, the Pashtun tribes in the borderlands are marginal to the state because of their mixed character of being partly pastoral, partly settled/segmented and partly decent groups interspersed in urban populations.[10] They have transformed themselves as farmers and traders, but also owing to the imperial and Pakistani policies of extending education and services, they have become soldiers, bureaucrats, businessmen and politicians. In a strict sense, however, this segment of the tribes is not strictly tribal any longer, rather settled and urbanised by retaining relationships and identity as tribal descendants. In new age of democratic politics, this is the class that has assumed the role of intellectual leadership for the borderlands.

There are two major streams of thought on interaction between the tribe and the state and the outcome of this interaction that rests on two different readings of empirical reality. The first is somewhat a static view of the borderlands as autonomous, spatially bounded and managed by an internal political order – leadership, institutions and norms – jealously guarding the boundaries of the tribal political system. Akbar S. Ahmed explains the relationship of the tribe and state as centre-periphery relationship and argues that attempts to enforce any change by the centre have been historically resisted from Mughal to colonial and post-independence times.[11] This view places the state and the tribes in a dichotomous position on the assumptions that social, political order and interests of the two are divergent. Tapper who argues that the tribe and the state are two different 'cultural categories' shares this view.[12] But the dilemma of the tribes is that they are not a territorial unit but a part of large geography of the modern nation state. It is this new and broader ecology that as a matter of principle brings them under the authority of the state. The question however is, how is this authority exercised and what consequences does it create for the tribes and the state? The answer to this question lies in the second view of the interaction between the two, which argues that the tribe is inferior, unsustainable to the superior power of the state.[13] The state has resources, power and policy tools that tribes cannot match. Therefore, being in a hostile situation would never work to the advantage of the tribe. Sooner or later, it will have to give way to the power and needs of the nation state.

Among these tools are policies of economic, social and infrastructural modernisation that have been at play since the British colonial order in the borderlands. But effectiveness of the state will depend on many factors, not just the structural elements of being a state but its penetration into the tribal areas though extension of institutions, social development and assimilative policies. The reason tribal structures have endured in some places is that either the state left the tribes alone or it was not effective enough to bring about a social change. In case of the borderlands, three interlocking processes have generated change as well as conflict, which are centralisation, extension of patronage system and integration of the borderlands into the geopolitics of national security. For the past ten years, the geopolitics of security has transformed the economic, social and political landscape of the borderlands that are 'in danger of being turned upside down'.[14]

My argument is that geopolitics of security for the past four decades has in many ways brought the region into a centralised strategic apparatus, reducing significantly its traditional autonomy, if there is any left in the wake of 'war on terror', drone strikes and march of the Pakistan military into the borderlands to evict and destroy the TTP and its affiliate groups. The question of Islam and *jihad* within the borderlands has been an important one for well over a century among the Islamist ideologues during the nationalist struggle against the British, and during the Soviet-Afghan war by the state of Pakistan. Both have idealised the free-spirited mountain Islamic man in the borderlands as a model of good Muslim and the Pashtun tribal society as a model of good Islamic society.[15] Pakistan and its Western allies employed the tribesman as a warrior in the cause of Islam, nationalism and against the Soviet powers intruding into Afghanistan. In furthering the national security interests of the state, Pakistan has since then turned the borderlands into a strategic landscape for pursuit of its intervention into Afghanistan. This in many ways has redefined the centre-periphery relations, tilting the balance in favour of the Pakistani state. But this has also produced resistance, turmoil and conflict with enduring effects on national security and the stability of Afghanistan.

The Northwestern Borderland of Colonial India and Pakistan

The British imperial rule in India began to expand in the direction of Afghanistan from the middle of the nineteenth century, and it soon annexed territories of the former Punjab state of Ranjit Singh in the British Raj.[16] It was the emergence of Russia as an expanding imperial power in Central Asia that impelled the Raj to politically intervene in Afghanistan and transform it from an 'ancient kingdom' to a buffer state by drawing its borders in the north with the Russians and settling its boundary with the Indian Empire under the 1893 Durand Line agreement.[17] Pakistan, as a successor state, has inherited this legacy of the British power in the border regions.

Geographically, this borderland stretches from the coast along Arabian Sea in Balochistan province to the foothills of Karakorum ranges in the north. This stretch of borderland runs along the international borderline between Pakistan and Afghanistan and includes larger parts of western side of Balochistan and Federally Administered Tribal Agencies (FATA). This borderland has remarkable topographical, social and political characteristics: it is rugged, barren and mountainous and has tribal social structures. The tribal society has a segmentary lineage system, which is dominated by the elders, who are often chiefs of their respective tribes and sub-tribes.[18] The borderland, or part of it, was referred to in the British records as independent territories but subject to administration and security of the colonial government.[19]

Although the term borderland has an imperial, sub-continental context of political usage during the British Raj, my preference for the same rests on the assumption that Pakistan's policy towards this borderland has been shaped by a similar framework of administration and security outlook as that of the Raj. It has included a mixture of 'close' and 'forward' policies that the British pursued for approximately one hundred years to create a buffer zone inside the boundaries of the imperial territories. By 'close' policy, the colonial administration isolated this borderland from the settled districts of the British India to protect the latter from violent troubles arising on the borderland. Their 'forward' policy had two connotations: first, pushing the border to the farthest possible point to turn Afghanistan into a buffer zone against the expanding Russian imperial power. It is worth noticing that the 'close' policy was an integral part of the 'forward' policy (seldom discussed in the contemporary literature), which reflected a 'moral' obligation toward colonial subjects to be safe and secure from the so-called violent tribesmen. On the other hand, the 'close' policy sought to keep the tribesmen within the confines of their tribal territories so that they live by their traditions. The policy thought of them as subjects of security and order for the adjoining regions.

The border between Afghanistan and British India was drawn in 1893 after three months of negotiations between Amir Abdul Rahman (the ruler of Afghanistan) and Sir Mortimer Durand (the representative of the British Government). Before this, the British had worked with Russia to define the boundary and demarcate it from the northern parts of the country in 1891 and further demarcated in 1895.[20] The British came to own and control all the territories west of the Indus river that the Punjab state had taken from the control of Afghan kings extending from Chitral in the North to the Pashtun regions in the north of Balochistan province.[21] The region formed a strategic frontier and a 'frontline' in the 'Great Game'. The region's carving out as a separate territorial unit with different laws, institutions and direct relationship with the central authority was a well-thought-out geostrategic policy. In this policy, one can see that the British put together a delicate balance between the autonomy of tribes, self-rule and recognition of their individuality on the one hand and the strategic needs of the empire, its order and stability on the other.[22]

The borderland along the 2,400 kilometre Afghanistan–Pakistan border has two territorial components. The first component is the seven tribal agencies – Bajaur, Mohmand, Khyber, Orakzai, Kurram, North Waziristan and South Waziristan. The second is the six Frontier Regions (FRs), which are located between the agencies and the settled districts. Up until late 1960s, the princely states of Dir, Swat, Chitral and Amb were also part of the borderland. However, these states were merged with settled territories of Pakistan and redefined as provincially administered tribal areas (the PATA).[23] In Balochistan, the British policy toward the borderland related to a different scheme of ideas. Instead of separating and closing the borderland, the British negotiated agreements with tribal chiefs and incorporated the territories in the British Balochistan. These contained four tribal agencies – Dera Bugti, Kohlu, Chaghi and Zhob. The first two were Mari and Bugti Baloch areas, and the other two were mainly Pashtun regions. In the south of Balochistan are territories that formed the princely states of Kalat, Kharan, Las Bela and Mekran. These territories were later settled into regular districts of the Balochistan province but still remain under different policing and administrative setups. For the purpose of this essay, my focus will be on the Pashtun tribal areas between Khyber Pakhtunkhwa and Afghanistan because of the different nature of conflict there and their connectivity with the troubles in Afghanistan. While regions comprising the FATA are generally treated as a single entity, a closer look would reveal that this conception is misleading.[24] Each of the seven agencies of this region has its own specific tribal, geographic, socioeconomic and religious characteristics, and these have varying relationships with the conflicts and the militant groups within and outside the region.

In this regard, there are three historical facts that we need to contextualise for understanding the regional dynamics of the conflict and how and why they spill over borders. First, the border drawn by the British was not a natural border in the ethnic sense. The Durand Line 'cut through cultural areas' by dividing tribes and leaving them in two different countries.[25] The same tribes with family links, common ancestry and social linkages inhabit lands across the border. For this reason, the British and Pakistani governments have deliberately kept the borders porous, allowing tribesmen to cross without any formality and leaving it mostly unattended and without effective control, for more than a century.

Second, tribes on both sides of the border have remained connected through the two powerful forces, Islam and nationalism. For instance, when the tribes on one side of the border faced some problem, then the tribes on the other side were also affected. Even during the colonial rule on the borderland, the tribes on the British side participated in conflicts in Afghanistan to support the resisting movement, a king or a rebellion. For instance, Nader Khan raised his army in North and South Waziristan to march on Kabul in 1929 and wrested power from Amir Habibullah Kalkani, who he labeled as the 'bandit' king – the first non-Pashtun ruler who briefly held power after the ouster of Amir Amanullah Khan.[26]

Finally, the tribes have maintained internal coherence and stability through their social code of Pashtunwali – equality, self-respect, hospitality and revenge.[27] Part of this code of life is also known as *rewaj* or custom. This code of life and *rewaj*, however, should not give an impression that Pashtun areas became a proto-state or had a unified sense of any political solidarity at some point of time in history. They have so far lived by their code of life in social matters, but the matters that related to legal, administrative or political aspects of the state were always negotiated with or imposed by the British, and later by Pakistan. Furthermore, they have principally accepted the international border between Afghanistan and Pakistan, and it is expected that they 'will not allow one to encroach upon the territory of the other'.[28] Despite ethnic and cultural similarities, the Pashtuns have evolved different identities – they are known as Pashtuns on the Pakistani side of the border, while those across the border are called the Afghans. However, these are two identities, which are often used interchangeably.

Administering the Borderlands

The colonial administration in the Northwestern borderland rested on three pillars — the political agent as the representative of the government, the Frontier Crimes Regulations (FCR) and the *maliks* (the tribal chiefs). After independence, Pakistan adopted this administrative system without making any changes, and it delivered on maintaining social order. The question is how and why did the borderland lose stability and social balance in recent times? Typically, we get a variety of answers to this question. However, the first thing to bear in mind is that the often-made general portrayal of the border as always 'lawless', the 'most-dangerous place' or 'wild-west' of colonial India or Pakistan has little to do with the everyday reality on the borderland. These depictions are arbitrary, subjective and contentious. The low presence of the state or even its benign absence has hardly been a factor in the local or trans-border conflicts. I agree with Thomas Johnson and M Chris Mason that it is mainly the foreign wars that have affected Afghanistan's and the borderland's stability and order. They argue:

> ...To be sure, parts of the region, particularly those dominated by the Pashtuns, are often witness to bloodshed and are not infrequently hobbled by feuds. Yet despite poverty, unemployment, illiteracy, maternal and infant mortality, and human

longevity rates at or near the worst in the world, when not subjected to external pressure, most of the Pashtuns are peaceful pastoralists and subsistence farmers in a feudal economy.[29]

A protracted war in Afghanistan has adversely affected the borderlands of Pakistan more than any other adjoining region. As alluded to in foregoing discussion, this borderland has been at the 'frontline' of conflicts in Afghanistan as well as the subcontinent, with disregard to the policies and preferences of the powerholders on either side of the border. Historically speaking, the borderland's role as the frontline territory has two major aspects. First, neither the Afghan state nor the British imperial power and its successor state, Pakistan, were keen to control the border the way a border is normally controlled as in other parts of the world. It has been the tacit allowance for maintaining the trans-border connectivity of the tribes across the borderland that impelled the states to avoid imposing strict control and regulation. The states remained at peace with the tribes as long as the latter remained peaceful. The state-tribe relationship developed on the pattern of soft sovereignty, and it worked well for more than a century. The pattern began to change due to several factors: initially due to the Soviet invasion (1980s), then the civil war between the Taliban and the Northern Alliance (1990s) which took an ethnic form and finally the American intervention and continual war (2000s). It is worth mentioning that in these time periods of wars, some Pashtun tribes were actively engaged in taking sides with conflicting parties and thereby interfering across the border inside Afghanistan. They did not care about the logic of non-interference in another independent state. This attitude is partially supported by certain ultra-nationalist Pashtun ideologues who consider Afghanistan as their 'own' country or the country of their origin and therefore feel some kind of ethnic obligation to assist the Afghans in their struggles.

In fact, the *jihad* transformed the social and religious thinking of the people of the borderland. This is however not to say that historical calls for *jihad* were never made. Rather the invoking of *jihad* in the Afghan tradition is not new. The call for *jihad* has often been made as a war cry for engaging in internal and external conflicts and also as a way of expressing self-righteousness and rationalisation in causing bloodshed. During the Soviet–Afghan War, the United States found *jihad* as a powerful ideology to incite the tribesmen on both sides of the borderland to defeat the Soviet intervention in Afghanistan. The *jihadi* ideology proved to be an effective tool in mobilising the tribesmen as well as tens of thousands of Muslim youth from other parts of the world. Thus, igniting the fire of *jihad*, the United States achieved its Cold War end – the retreat of the Soviet Union from Afghanistan.

The collapse of the Communist giant four years later in 1992 may partly be attributed to its fatigue and defeat in Afghanistan. One thing that the sponsors of *jihad* in Afghanistan did not realise was that once the *jihadi* ideology became strongly ingrained in the minds of the Muslim youth and as it gave birth to militant organisations in various Muslim countries, it was not possible to easily restrain this ideology and organisations from causing more conflicts and violence. The Afghan *jihad* became a social movement within the concentric cycles of political Islam throughout the region. Having defeated a superpower, the *jihadists* evolved a mythology of religious resistance, sacrifice, martyrdom and confrontation with the 'evil' that often meant the pro-Western local forces and the West. They began to believe in *jihad* as an article of faith as well as an effective tool of regime-change in the Muslim world. The similar mindset, it can be argued, visited the United States in the tragedy of 9/11. On the other hand, Pakistan had to face greater and enduring troubles arising from the wars in Afghanistan and the connectivity of Northwestern borderlands with these wars.

Geopolitics of Militancy

In the last decade, the rise of the Taliban insurgency in the Northwestern borderland on the one hand and ethnic nationalism in Balochistan on the other demonstrate a strained relationship between the imperatives of governance in a less-governed borderland and the security demands of the state of Pakistan. There is no denying the fact that Pakistan was involved in making the borderland a frontline strategic territory to fight against the Soviet forces in Afghanistan. In this process, the United States gave express support to Pakistan. It turned out to be a long war fought under the banner of international *jihad*, and it spawned three more cycles of violent conflict in Afghanistan. During this *jihad* (of 1980s), the *jihadi* groups from Afghanistan, the Middle East, Central Asia and Pakistan took strong roots in this region, even though a *jihadi* culture did not flourish much in other parts of Pakistan. In the aftermath of the Afghan War, the *jihadi* groups stayed back in Afghanistan. Their *jihadi* struggle in the long run culminated in the formation and rise of the Taliban in 1996.

In the 1990s, the Taliban movement in Afghanistan capitalised on the legacy of Mujahedeen who fought and won the Afghan War. It can be argued as such that the Taliban movement in Afghanistan was the ideological child of the Afghan War. The web of transnational linkages the war created survived and flourished in many forms, especially in the shape of the various militant organisations. However, when Pakistan withdrew its support from the Afghan Taliban under the pressure from the United States, the Taliban regime began to collapse. Militants of all varieties began to flee Afghanistan, and many arrived in the Northwestern borderland. The refuge of the militant groups in the borderland was facilitated further by the low presence of the state and the cultural changes – *jihadi* ideology and international linkages – that the Afghan War had already brought about in the borderland.

The power relationships of the Northwestern borderlands changed with the arrival of militant commanders, the flow of weapons and fighters, which began to stress the colonial administrative system maintained by Pakistan. The change became visible as the traditional role of elders, the institution of *jirga* (council of elders) and the office of the political agent began to become increasingly ineffective. The borderlands' administrative system was no longer capable enough to ensure peace, stability, order and writ of the state. Nor was it possible to contain the militants and their *jihadi* designs to the borderland. Within few years after the beginning of the War on Terror (2002), the resident militants emulated the Taliban movement, which appealed many smaller and splinter groups at the local level. Soon they challenged the authority of the state of Pakistan in the borderlands, especially to show their resentment on latter's aligning and assisting the United States in Afghanistan. In the long run, they aimed to capture state power starting with its weak periphery. The Taliban along with several other militant groups put together a parallel state structure with basic state institutions of administration and justice and began to govern the local population in parts of the borderland. They challenged the authority of the Pakistani state with their invasion of Swat valley and infiltration in most of the tribal agencies. It needs to be noted that the rule of the coalition of religious parties called Muttahida Majalis-e-Amal (MMA) (the United Action Front) in the Khyber Pakhtunkhwa province proved to be one of the major factors in the expansion of the TTP because the religious parties resisted military operations in the tribal agencies.

When the TTP and its affiliated group TSNM took control of the Swat valley and neighbouring areas, the military operations could not be avoided and delayed any longer. The fall of valley can be attributed to a long-standing demand of the local people who were discontent with the administration and local judiciary since the time of merger of Swat with the state of Pakistan. It was in the backdrop of this dismay among the people that the TTP's call for speedy justice based on *Sharia* law received sympathy and support among the local population. However, once they came into power, they were able to maintain their rule by spreading fear and giving threats of violence, which they enacted against the local elite (*maliks*). On the other hand, the Pakistani state failed the local population in Swat by leaving them alone under the harsh, inhuman and violent rule of the Taliban.

There are a number of explanations pertaining to why and how the Pakistani state failed and the militants took over the empty territorial spaces created by the low presence of the state or its retreat. In the existing literature on the borderland, Pakistan's policy and the rise of militancy may be roughly divided into three strands of arguments. First, there have been linkages between the Pakistani militant groups and those across the border in Afghanistan. There are multiple connections, such as Pashtun ethnicity,

Islam and the sense of collective responsibility to fighting against foreign intruders, which bind these groups together.[30] It should be noted that the Taliban movements both in Afghanistan and Pakistan have the element of Pashtun nationalism that is often overlooked by scholars who attempt to explain the Taliban movement more in terms of religious extremism than ethnicity.[31] Second, the conflict in the borderland has been explained with reference to Pakistan's Afghanistan policy, as one of its unintended consequences. The argument is that Pakistan was interested in achieving 'strategic depth', and for that reason, it used the Mujahedeen and later the Afghan Taliban as proxies in the Afghan conflict. A third explanation is that the borderland has been a neglected periphery of the state, especially by the federal government. Besides these views, the backwardness and low level of social and economic development of the borderland also created social space for the militant groups to emerge.[32]

Geopolitics of the New Great Game

The stability and order in the Northwestern borderland began to erode with the Afghan Jihad, when tens of thousands of Afghan *Mujahedeen*, Arab *jihadists* and Pakistani extremists arrived there. It was one of the most broad-based modern insurgencies that was supported by the United States and its allies. There was a sort of tacit alliance between the ideologues of *jihadist* Islam and the United States, who today are on opposite ends. In this tacit alliance, Pakistan served as a strategic bridge, while its border region served as strategic territorial bridge. At the end of the war, the United States withdrew its investment in the region, and the *mujahedeen* it had brought here and supported were left alone. Feeling betrayed and purposeless at the end of the war, the *mujahedeen* took up arms against their own states or became part of larger regional networks of Islamists. The Afghan war gave them valuable experience, skills in leadership, propaganda, organisation and in establishing transnational networks. The establishment of Al-Qaeda by Osama bin Laden was one of such ventures with a focus on global Islamic revolution through an armed struggle. The Muslim states that had encouraged the leaders and foot soldiers of the Afghan *jihad* became concerned about *mujahedeen*'s plans and activities. *Mujahedeen*'s ideology of radical Islam and *jihad* was seen as a grave security threat by these Muslim states. As they adopted counter-insurgency measures against the *Mujahedeen*, the latter looked for places where the writ of the state was either weak or the state authorities were willing to tolerate their presence. They found Sudan, Somalia, Yemen, Afghanistan and the Western borderlands of Pakistan secure to hide in and to plan their future wars.

The inter-*Mujahedeen* conflicts in the 1990s and later the rise of the Taliban in Afghanistan created opportunity for these *Mujahedeen* to conceive and execute new *jihad* plans. They traveled back to Afghanistan along the same routes through the border regions, met old friends and made new ones on the way. The seeds of the religious and ideological change that the *jihadists* had sown in the tribal region during the Afghan *jihad* along both sides of the border earned them local allies. The young recruits with the experience of Afghan War, transnational connections, weapons and money began to assert themselves in local and regional matters. The rise of the militant local commanders with their tribal base and organisation, that is, the *lashkar* (militia), was a new phenomenon, which had earlier emerged in every part of Afghanistan, now emerged, although on a lesser scale, in the tribal regions of Pakistan. The local militants had played a great role in providing a transit route during the Soviet-Afghan war and assisting in the war to oust the Soviets from their imagined, and historically claimed, homeland – Afghanistan. The Pakistani state therefore tolerated them and even encouraged them to align with the Kashmiri militant groups fighting against the Indian forces. At local levels, they developed a cult of *jihad* and militancy that attracted unemployed youth to join their service. A number of groups like the Taliban, and named after their leaders, emerged in every agency of the tribal region. With armed manpower, the militant commanders exploited the illegal economy of drugs, smuggling, extortion and kidnapping for ransom. They got their share along with other regular beneficiaries – the tribal chiefs and the corrupt administration of the agencies. The militant commanders and their militias were a new player in the power politics of the borderland with a greater capacity to set new rules of conduct and enforce these on the local populations.

The *mullah* or the clergyman has been a vital part of the Pashtun and tribal social structure – traditionally as a client of khans and socially at a lower rung of the hierarchy. However, not all *mullahs* would fall in the same lower rung, as historically some rose to prominence, assumed leadership positions, took up arms and resisted the British and Pakistan's authority. The local populations gave the *mullah* respect and resources to run mosques and madrassas (religious school) and even approached them for the settlement of minor disputes and to act as a counselor in family affairs.[33] Compared to other parts of Pakistan, the *mullah* in Pashtun society has enjoyed far greater veneration and wider social role. He attends the committees of elders and issues religious edicts when requested and takes care of the religious affairs of the community – solemnising marriages, births and circumcisions. The Afghan War and the ideology of *jihad* further transformed the role of the *mullah* from leading prayers to leading the *jihad* against 'infidels' in Afghanistan. Many of these *mullahs* mobilised local populations and became leaders of their militias. There were two other factors that contributed to the power of the *mullah*. First, it was the funding and proliferation of the madrassa networks with the support of Arab countries that hundreds of religious schools were established along the border in Pashtun areas, including northern parts of Balochistan, to enroll the children of Afghan refugees as well as to provide basic education to the local population. Foreign funding changed the dynamics of the relationship of the *mullah* with the traditional power structure in the borderland. He emerged as an autonomous, powerful actor on the tribal social stage, less dependent on the local chieftains, and populations. He was able to accumulate more resources, power and influence than he could at any other time in the past.

The foreign militants were a third new actor in the borderland after the American war began in Afghanistan (2001–2014). However, seen in their historical context, they were not entirely new, as many a times in the past, militant leaders and movements sprang up in the borderland, for instance, against the colonial power. The uprisings stirred by the Faqir of Ippi and Mullah of Hadda, and before that Mujahedeen movement against the Sikh rule, are just a few examples.[34] The rise of the present militant groups and their influence however depended on the political situation in Afghanistan. With the emergence of the Taliban movement, the foreign fighters from Central Asia, the Middle East and parts of Pakistan found refuge in the vacuum left by the Afghanistan state. But when the United States and its allies intervened in Afghanistan to oust the Taliban regime, the global *jihadists*, including the leadership of Al-Qaeda, moved into the borderland. The remoteness, difficult mountainous terrain, hospitable social conditions and the thin presence of Pakistani security forces made the borderland an ideal sanctuary for the militants.

The Pashtun cultural mores based in *Pashtunwali* (the social code of egalitarian life) worked to the advantage of the militants. The United States did arrest some of the top leaders of Al Qaeda, but hundreds of these militants were able to successfully escape to the borderland and found support within the larger region and began to live there. The question whether foreign militants remained free to move about in the borderland is a critical one. Different scholars and journalists have provided different answers and explanations to it. In my assessment, the militants depended on local support networks of militia leaders by assuming the role of mercenaries in local rivalries and feuds of the warlords. Being between the deep sea and the devil, it was their survival strategy. They were linked to the global *jihad* of the Islamic Movement of Uzbekistan and Al-Qaeda. Their presence in the border region and carrying out ruthless attacks against the security forces to avenge Pakistan's policy to align with the United States in the War on Terror turned out to be a grave threat to the national security.

With the three new actors – *mullah*, militia and the global *jihadists* – the old colonial structure of power of *maliks*, the FCR and the political agent began to weaken.[35] The Pakistani state began to lose its monopoly over means and institutions of carrying out legitimate violence in the borderland. With this, the tribesmen also lost their traditional sources of power to the new actors. The militants targeted *maliks* first and then those who were most vulnerable in the society to terrorise the local population and send them a message about the power of the militants.[36] Several local militant groups under the banner of the Taliban launched a campaign of targeted killing to eliminate *maliks* and their traditional social influence. According to official sources, these groups killed over 113 *maliks*.[37] According to private sources, the public intellectuals and former bureaucrats from the FATA, the figure is much higher and stands around 700 to 1,500. The targeted murder of *maliks* is a big loss to the traditional institutions and leadership in the area.[38]

The political agent and the security force having a thin presence in their fortified positions also came under militant attacks. In many areas, the two symbols of sovereignty in the borderland lost their effectiveness, credibility and capacity to enforce order. The balance of power shifted in favour of the Taliban and their affiliated groups. This also rendered the legal framework of the FCR questionable to the new situation. The militants questioned the legitimacy of the colonial system (of the FCR), which had become inefficient, corrupt and manipulated by the *maliks*. They replaced the system with their own administration of justice through *shuras* (consultative assembly). *Shuras* were voluntary and inexpensive institutions dispensing speedy justice based on *Shariah*. Therefore, the local tribal population viewed the *shuras* as fair and trustworthy institutions. On the other hand, the strategy of capturing border territories and keeping the local population under hostage in one tribal agency encouraged the militants in other tribal agencies to follow suit. From 2004 through 2008, the state of Pakistan practically lost control of Waziristan and then one by one of other agencies. Eventually, it lost control of the valley of Swat, which is a settled territory. From their bases in the borderland, the Taliban succeeded in terrorising the state and society of Pakistan by carrying out a campaign of violence in different cities of the country. They also prepared and sent suicide bombers who attacked mosques, religious congregations, parks, public spaces and security check posts.

Geopolitics of the War on Terror

The brief historical narration above demonstrates that the militant culture and radical mindsets, which challenged the state authority, are the product of the past four decades. The Pakistani state kept accommodating, conceding and negotiating power relationships with the Taliban and other organisations, which often weakened territorial control of the state. The appeasement by the state didn't work in its interest for long. The peace deals and agreements it negotiated several times with the Taliban were violated on one pretext or the other.[39] While the spread of the Taliban went on unabated, there emerged a rift between the civil governments and the military whether to use force or negotiations as a policy.[40] Indetermination, policy clashes and inconsistency in approach were also some factors encouraging militants to resist the state authority.

Pakistan's policy of flexible response to the conflict in the border regions proved to be ineffective. The conflict has caused fifty thousand civilian deaths. This number is more than the number of deaths for all conventional wars with India. The security forces, including the military, intelligence agencies, border security forces and police have lost more than five thousand personnel. The economic cost in terms of loss of investment opportunity and destruction of infrastructure is estimated at USD 106.98 billion.[41] It belatedly realised that since the ideology of the Taliban was driven by religious fanaticism and their ambitious agenda included capturing the Pakistani state, engaging them in negotiations was useless. Furthermore, there is one other important aspect – the subject of negotiation and its negotiability. For instance, the subject of negotiation in the talks with the Taliban was to seek ways to end the insurgency. What the state was not ready to talk about was any compromise on democracy, the constitution or the territorial sovereignty of the state. The government for political reasons wanted to exhaust the strategy of talks while at the same time get prepared to use force. The moment for the use of force came when the Taliban took over the valley of Swat. This was the beginning of a new strategy against militancy that rested on the understanding that the centre of the Pakistani state and society will remain in turmoil until the periphery – the borderland – was taken back from the Taliban's control.

In 2009, in order to remove the Taliban from the Swat valley, the government carried out a military operation, which was the largest in history of its kind as it involved tens of thousands of troops and all different units of the armed forces.[42] However, removing the Taliban became only possible after evacuating the civilian population from the valley. Hundreds of thousands of people were asked to leave their homes, towns and villages. This evacuation caused a humanitarian crisis for the local population. However, it can be argued that the evacuation on the part of the people was a relatively small price compared to the loss of their self-rule and popular sovereignty, which could have spread to neighbouring districts. The rise of the Taliban in Swat encouraged other militant groups to encroach upon the tribal territories.

Beginning with the valley of Swat, Pakistan's armed forces have remained engaged in the borderland against the militants over the past decade. Even before the operations in Swat, the Pakistan Army carried out a major operation in South Waziristan in 2004.[43] Determined to recover the borderlands, the Pakistan Army launched a much bigger operation named Zarb-e-Azb in June 2014 in North Waziristan. This operation came at the end of four other major operations in different parts of the tribal agencies, which were only partially successful. Unlike earlier operations, Zarb-e-Azb targeted all different types of militant groups present in North Waziristan. It took a year before the army could flush out militants from the agency. The operation, as expected, resulted in the displacement of local population and destruction of infrastructure, including hundreds of schools. After the operation, however, the army invested considerable money and energy in the reconstruction of infrastructure and resettlement of IDPs in the agency. In this way, the army was able to regain the trust of the local population.[44]

Geopolitics of Reforms

Well over more than two decades, a debate has been going on in the FATA, and generally within the country, to introduce political and administrative reforms in the border regions and integrate them with the rest of the country. The historical roots of this debate go back to the colonial times. Under the British rule (1849–1947) for about a century, the tribal agencies were administered by the Chief Commissioner of NWFP who reported to the Viceroy of India.[45] After the independence, the tribal agencies were placed under the direct supervision of the federal government of Pakistan. They were given 'special status' after several treaties were signed between the tribal chiefs and the colonial administration and then with the Government of Pakistan. The special status was maintained under different constitutions of Pakistan – 1956, 1962 and 1973. However, they were kept outside the mainstream government of NWFP (now KP) and directly governed by the centre.

In the initial years of independence, there were some voices that were in favour of merging tribal areas with settled districts of then NWFP. These voices included that of the voice of the influential political leader Khan Abdul Ghaffar Khan.[46] The 1962 constitution provided for one member from the tribal areas to represent in the provincial assembly of NWFP and one member to represent in the national assembly. These members were to be elected by the electoral college of basic democrats.[47] Under the current 1973 constitution, the federal government exercises its authority in the tribal areas through the Office of the President and that of the governor of KP.[48] Several commissions and committees have been formed over the past decades to reform the administrative and political system of the borderland, but little progress has been achieved to end the 'special status' of the agencies because of the resistance of the vested interests, mainly the *maliks* and bureaucracy. As I mention above, the *maliks* constitute the traditional leadership in the tribal areas. The tribe confers the position/status of a *malik* though a *jirga*, which considers the candidate's ability to lead the tribe, along with the consideration of hereditary factors. Once the *jirga* has named a *malik*, the political agent of the tribal agency officially recognises his status. The *malik* and the political agent are the two main powerhouses in the tribal areas.[49] They use the FCR and the *rewaj* to create their power and privilege.

One of the most significant political reforms introduced in the FATA was the introduction of adult franchise in 1996. The reform in fact recognised political equality and citizenship right of the tribal person for the first time. However, the reform has yet to take roots with wider popular participation. Compared to other regions of the country, the turnout in 2013 election in the tribal areas was only 36%. It was the lowest turnout.[50] Women are generally excluded from voting by the tribesmen due to the factor of strong patriarchal culture.[51] Since the introduction of adult franchise, the borderland has seen four general elections compared to a total of ten general elections of the rest of the country. Although the borderland has adequate representation in the two houses of national parliament, there is a contradiction in the system: the FATA representatives don't have the power to influence lawmaking about the FATA. This is partly because the national Parliament has no constitutional jurisdiction regarding making laws and policies for the borderland/tribal agencies. This power rests with the president, and he exercises it in consultation with the governor of KP and the FATA secretariat.

Another major reform introduced to bring coherence in the administrative and bureaucratic structure was the establishment of the FATA Secretariat in 2002. Later in 2006, the FATA Development Authority was established to initiate large-scale developmental projects in the borderland. Over the past decade, billions of dollars have been spent for the development of the borderland, which critics argue have not made much impact.[52] Then in 2011, two more major reforms were introduced: one amended the FCR and the other introduced political parties to the borderland, the Political Parties Order of 2002. The amendment in the FCR discontinued collective punishment and the interment of women and children under the age 16 or elderly men above the age of 65. The amendment also introduced three-member tribunal to act as an appellate court to hear cases decided by *jirgas* and political agents. The tribunal has powers equal to that of the high court under article 199 of the Constitution.[53] On the other hand, the introduction of political parties to the borderland was complementary to the introduction of adult franchise earlier. For a long time, tribal people could not participate in the political process. Tribal elders or *maliks* monopolised the political arena. The permission to political parties to nominate their candidate and carry out election campaigns was a big step toward politically mainstreaming and integrating the tribal areas.[54]

The government's geopolitical strategy advocated three aspects in the fight against militants – to defeat the militants, hold the territory, rebuild it and transfer the power to local government. In this geopolitical strategy, the aspect of defeating the Taliban and their affiliated groups proved easier than other aspects of achieving developments and transfer of political power to local civilian government. For instance, the projects of rebuilding in South and North Waziristan are under way and have been taking considerable time. The rehabilitation of the internally displaced persons is also under way, but not complete yet.[55] The army has launched big development projects to build roads, communication networks, irrigation dams and installments for extracting clean drinking water. From the point of view of National Action Plan, the building of roads in the borderland is a part of the larger project of modernising the borderland. As Chad Hains has argued, roads 'landscape the nation state', contribute to economic development and 'integrate diverse communities'.[56] Never have so many development projects been initiated in the borderland – and with so much speed – in the past as we have seen during the past seven years.[57]

In recent times, there has emerged national consensus that the old administrative system in the tribal areas cannot work any longer. The Afghan wars and the local conflict within tribal areas have changed the social and security dynamics forever. It is only the beneficiaries of the old order – the *maliks* – who insist on keeping the colonial system, after introducing certain amendments in the FCRs. In the past, they have successfully resisted major reforms, like the one for merging the FATA with the adjacent province of KP. Presently, all the major political parties, including the religious ones and the ruling party, the Pakistan Tehreek-e-Insaf (PTI), support integration of FATA into KP.[58] While the tribal chiefs oppose reforms, the emerging middle class from the borderland not only desires reforms but is also open to different political choices for the future of political integration: integration with KP and a separate province consisting of the tribal agencies.[59] The people at the grass-roots level, about 54 percent 'fully' and 20 percent 'partially' support merger of their agencies with the KP.[60] It is one of the positive gains of reforms like extension of adult franchise, allowing political parties to operate in the borderlands and development work by the non-governmental organisations that the tribesman has found his voice. The old system didn't allow him opportunity or freedom of self-expression. The region in post-conflict situation is still in transition, and the voice of the tribesman is yet to be heard and accommodated. But it is filtering out, as in surveys, group discussion and through political participation that the reforms have promoted.

As pressure for reforms and implementation of NAP increased, which included integration of FATA with the settled territory of the state, and end colonial administrative system, the Federal Government constituted a committee on FATA reforms.[61] After eight months of deliberation, the committee submitted its report in August 2016 with a plan to integrate the tribal areas with the KP over the next five years. The committee recommended that a) the FCR should be repealed and substituted with a 'Tribal Areas *Rewaj* Act' b) the *jirga* system should continue to work with addition of a regular judge in it and c) the jurisdiction of the Peshawar High Court and Supreme Court of Pakistan should be extended to these areas. Apart from these recommendations report presented a comprehensive reforms package addressing security, political, economic and administrative institutions.[62] The driving idea behind the reforms is reconstruction, resettlement, development and integration of the tribal areas with the province of KP. This is the most comprehensive reform package and has much wider national consensus than any such reforms proposed in the past. The Government of Pakistan has yet to implement the recommendations of the reforms though. It is facing resistance from the minor parties – Jamiat-e-Ulem-e-Islam and Pakhtunkhwa Milli Party – which are allies of the Pakistan Muslim League (Nawaz Sharif Government).[63] These parties argue that the FATA's historical status be retained, and if any change has to take place, it must reflect people's wishes that can be ascertained by referendum. Some of the tribal leaders have also opposed any change in the status of the borderlands.[64] On the other hand, the peoples' representatives in the parliament have consistently demanded merger of FATA with the KP.[65] For now, it seems, government's indecision on such a vital issue undermines the momentum to mainstream borderlands with the rest of the country. In my assessment, it is only a matter of time before the status of the borderlands changes, which has much broader political support and endorsement of state institutions, including the powerful security establishment.[66]

Conclusion

For its geopolitical purposes, Pakistan has deeply involved the Pashtun borderlands in the Afghanistan wars. An extended view of national security and geopolitical interests of Pakistan have highly destabilised the borderlands, especially its tribal culture, social networks, local economy and the role of religion.[67] The balance of power among the traditional social institutions of society also underwent major transformation. The continuation of conflict, flow of weapons and entry of foreign militants in the borderland are some of the factors that created conditions for this transformation.

The ongoing War on Terror, including military operations by Pakistan and use of combat drones by the United States against the terrorists, continues to adversely affect the borderlands. It is widely understood that the drone warfare has tacit consent of Pakistan. The drone war has heightened fear, insecurity and anxiety among the tribesmen. The claims of successful targeting of the wanted terrorists have come at the cost of lives of local people, including children, women and elderly. Civilian casualties that are ignored as 'collateral damage' of war are estimated to be in thousands. The push-button drone warfare is not sensitive to the human tragedy on the ground and physical rubble it leaves behind. While the villagers pull out the loved ones and rush them to expanding graveyards, the drone-warfare commanders, having done their job, move on searching for the next targets.

No doubt it is hard to escape human tragedies in wars, but those who wage wars should also be made subject to laws of war and should take the responsibility for decisions affecting local populations in the border regions. The tribesman is voiceless, helpless and has turned angry at Pakistan for its failure to protect him against both the militants and the drones. Pakistan itself has moved its forces into the region for securing the borderlands, which the tribesmen see as violation of their 'autonomous' status.

The tribesmen are faced with three different dangers – the militants, the American drone warfare and military operations. They have been fending for themselves. The military operations have resulted in increased trans-border mobility of the militants – back and forth across the border from Afghanistan. Some of them have also moved inside Pakistani society. The tribal population, now displaced internally everywhere in the country and with their livelihood damaged or lost, are faced with challenges of rehabilitation.

Once the dust of the War on Terror in and around Afghanistan settles, the world will be able to see the scale of the damage inflicted on the local populations. I argue that there will be no winners in the war. Each side will leave the battleground after having suffered tremendous damage.[68] At the moment, what is not being thought are the losses that the local population is bearing. The primacy of geopolitical interests of Pakistan has pushed the local peoples to the margins. As a reaction, they have developed feelings of hate and revenge, against both the state of Pakistan and the United States, which may last for generations. Instead of prolonging the war, what is needed on the part of the Pakistani state is to introduce reforms in the tribal areas, both political and developmental, and a sense of empowerment among the people of the borderlands. The long-term success of the military operations will depend on how quickly the borderlands are rebuilt and reformed, reflecting wishes and desires of the tribesman. If not done this way, the tension between the centre of the state and the periphery of the borderlands will continue in one form or another.

Notes

1. Daniel Seth Markey, *Securing Pakistan's Tribal Belt* (New York: Council on Foreign Relations, CSR No. 36 2008) pp. 1–27.
2. Sana Haroon, 'Competing Views of Pashtun Tribalism, Islam, and Society in the Indo-Afghan Borderlands', in Nile Green (ed.), *From Conversion to the Taliban* (Berkeley: University of California Press 2017) pp. 145–62.
3. Peter Tomsen, *The Wars of Afghanistan: Messianic Terrorism, Tribal Conflicts, and the Failure of Great Powers* (New York: Public Affairs 2011) pp. 23–44.
4. Kaushik Roy, *War and Society in Afghanistan from Mughals to the Americans, 1500–2013* (New Delhi: Oxford University Press 2014) pp. 37-55; Gregory Feifer, *The*

Great Gamble: The Soviet War in Afghanistan (New York: HarperCollins 2001) pp. 1-14.

5. Haroon (note 2) pp. 145–6.
6. Akbar S. Ahmed, *Millennium and Charisma among Pathans* (London: Routledge, Kegan & Paul 1980); Fredrik Barth, *Political Leadership Among Swat Pathans* (London: London School of Economics 1959).
7. Richard Tapper, *The Conflict of Tribe and State in Iran and Afghanistan* (London/Canberra: Croom Helm 1983); Philip S. Khoury and Joseph Kostiner (eds.), *Tribes and State Formation in the Middle East* (Berkeley: University of California Press 1990); Brad A. Bays and Erin Hogan Fouberg (eds.), *The Tribes and States: Geographies of Inter-Governmental Interaction* (Lanham: Rowman and Littlefield Publishers 2002).
8. Akbar S. Ahmed, *Thistle and the Drone: How America's War on Terror Became a Global War on Tribal Islam* (Washington, DC: Brooking Institution Press 2013) p. 13.
9. Richard Tapper, 'Tribe and State in Iran and Afghanistan: An Update', *Études Rurales* 184 (2009) pp. 33–46.
10. Ibid.
11. Ahmed (note 8) pp. 43–95.
12. Tapper (note 7) p. 38.
13. Patricia Cone, 'Review: Tribe and State in the Middle East', *Journal of Royal Asiatic Society* 3/3 (1993) pp. 353–76.
14. Ahmed (note 8) p. 56.
15. Haroon (note 2) pp. 145–62.
16. Mortimer Durand, 'Mission to Kabul: A Confidential Report', Afro-Asian Collection, British Library, p. 8.
17. Muhammad Mushtaq Jadun, 'Durand Line Status', *Dawn*, 31 July 2016.
18. F. Fredrick Barth, 'Descent and Marriage Reconsidered', in Jack Goody (ed.), *The Character of Kinship* (Cambridge: Cambridge University Press 1975) pp. 3–19.
19. *Report of the Punjab Frontier Administration for the Year 1891–92* (Lahore: Punjab Government Press 1892) p. 5.
20. Zalmay Ahmad Gulzad, *The History of the Delimitation of the Durand Line, Development of the Afghan State (1838–1998)*, 2 vols. (Madison: University of Wisconsin 1991).
21. E. P. Singhal, *India and Afghanistan, 1876–1907* (St. Lucia: University of Queensland Press 1963) pp. 80–110.
22. Ainslie T. Embree, 'Pakistan's Imperial Legacy', *Pakistan's Western Borderlands* (Durham: Carolina Academic Press 1977) pp. 24–39; Richard Tapper (ed.), *The Conflict of Tribe and State in Iran and Afghanistan* (London: Croom Helm 1983).
23. Sultan-i-Rome, *Swat State (1915–1969) from Genesis to Merger* (Karachi: Oxford University Press 2008) pp. 20–57.
24. Magnus Marsden and Benjamin D. Hopkins, *Fragments of the Afghan Frontier* (London: Hurst Publishers 2014) pp. 34–56.
25. Louis Dupree, *Afghanistan* (Karachi: Oxford University Press 1973) p. 425.
26. Nabi Misdaq, *Afghanistan: Political Frailty and External Interference* (London/New York: Routledge 2006) pp. 52–71.
27. Thomas H. Johnson and Barry Scott Zellen, *Culture, Conflict and Counterinsurgency* (Stanford: Stanford University Press 2014) pp. 244–5.
28. Brig Mahmood Shah (Retd.), 'Tribal Areas of Pakistan, Afghanistan: Interconnectivity and Spillover Effects' (Unpublished paper), 15 June 2017.

29. Thomas H. Johnson and M. Chris Mason, 'No Sign until the Burst of Fire: Understanding the Pakistan and Afghanistan Border', *International Security* 32/4 (2008) p. 55.
30. Shuja Nawaz, *FATA – A Most Dangerous Place: Meeting the Challenge of Militancy in the Federally Administered Areas of Pakistan* (Washington, DC: Centre for International and Strategic Studies 2009) pp. 1-54.
31. Ahmed Rashid, *The Taliban, Militant Islam, Oil and Fundamentalism in Central Asia* (London: I.B. Tauris 2001) pp. 1–15.
32. Ijaz Khan, 'Challenges Facing Development in Pakistan's FATA', *The National Bureau of Asian Research* 19 (2008) pp. 13–20.
33. Akbar S. Ahmad (note 6).
34. Milan Hauner, 'One Man Against the Empire: The Faqir of Ipi and the British in Central Asia on the Eve of and during the Second World War', *Journal of Contemporary History* 16 (1981) pp. 183–212.
35. Brian R. Kerr, 'A Progressive Understanding of Pashtun Social Structures Amidst Current Conflict in FATA', *Conflict and Peace Studies* 3/4 (2010) pp. 1–10.
36. Malik Akbar Muhammad, 'Role of Malik in Tribal Society: A Dynamic Change After 9/11', *Pakistan Annual Research Journal* 49 (2013) pp. 103–13.
37. This information has been obtained from FATA Secretariat, Peshawar, 10 June 2016.
38. Author's interview with Ayaz Wazir, former diplomat from FATA, 9 Feb. 2017 and an interview with Mansoor Khan Mahsud, Islamabad, 10 Feb. 2017.
39. Daud Khattak, 'Reviewing Pakistan's peace deals with the Taliban', *Combating Terrorism Center*, 26 Sep. 2012, available at <https://www.ctc.usma.edu/posts/reviewing-pakistans-peace-deals-with-the-taliban>, accessed 16 Sep. 2016.
40. Susannne Koelbl, 'Islamist Triumph in Swat Valley: Bowing Down to the Taliban', *Der Spiegel*, 21 Feb. 2009, available at <http://www.spiegel.de/international/world/islamists-triumph-in-swat-valley-bowing-down-to-the-taliban-a-609575.html>, accessed 16 Sep. 2016.
41. Government of Pakistan, Ministry of Finance, *Economic Survey of Pakistan* (2016) p. 280.
42. 'Operation in Swat intensified: ISPR', *Dawn*, 11 May 2009.
43. Babar Sattar, 'The Revenge Argument', *Dawn*, 30 Sep. 2013.
44. Muhammad Amir Rana, 'Zarb-i-Azab, One Year On', *Dawn*, 14 June 2015.
45. FATA Secretariat, available at <https://fata.gov.pk/Global.php?iId=28&fid=2&pId=23&mId=13>, accessed 15 Feb. 2017.
46. Noor ul Haq, et al., *Federally Administered Areas of Pakistan* (Islamabad: Islamabad Policy Research Institute 2005) pp. 3–15.
47. Sarfraz Khan, 'Special Status of Tribal Areas (FATA): An Artificial Imperial Construct Bleeding Asia', *Eurasia Border Review* Part II (2010) p. 71, available at<http://src-h.slav.hokudai.ac.jp/publictn/eurasia_border_review/no1/06_Khan.pdf>, accessed 15 Feb. 2017.
48. *The Constitution of the Islamic Republic of Pakistan* (Islamabad: National Assembly of Pakistan 12th April, 1973) pp. 118–9.
49. Sartaj Khan, 'Changing Pashtun Society', *The News*, 14 Jan. 2010.
50. *KPK and FATA: Nature, Sources, Forces and Implications* (Islamabad: FATA Research Centre 2013) p. 11.
51. Faisal Bari, 'Missing Women Voters?', *Dawn*, 7 May 2013.
52. Erum Ayaz, *Peace and Development in FATA through Economic Transformation* (Islamabad: FATA Research Centre 2001), available at <http://frc.org.pk/wp-content/uploads/2012/08/Peace-and-Development-in-FATA-through-Economic-Transformation.pdf>, accessed 15 Feb. 2017.

53. 'Major Changes Made in FCR: Fata People Get Political Rights', *Dawn*, 12 Aug. 2011.
54. "Extension of Political Parties Act to Fata", *The News*, 10 Aug. 2011.
55. 'Nearly 40 PC IDPs Have Returned to North Waziristan, Army Chief Told', *Dawn*, 19 December 2015.
56. Chad Hains, *Nation, Territory and Globalization in Pakistan: Traversing the Margins* (Lanham/New York: Routledge 2012) p. 2.
57. FATA Development Authority and FATA Secretariat, available at <http://fatada.gov.pk>.
58. 'ANP, JI, PPP in Favor of Fata's Merger with KP', *Dawn*, 12 Sep. 2015; 'Government Asked to Merge FATA with KP without Delay', *Dawn*, 25 Aug. 2016.
59. 'People Back PKMAP Call for Separate Fata Province', *Dawn*, 8 May 2016.
60. Sadia Sulaiman and Syed Adnan Ali Shah Bukhari, *Governance Reforms in FATA: A People's Perspective* (Islamabad: FATA Research Centre 2016) p. xix.
61. '20 Points of National Action Plan' (Islamabad: National Counter Terrorism Authority Pakistan (NACTA)), available at <http://nacta.gov.pk/NAPPoints20.htm>, accessed 15 Feb. 2017.
62. *Report of the Committee on FATA Reforms, 2016* (Islamabad: Government of Pakistan 2016); Mubarak Zeb Khan, '10—Year Timeline to Bring Fata on a Par with KP', *Dawn*, 25 Aug. 2016.
63. 'PMLN ally Fazl Opposes Fata Reforms in NA', *Dawn*, 16 May 2017.
64. 'Tribal Leaders Challenge Govt Plan to Merge Fata with KP', *Dawn*, 10 March 2017.
65. Kalbe Ali, 'Fata MPs Agree on KP-tribal Areas Merger', *Dawn*, 2 April 2017.
66. 'Commanders Moot Stresses Need for Fata Reforms', *Dawn*, 24 May 2017.
67. Razia Sultana and Saira Aquil, 'The Pakistani Pashtuns and the Endgame in Afghanistan' *International Journal on World Peace* 29/4 (2012) pp. 13–36.
68. Milton Bearden, 'Afghanistan, Graveyard of Empires', *Foreign Affairs* 80 (November-December 2001) pp. 17–19.

Of Pious Missions and Challenging the Elders: A Genealogy of Radical Egalitarianism in the Pashtun Borderscape

Jan-Peter Hartung

ABSTRACT
At the core of this article lies the attempt to consider "radical egalitarianism" a defining feature of "borderscapes", that is the space in which distinct socio-spatial identities between territorial claims and counter-claims at the margins of larger political entities are negotiated. These more general considerations are exemplified by a genealogical excursion into the dominantly Pashtun-inhabited regions around the Hindukush and its foothills. In a first step, the emergence of distinct ethnicities and religiosities as result of such asymmetrical negotiation processes, which are also strongly informed by the urban-rural divide, is highlighted by a historical recourse into the later seventeenth century. In the two successive steps, then, the further modifications of those ethnicities and religiosities since the late nineteenth century are indicated, painting an image of the "Pashtun borderscape" in which even militant movements like those of the present time can be understood as just a manifestation of such kind of negotiation processes that limit the scope of "us" and "them" ever further. It will be illustrated how an ever changing semantics of "egality", which nonetheless is construed as entirely static, is established as a core benchmark of belonging.

Much has been written on who or what the *Ṭālibān* – a virulent force in the region between today's two nation states Afghanistan and Pakistan since the early 1990s – are; yet, unfortunately we still know fairly little about them. Even the standard notion of them as a 'fundamentalist' movement, radiating predominantly from investigative journalist Ahmed Rashid's (2008) influential work, is incorrect with regard to their epistemology.[1] Moreover, many writings that approach them from a security angle, for example by Gustozzi (2007) and Schetter and Klußmann (2011), neither acknowledge their complex regionally determined cultural specifics, nor do they try to explain them within a historical continuum on the Afghanistan–Pakistan border, which I – following Chiara Brambilla (2015) – conceptualize here as a 'borderscape.'[2] Against the widely used notion of 'borderland' in the study of the Afghanistan–Pakistan spatial nexus, which does not really challenge the reality of physical political boundaries, the advantage of the concept of 'borderscape' is that it highlights the discursiveness and resulting fluidity of this political border depending on the respective vantage point.

What I am interested in is how actors, discursively framed by others as 'borderlanders,' adapt to these external designations and produce a 'borderland' discourse of their own by conceptualizing themselves as distinct ethnic and political entity. A prominent feature of these self-conceptualizations appears to be a notion of 'egalitarianism,' informing also the ethnic self-understanding of 'Pashtun-ness.' Without necessarily accepting 'egalitarianism' as an empirically grounded reality in the region under consideration, I highlight the strong possibility of a thread in the debates and literatures produced in the region that substantially pivots on the idea of 'egalitarianism' as a distinct feature of Pashtun borderland culture. As such, my approach is necessarily that of a historian, though with a keen interest in making conceptual advances.

Nonetheless, this article is not an immediate contribution to a theoretical debate in the academic field of geopolitics. Instead, it should be regarded as a part of the necessary groundwork for an eventual reconsideration of the implications of the approach presented here for prevalent geopolitics theory. Therefore, I will predominantly be concerned with primary literature historically produced in and around the region under review, rather than critically engaging with existing academic contributions. That, of course, is not to imply that I have deliberately decided to ignore existing scholarship. In particular, more recent historical works by authors like Robert Nichols and David B. Edwards are certainly conducive (see, e.g., Edwards 2002; Nichols 2001). Still, I am slightly suspicious that the bulk of the existing literature may have contributed to shaping the heavily security-oriented discourse on the borderland between today's Afghanistan and Pakistan, which, historiographically, is strongly informed by hegemonic archives, both pre-modern and more contemporary.[3] It appears therefore legitimate to go beyond the existing scholarship and, once again, engage with the texts produced by the 'borderland communities' themselves. As such, I aim at providing an alternative historical backdrop to that which has so far been prevalent, with which more theory-oriented or contemporaneous contributions in this special issue could be brought into meaningful conversation.

One of my primary arguments in this article is that the notion of egalitarianism is often used to categorize the historically evolved 'border-culture' of Pashtuns, especially taking into account their engagement with or sympathies for a number of religious movements in the past. In fact, the intersection of 'borderscape' and '(radical) egalitarianism,' producing what one may call 'border egalitarianism,' remains understudied, especially in a historical perspective. The majority of more recent deliberations put forward for discussion on the most relevant publication platforms[4] do not engage in a historical investigation into the origins and developments of egalitarian traits in borderland societies, while those that do seldom do so in much depth.[5] The present article therefore constitutes an experiment: by venturing seriously into the past I shall try to present in an (admittedly modified) *longue durée* perspective[6] – an alternative narrative of Pashtun 'border-culture,' one that revolves to a great extent around the notion of 'egalitarianism' (*musāwāt*, or *barābarī*) as its defining feature. Bringing the general discussion and the regional case study into dialogue, the overarching question for me in the following pages is whether or not 'egalitarianism' can – as suggested elsewhere (see, e.g., Eilenberg 2012, 28–29 and 61) – be considered as an essential feature of border cultures at all, and thus whether we can, indeed, theorize to inherent relationships between certain types of spaces and personal dispositions.

As a next step, I will indicate that the discursively constructed narrative of 'egalitarianism' has recently gained new momentum, which poses a new challenge to the established social fabric in the Pashtun-inhabited border. It will be argued that the various trajectories in the 'egalitarian' discourse, developed over time, became expanded beyond the socio-economic and political to the religious field, challenging the foundations of prevalent authority in this realm, and culminating in claims to the monopoly of definition in all religious matters by new actors.

Framing 'Radical Egalitarianism' as a Borderscape Feature

The concept of 'egalitarianism' in general, with or without any further attribution, belongs in the field of political philosophy, and as such it is heavily dependent on the anthropological premise of generic equality of all human beings. This axiomatic determination, however, is rooted entirely in beliefs, be they explicitly religious or pseudo-secular and is therefore by definition dogmatic: all humans, either by virtue of divine creation or the assumption of universal human rights, 'should get the same, or be treated the same, or be treated as equals, in some respect, (Arneson 2013, 1). From such a rather general framework scholars in the field have derived two chief notions of 'egalitarianism,' an instrumental and a non-instrumental one (see Arneson 2013, 2–3). The former is quite utilitarian insofar as it considers the moral imperative either an end or a means towards a greater good, usually the 'common good' of a given community or society. The non-instrumental form of 'egalitarianism' meanwhile posits 'equality' and its derivatives, such as 'justice,' as ends-in-themselves; in this regard, much reference is made to prominent theorists like John Rawls (1999, e.g. 3–46, 102–105, 347–396, and 506–514; Rawls 2001, 5–38).

In reality, however, both forms seem to overlap. While 'instrumental egalitarianism' is a dominant driving force of social movements that demand economic, social and political equality – very often manifest in a demand for independence from the hegemony of superstructures – it is the non-instrumental variety of egalitarianism that provides the argumentative framework by which such claims can be rationally maintained. It is this combination of both forms of 'egalitarianism' that shall be defined here as 'radical egalitarianism': a metaphysically sustained and thus all-encompassing socio-political agenda that aims at challenging any form of hegemony in human affairs.

The respective dynamics in the region between today's nation states of Afghanistan and Pakistan appear as a good example of this notion of 'radical egalitarianism.' In this region, the local constituents – real or imagined – are combined with trans-local anthropological concepts that are normatively rooted in Islamic precepts. This, of course, poses the question to what extent 'egalitarianism,' not to speak of its radical variety, is a constitutive feature of borderscapes, as oftentimes suggested. Eilenberg, for instance, speaks of 'social egalitarianism' as a 'central principle' of the Indonesian–Malaysian borderland of Borneo, defining it as 'everybody is equal to compete and follow economic opportunities as they appear' (Eilenberg 2012, 28). He locates the reason for its existence in the relatively low degree of social stratification of borderscape communities, and the communal recognition of 'various informal levels of status or class based on achievement and on an individual's personal ability to accumulate wealth' (Eilenberg 2012, 28). Indeed, the impassability of mountainous regions that have more often than not constituted frontiers of larger political entities – states or empires – appears to contribute significantly to the somewhat stubborn persistence of alternative forms of social, economic and political organization, which time and again have clashed violently with attempts to streamline them in the course of state- and empire-building.[7] Yet, we still need to be aware of the discursiveness of 'egalitarianism' here. After all, an appraisal of the realities in the region under consideration easily disenchants this egalitarian claim at least as a heavily gendered one. Thus, females are very much denied a voice in this discourse, not to speak of having significant agency at any time. They rather form a passive constituent in the male-dominated discourse, as most negotiations of values revolve around the necessity to preserve the honour – or in other words the moral integrity – of a community with regard to the ability of its male members to control the public exposure of females (see, e.g., Glatzer 1996; also Tapper 1991, 103–107, 142–149 and 207–239).

It is especially this gender aspect that indicates that any activism in the borderscape that is considered egalitarian usually goes hand in hand with processes of self-conceptualization and -affirmation, designed to assess whether and to what degree one needs to delineate the 'own' from 'alien,' and with potentially conflicting patterns of social and political organization, regarding which gendered rhetoric is no rarity (see, e.g., Glatzer 1996, 111–117). Such incongruities are highly complex, since they have mainly developed over longer periods and have therefore formed multi-layered encrustations. In addition, these processes of self-conceptualization and -affirmation are also informed by the attempts of states, political parties and ethnic movements to distinctly define and/or identify these border communities.[8]

Therefore, in an attempt to map the borderscape of/between today's two nation states Afghanistan and Pakistan as a distinct cultural entity, I deem it important to dig deeper into the various 'layers of time'[9] and to analytically separate indigenous structures from those that have penetrated the region over various periods and forced its people time and again to re-position themselves. As such, the present article contains an – in Foucauldian terms – 'archeology of borderscape,' focusing on 'egalitarianism' as a constitutive element in the discursive constructiveness of 'borderland' beyond its narrower definition as an entity of physical and political geography only. The regional example of the Pashtun-dominated areas around the current political border between Afghanistan and Pakistan may then inspire the consideration of 'egalitarianism' as a constitutive feature of 'borderland discourse' in other geographical and cultural contexts. Only following such a comparative approach, we may advance to a more theoretical level where we can reconsider whether the existing conceptions of 'borderland' in theories of geopolitics and beyond could – and perhaps should – be re-thought.

In the discussion that follows, I identify three different layers in time that inform the complex and multidimensional discourse regarding the predominantly Pashtun border between the contemporary nation states of Afghanistan and Pakistan. Each of these temporal layers' constitutive political, economic and socio-religious features will be highlighted to indicate the extent to which the actual context – always contingent on time and space – informs the overarching discourse on 'egalitarianism' as a defining feature of 'the Pashtun borderland.' Honesty, however, demands the acknowledgement that the historical research that recognizes literary production within the Pashtun communities, including localizing the contemporaneous source material, is still in its infancy, and much of the following remains necessarily tentative.

A Layer Deep Below: Negotiating the 'Own' and the 'Alien'

(a) *The Ethnic Denominator*

The first historical layer I identify is situated in the adversarial negotiation of the 'self' and the 'other' that has shaped the socio-political imaginary of today's border between Afghanistan and Pakistan. What is significant in this regard is the fact that this region has constituted the political frontier since the Mughal era. Accordingly, it has clearly contributed to the self-conceptionalization and -affirmation of its local people, *vis-à-vis* the various imperial powers for whom their mountainous territory proved to be a hard-to-navigate buffer zone. Leading personalities from the region have contributed to cement this image, one of them the celebrated Pashto poet and tribal chieftain Khūshḥāl Khān Khaṫṫak (d. 1100/1689), an officer with command over five thousand troops under the Mughal ruler Shāh Jahān.[10] Khūshḥāl's eventual unhappy change of fortune at the hands of the Mughals, which resulted in him becoming an ardent opponent of imperial policies in the region,[11] is indicative of the *divide et impere* politics of the Mughals, whereby alliances were forged and dissolved strategically and in view of Mughal interests only. On the other hand, Khūshḥāl's violent break with the Mughals ensued in the somewhat disproportionate appraisal of his wider significance by local Pashtun historians:[12] yet, with Khūshḥāl the establishment of a conscious 'own' that demands equality in opposition to the hegemony of powers alien in almost every regard gained a critical momentum, the ripples of which are still underlying the current manifestations of the 'egalitarian' discourse in the region.

However, the perception of a given situation as one of conflict between an 'own' and a radically different 'alien' usually requires a trigger. Initially the relationship of the tribal elites in the mountainous region that would much later form the borderscape between Afghanistan and Pakistan with the Mughals appeared rather harmonious. Thus, the alleged conferment of chieftaincy over the Khaṫṫak to Khūshḥāl's grandfather Malik Akoṛ Khān (assassinated 1008/1600) by Akbar, which is nowhere mentioned in the standard Mughal historiographies of that period,[13] somewhat epitomizes the notion of *sulḥ-i kull*, which is often romantically rendered as 'peace with all.' In reality, however, it indicates the pragmatic approach of the Mughal ruling establishment to governance: The Khaṫṫak tribe was a necessary ally for the Mughals in channelling the perpetual conflict with the Yūsufzəy into a regional one between rivalling Pashtun tribes, thus keeping conflict locally contained and away from the imperial centre that had meanwhile shifted to Lahore.

While Khūshḥāl was recognized by the Mughals, and aptly granted power and prestige, things were fine, thus purporting an illusion of equality between the Mughals and the Khaṫṫak chieftain.[14] Only when Awrangzīb rescinded his own father's earlier position towards Khūshḥāl did the latter – disgruntled by a treatment which he regarded unfair towards a faithful vassal[15] – break off all relations and establish the Mughals as first prototype of the ultimate 'Other': the oppressive and ethnically different city-dweller who, not least because of the features that define him, is no peer to the ability of the males in rural Pashtun communities to safeguard the chastity of their females and, thus, ensure the preservation of collective honour. Such a radically altered view on these grounds is, of course, a vivid indication of Khūshḥāl's rather naïve perception of the highly complex imperial politics of the Mughals, one that resonates in his versified understanding of the religious precepts which would ultimately feed into the concept of 'good governance' (*siyāsat sharʿiyyah*) (see Khaṫṫak 2001, 801–972 [*Faẕl'nāmah*]). The resulting, highly value-loaded binary of 'own' and 'alien,' however, provided the Pashtuns with a mighty stimulus for their self-affirmation, proven by the esteem that Khūshḥāl enjoys among them until today.

(b) *The Religious Denominator*

At around the same time we encounter yet another indigenous development, one that Khūshḥāl, in his privileged socio-political position, ostensibly ignored, but which adds an important flavour to the emerging discourse on 'egalitarianism' in the region: the so-called *Rawshāniyyah* movement of Bāyazīd ibn ʿAbdallāh Anṣārī, the 'Rawshān Pīr,' who died around the time when Khūshḥāl was just beginning to forge his allegiance with the Mughals. In the *Rawshāniyyah* we have a regional expression of egalitarian demands by a subaltern force that derived its legitimacy not, like Khūshḥāl and other tribal leaders, from the fulfilment of a privileged contract with another political force, but from a self-defined moral superiority, rooted very much in religious precepts. Bāyazīd's own life context seems to have greatly facilitated this.

Descending from the Barakī, or Ormuṛ tribe, Bāyazīd moved from his native Jālandhar in north-western Punjab to the ancestral territory of the Barakī in South Waziristan's Kānīguram, where his father had served as *qāẕī*.[16] Bāyazīd's religious orientation appears to have been quite literalist; even his take on Sufi spirituality was shaped by a stern anti-ritualistic sentiment that strikingly echoes the thoughts of the celebrated Naqshbandī *shaykh* Aḥmad Fārūqī Sirhindī (d. 1034/1624) at around the very same time, as titles of his works, such as the Persian *Ṣirāt-i Tawḥīd* and the Arabic *Maqṣūd al-Muʾminīn*, indicate.[17] Unlike a tribal notable such as Khūshḥāl Khān, the normativity of Bāyazīd's approach hardly allowed for pragmatic compromises with imperial ideologies; the strategically lesser importance of South Waziristan for the Mughals may well have contributed to the maintenance of Bāyazīd's uncompromising stance, which eventually resulted in open confrontation with the Mughal establishment.

In the case of Bāyazīd and his followers, it is important to recognize the opposing narratives of the activists themselves and of the Mughal centre, as these seem indicative of the asymmetries of mutual perception that carry well into the present. In the view of Mughal officials, namely, Bāyazīd was considered an 'Indian soldier' (*hindūstānī sipāhī*), who styled himself 'enlightened elder' (*pīr-i rawshānī*) and initiated among the Afghan tribesmen a 'sect of heresy and unbelief' (*maẕhab-i ilḥād wa zandaqah*) (Badāʾunī 2001, 243).[18] Elsewhere, his son and successor, Miyāṇ Jalāl al-Dīn (d. 1009/1601), was described as 'an Indian of little knowledge,' who is now known as 'Pīr of Darkness (Badā'unī 2001, 241).[19] It is perhaps revealing that the British, more than two centuries later, embraced this imperial imaginary, when the orientalist David Shea (d. 1836), in his synopsis of the relevant section of the *Dabistān-i Maẕāhib*, stated that 'at first a strict observer of Muhammedism, he [i.e. Bāyazīd] abandoned afterwards the exterior practices of this religion, and devoted his mind to contemplation (Shea and Troyer 1843, cxlvi).[20] In the *Dabistān-i Maẕāhib* itself, written in the mid-seventeenth century by an anonymous Zoroastrian author – although for a long time wrongly attributed to Muḥsin 'Fānī' Kashmīrī (d. 1081/1670) – a slightly more sympathetic image of Bāyazīd and his followers is conveyed; we shall return to this in due course. The portrayal by the Mughals and their imperial successors, however, served purposes of legitimization: on the basis of such assessments, the Mughals were entitled to persecute Bāyazīd and his followers, soon to be known as *Rawshāniyyah*, for their assumed insubordination as imperial troopers as well as for their deviation from what the centre proclaimed as sound and therefore officially valid religiosity.

Against such images stood the self-perception of Bāyazīd and the other Rawshānīs as upright defenders of a *sharī'a*-conformant religiosity, whose task – in conformity with the Qur'anic injunction of 'enjoining the commendable and preventing the reprehensible' (*al-amr bi'l-ma'rūf wa'l-nahy 'an al-munkar*)[21] – was to serve as admonishers to those who were not in full compliance, regardless of their respective social, economic or political status. It is therefore no surprise that, prior to military engagement, Bāyazīd had his *Ṣirāt-i Tawḥīd* – interestingly one of his still unpublished works – presented to Akbar, who he saw as deviating from this most crucial of all Islamic doctrines (see Ikrām 1967, 26).[22]

Crucial for an understanding of the egalitarian persuasion of the Rawshānīs is Bāyazīd's *Khayr al-Bayān*, presumably one, if not the, oldest extant Pashto text. Though a rather short text that revolves mainly around spiritual perfection in the footsteps of the Prophet (see Anṣārī n.d., 152–157, 209–211, and 359–360).[23] it carries a number of particularities that point towards a counter-hegemonic argument. First, its languages of composition are significant. Rather than subscribing to one of the imperial languages – Persian in the more mundane circles and Arabic in the religious ones – the *Khayr al-Bayān* appears in four languages, thus privileging colloquial ones, such as Pashto and Hindawī, as equal to Arabic and Persian.[24] Moreover, Bāyazīd stressed the superiority of spiritual advancement over social, political and economic status – here employing the Qur'anic terminology of 'riches [and progeny]' (*māl-mulk* [*wa awlād*]) – thus implying that spiritually accomplished subalterns are, in fact, superior to the holders of worldly power. The ultimate benchmark is the correspondence of individual piety and practice.[25]

Based on such messages of individual spiritual refinement, the *Rawshāniyyah* seemed to emulate – a least to an extent – the early Islamic notion of *futuwwa*, that is, a fraternity of chaste young men (*fityān*; sg. *fatá*) at the frontiers of the Muslim lands, who have vowed to protect these lands from any violation of their sovereignty, as well as from threats to its fidelity. These same fraternities, which soon tended to merge with Sufi communities as well as (albeit predominantly in the Ottoman context) professional guilds (see Taeschner 1979, 229–241 and 405–423),[26] were often seen by the political centres as a peril to wider communal harmony, their religious fervour leading them on occasion to drastic measures that were not in line with political and economic pragmatics. For the early *fityān* – the *jawān-mardān* of the Persianate world (see Taeschner 1979, 50–51) – such political manoeuvring was seen as somewhat compromising to the tenets of faith, according to which the divine revelation constitutes the sole supreme benchmark for all human endeavours.

Consequently, the Rawshānī message, carried mainly by subalterns, would soon be perceived as a threat to a variety of worldly hierarchies. While not yet resorting to militancy as a form of protest, they combined a rural version of piety, strongly shaped by individualistic and non-hierarchical notions of Sufism, with the righteousness of young men in opposition to what was seen as the concession of the tribal elders and religious dignitaries to the conveniences of worldly life, even if this lead to compromise of religiously sustained norms and values. This, in fact, resonates well with the *Ṭālibān* of the twentieth and twenty-first centuries, in whose case the generational conflict foreshadowed here gains momentum, as will be discussed further below.

For now, another line of conflict in the 'egalitarian' discourse in the Pashtun-inhabited borderscape shall be put under the spotlight: that between traditional forms of social and political authority in a tribally organized society, oftentimes bolstered by local forms of religious authority, and alternative subaltern conceptions which foreshadowed the developments to come. Here the earlier dichotomy of 'own' and 'alien' was applied to a moral review of the 'own,' enacting a renegotiation of what was to count as its basic norms and values, thus allowing, indeed necessitating the rejection of ideas and practices that existed within the 'own' but were now rendered 'alien' on moral grounds. Indeed, Khūshḥāl Khān and Bāyazīd Anṣārī could well be seen as representatives of the two opposing positions within Pashtun society: the one firmly established in the hereditary tribal leadership of the Khaṫṫak and therefore willing to pair up with other societal elites, the other with 'no respect for descent [*nisbat*], but only for knowledge and manners [*'ilm wa adab*]' (Anonymous 1877, 305), thus putting spirituality above worldly matters, as emphasized by the Prophet Muḥammad: 'Verily, God does not regard your forms, nor does He regard your wealth, but He regards your hearts and your actions' (Anonymous 1877, 307–308).[27] As a matter of fact, the benchmark of religious precepts for the evaluation of all human endeavour is rooted in a worldview that claims universal validity and must therefore transcend regionally confined cultural specifics. From such a perspective, those specifics need to integrate themselves within such a normative framework; where they appear irreconcilable they need to be eradicated.

(c) *The Significance of the Rural Setting*

Rurality plays a significant role in this dynamic, since such a sustained deep suspicion in the prevalent socio-economic and political frameworks seems to thrive exceptionally well in the rural setting.[28] Usually seen as a stable reservoir of traditional values, it stands in stark contrast to effervescent urbanity, where the ability to adapt to temporary fashions assumes priority over stability in all walks of life. Not just by accident did the *Ṭālibān* during their reign over Afghanistan appear deeply apprehensive of the 'den of iniquity' of Kabul, perhaps best epitomized in the anxious concerns of their first supreme commander Mullā Muḥammad ʿUmar (d. *c.* 1434/2013; see, for example, Rashid 2008, 54)[29] that made him ever reluctant to enter the city. Besides the emphasis on stability in a rural setting, another extremely important factor here is economic deprivation and resulting subaltern 'theologies of liberation.'[30]

Here it was not only the political hegemonies held by forces from outside the region and those from among the Pashtun who were perceived as their wilful stooges came under fire, but increasingly also the local social, political and economic elites, subsumed under the term *mashar* (lit.: senior).[31] While the opposition against alien political hegemony was oftentimes rooted in regionally and even ethnically confined frameworks, as the example of Khūshḥāl Khān Khaṫṫak indicates, the next discursive layer under investigation introduces a new frontline: no longer between the 'own' and the 'alien,' but between the *masharān* and *kasharān* (lit.: juniors; i.e. 'political "have-nots"') (see Ahmed 1980, 144) within the 'own.' When exactly this new discursive layer emerged is difficult to tell. However, Pashto folk literature, prominently including poetry and also jokes, suggests that a sensitivity for economic and, subsequently, social and political injustices within the Pashtun communities was developed from quite an early point in time.[32] I would nonetheless argue that geopolitical developments since the nineteenth century have contributed significantly to the intensification of an increasingly antagonistic relationship between *masharān* and *kasharān*: since the Great Game the former faced being drawn into the spheres of influence of the imperialist powers as those powers sought to serve their own ends,[33] and this irreversibly changed the fabric of the Pashtun-dominated borderscape. *Masharān*, like Khūshḥāl Khān Khaṫṫak when he collaborated with the Mughals, would now be regarded as 'alien' to the increasingly romanticized egalitarianism of Pashtun society – the later *Rawshāniyyah* are a case in point here[34] – and could thus be legitimately opposed from within.

However, as the frame of reference became increasingly global since the Great Game, in attempting to defend the changing role of the *masharān* as necessitated by an ever changing and increasingly interconnected world, the *kasharān* had to develop a narrative that would befit the changed geopolitical landscape of the nineteenth and early twentieth century equally well. While an attraction to anti-imperialist Marxist models of explanation was clearly discernible also in the Pashtun-inhabited borderscape (see, e.g., Caron 2016, 135 and 145–148) in the context under review here, it was above all 'Islam' that had to provide a backdrop against which 'liberation theologies' – including Marxism in its many varieties – could eventually be conceptualized.

Those 'theologies,' in turn, would have to claim similar universal validity; because of this there was no obvious need for them to originate from within a specific local context. In fact, an extra-regional provenance was even preferable, as this might help to sharpen one's sense of prevalent iniquities within one's own local community. This was the situation when, around World War I, an egalitarian – although not yet radical – message of some leading Deobandī scholars and students arrived in the Pashtun-inhabited borderscape, subsequently shaping the socio-religious borderscape irreversibly. The Deobandī mission in this Pashtun-inhabited region was much linked to the specific understanding of the 'Deobandī project' by the somewhat elusive Maḥmūd al-Ḥasan (d. 1339/1920), better known by his honorific 'Shaykh al-Hind,' that appeared to connect very well with traditional notions of anti-authoritarianism in the region, and was perhaps for that reason markedly successful in the long term.

A Further Layer: Embracing the Message of Equality

Institutional folklore regards Maḥmūd al-Ḥasan as the first graduate of the *Dār al-ʿUlūm* in Deoband, a small market town about a hundred miles north of Delhi.[35] A student of the two founding figures Muḥammad Qāsim Nānawtawī (d. 1297/1880) and Rashīd Aḥmad Gangohī (d. 1323/1905), as well as a Sufi disciple of ʿImdādallāh Thanawī, better known as 'Muḥājir Makkī' (d. 1317/1899), Maḥmūd became an ardent advocate of Muslim egalitarianism that stood somewhat counter to the *ashrāf*-centrism of reformist educationists and politicians like Sir Sayyid Aḥmad Khān (d. 1315/1898) in early British India.[36] The underlying plea for social and political activism alienated Maḥmūd al-Ḥasan and many of his students from others in the upper echelons of the institution at Deoband, and their activities therefore became increasingly distant from it.

Maḥmūd al-Ḥasan's understanding of egalitarianism was, like that of the above discussed Bāyazīd Anṣārī, grounded in a normative religious framework that was to be granted a higher degree of authority then anthropocentric pragmatics. Likewise, Maḥmūd al-Ḥasan derived his respective views from the many clear Qur'anic injunctions that emphasize piety over progeny and worldly possessions, and shift the focus from the here-and-now to salvation in the Hereafter as the supreme objective of any human existence.[37] The resulting disposition of such a worldview would culminate in what I have elsewhere labelled 'Islamic pietism': an other-worldly orientation that in this world translates into active community service without any constraint with regard to variant social, political and economic status, understood as an integral aspect of Muslim worship (see Hartung 2016a, 359–361). The metaphysical foundations of such a worldview has significant socio-political consequences: 'community' is not determined by territorial or ethnic belonging, but by adherence to an universalistic ethos, that is, by granting a deliberately adopted inner disposition a higher value than external factors that are usually beyond the control of an individual. As a result, indigenous norms and value are uncompromisingly put to the test and, being measured against the benchmark of their universalistic counterparts, are either affirmed as being in accordance therewith or rejected if deemed to conflict.

What was triggered by the Deobandī mission into the rural and peripheral regions of the British Raj, under the aegis of Maḥmūd al-Ḥasan, was no less than a conflict between a normative universalistic framework based on divine revelation and its regionalist counterpart, shaped by locally and ethnically defined traditions. This conflict, initially only *in posse*, would over time increasingly materialize and embrace the earlier rhetoric of 'own' and 'alien' – now framed as 'Muslims' versus 'English Christians' – as a rationale for homegrown opposition to what is framed as a disruptive foreign body that seeks to distort essentialized local customs and traditions.[38] While this certainly resonates with Partha Chatterjee's famous notion of the 'rule of (colonial) difference' (see Chatterjee 1993, 18–24), it should not be understood as an endorsement of this theoretical frame that has rightly been solidly criticized in recent times (see Chibber 2013). Rather, Muslim axiomatic superiority was derived from normative injunctions as well as the classical Islamic historiographical tradition;[39] its application in the colonial context was thus rather circumstantial. By employing the dichotomy of 'Muslim vs. non-Muslim' instead of 'own vs. alien' in the borderscape, however, the task emerged to define what makes a 'Muslim' proper. It is, in fact, this very tension between universalistic and local notions of 'Islam' that have shaped the Pashtun borderscape ever since.

Problematic in this context was – and still is – the fact that major impulses for defining 'Islamicity' came more often than not from outside the Pashtuninhabited borderscape, with variant degrees of success. The Deobandī excursion into the region appears to have been a more fruitful one, paying more heed to the importance of acknowledging local customs as Islamically inoffensive (see Hartung 2016a, 356–359). Earlier attempts had turned out to be more disruptive: already in the first decades of the nineteenth century the region came under the influence of the so-called *Ṭarīqah-yi Muḥammadiyyah*, with its roots in imperial Delhi and the plains of Awadh. In view of the general suspicion towards the ever-changing agendas of outsiders, Mahdist pretensions appear to have been consciously employed by the leading figures of this movement, Shāh Ismāʿīl of Delhi and Sayyid Aḥmad of Rāʾe Baraylī (both killed 1246/1831), as a sustainable 'sales proposition' (see Gaborieau 2010)[40]: it situated a concrete pietistic movement with clearly discernible local roots within a wider hiero-historical narrative[41] in which marginalized regions become elevated to points of departure for a cosmic battle between good and evil at the End of Times, manifest in rather contextualized political constellations.[42] On the other hand, however, both leaders of the movement came down rather harshly on many of the customs of their Pashtun allies, declaring them bluntly as contraventions of the *sharīʿa*, and thus ultimately alienating them (see Qadir 2015, 108–110).[43]

The fruitfulness of messianic rhetoric for popular mobilization[44] in the Pashtun-inhabited borderscape at grassroots level, however, had already been demonstrated by the *Rawshāniyyah* movement of the sixteenth century (see Malik 1993).[45] In an oft-repeated pattern, popular mobilization centred around an already charismatic figure, whose authority was boosted by the posthumous ascription of eschatological significance, and subsequently became routinized and frequently even hereditary. According to social anthropologist Anthony Wallace, the notion of 'charisma,' be it actual or institutionalized by routinization,[46] serves as a prime mover for socio-political activism (see Wallace 1956, 267, 270 and 273) and has therefore proven itself a powerful formula for mobilization especially in underprivileged rural communities. In this regard it may be observed how such inspired agendas were able to fall back rather easily on regionally dominant forms of communal authority, such as shrines, *khānaqāh*s and local mosques. This has certainly been the case with the Deobandī mission in the Pashtun-inhabited borderscape, as is amply indicated by the strategic alliance of Maḥmūd al-Ḥasan's chief deputy in the region, Faẓl Waḥīd of Turangzəy, better known as 'Ḥājjī Ṣāḥib Turangzəy' (d. 1356/1937), with important communal leaders on the ground.[47] Such a forging of strategic alliances between those from outside the region with local authorities was not confined to the borderscape; similar bonds were also established between the Deobandīs around Maḥmūd al-Ḥasan and leading Sufis in Sindh, prominent amongst them the Pīr Pagaṛo of Pīr Jo Goṭh (see Hartung 2016a, 356).

Personal charisma also played a significant role in yet another – this time purely indigenous – movement in the borderscape at more or less the same time that the Pashtun Deobandī deputies of Maḥmūd al-Ḥasan were spreading their egalitarian mission in the region. This was the movement led by Mīrzā ʿAlī Khān of the Torī Khel of North Waziristan, better known as the 'Īpī Faqīr' (d. 1379/1960). (On his biography, see Warren 2000, 84–85.) He and his followers, adherents of a religiously grounded radical socio-political egalitarianism, confronted both the British colonial establishment and the nation-building efforts of the Afghan ruling house of the Barakzəy.

Whether or not the confrontation between the followers of the Īpī Faqīr from among the Utmānzəy Wazīr and the Afghan royal forces in February and March 1933 in Khost (see Warren 2000, 66–68).[48] was actually a success for the former does not concern us here. Rather much more relevant in the context of the present discussion is its constituting an example of the general suspicion among the rural tribesmen in the Pashtun-inhabited borderscape of political hegemony of any kind.

Indigenous threads of egalitarian resistance to any kind of super-structure, like the movement led by the Īpī Faqīr, appeared to combine both forms of 'egalitarianism.' In its non-instrumental variety, it used universalistic religious precepts, just as the *Rawshāniyyah* had done some centuries earlier. In doing so, it joined hands with those efforts that permeated the region from the direction of Deoband at around the time of the first World War. However, being rooted in the specific socio-political environment of the borderscape and articulating egalitarian claims from the subaltern strata of Pashtun society, it clearly has also an instrumental aspect to it also.[49] Demanding equality in social, economic and political areas, based nonetheless on absolute and non-negotiable premises, changed the constitution of the borderscape irreversibly: it begot – as the newly reinforced prototype of the agent of change – the young subaltern religious warrior, with 'nothing to lose but his chains,'[50] who would form the vital base of the *Ṭālibān* movement to come.

A Layer of Radicalization: Step Aside, Old Man

The promulgation of an increasingly radical egalitarianism by the Deobandī missionaries turned out to be a double-edged sword, its repercussions very much noticeable in contemporary developments, developments that were certainly not anticipated nor necessarily aspired to by the 'Shaykh al-Hind' and his associates, or even the indigenous mobilizers like the Īpī Faqīr.

While namely the Deobandī mission in the Pashtun Belt and its eventual institutionalization throughout the region provided a firm framework for challenging traditional socio-political and economic authorities – their archetype being the so-called *khān*-ethics – increasingly the religious authority of the *akābīr*, including the Deobandī ones, also came under fire from an upcoming generation of students, or 'ṭālibān.'

Once again, one is reminded of the various constituents of the early Islamic *futuwwāt*, prominent amongst which youth and uncompromising fervour. 'Youth' here becomes an *epitomé* of innocence and humility, of purity from the stains of corruption by power and vain self-aggrandizement (see Taeschner 1979, 43–52). The literary trope of the 'ṭālib,' which gained a boost in prominence with the first publication of the romantic folktale of Ṭālib Jān and Gul Basharah around 1940 (see Nūrī 1318h, 235–271),[51] has recently been diligently analysed by James Caron. He emphasizes the image of 'a fluid masculine youth counterculture standing in opposition to the rigid voice of sober authority' (Caron 2012, 69) which seems to have had a considerable impact on the emergence of the actual *Ṭālibān* of the 1990s. What needs to be further investigated here, however, are the notions of 'fluid masculine youth counterculture' *vis-à-vis* 'sober authority,' as the latter especially may be subject to some contention. After all, we need to be clear whose authority is being challenged here and why; this then needs to be translated into the concrete contemporary context. Indeed, the 'ṭālib' of the folk romance does not so much stand out for erudite religious and worldly oriented knowledge, but for a certain ethical disposition that presents itself in distinct patterns of conduct. He is the uncompromising idealist, living very much in perception of this world as one to overcome in order to attain eternal bliss in the Hereafter; his opponent must therefore epitomize all that he does not stand for: social and political pragmatism, which more often than not means compromise, and this world as the primary reference point.

The embodiment of the morally upright and salvation-focused youth and the power-wielding landowner, or *malik*, which in the folk romance takes the shapes of Ṭālib Jān *vis-à-vis* Gul Basharah's father, is somewhat reproduced in the founding narrative of the *Ṭālibān* movement of the 1990s: after all, it was the outrage of upright and courageous young men around Mullā Muḥammad ʿUmar regarding frequent abuses of power by landowners and warlords in Southern Afghanistan that caused the movement to emerge (see Zaeef 2010, 59–65). Furthermore, the contrasting images of the 'ṭālib' on one hand, and the 'khān' and 'malik' – informally subsumed under the category of 'mashar' (see Ahmed 1980, 141–142) – on the other refer us back to the dichotomy of rurality versus urbanity. The archetype of 'ṭālib' also represents a romantically glorified imaginary of traditional nomadic mobility, which allows for social stratification only as far as division of labour is concerned. The archetype of 'khān' meanwhile serves as the counter-image of sedentary life which, in its worst manifestation, takes urban forms. In reality, however, both imaginaries of course appear as highly idealized, yet they are still powerful enough to shape collective perceptions and societal discourse.

While the conflict epitomized in the tropes of 'ṭālib' and 'khān/malik' as outlined so far refers to the challenges of indigenous social, economic and political structures from within Pashtun society, which received copious fuel from the egalitarian legacy of the *Ṭarīqah-yi Muḥammadiyyah* and the

Deobandī mission in the region, in more recent times, too, the authority of those learned in the religious sciences, including Deobandīs, came under scrutiny. In fact, I would argue that the strong plea for egalitarianism in the mission of the 'Shaykh al-Hind' Maḥmūd al-Ḥasan especially was expanded by more recent actors beyond the social, economic and political realms, beginning also to demand equality in the definition and administration of religious affairs. A new emphasis, however, was the relegation of extended religious education, with all of its social implications, to a lesser significance, a development that has various antecedents in other parts of the Muslim world.[52] The attitude of the younger generations of *ṭālibān* towards religious education – the oftentimes romanticized '*jihād* of the pen' – has increasingly become a sceptical one, and has as a result also begun to challenge the authority of the Deobandī learned establishment in the region and beyond. As case in point here might be Nek Muḥammad Wazīr (killed 1425/2004), one of the thriving forces behind the eventual formation of a *Ṭālibān* chapter in Pakistan (*Taḥrīk-i Ṭālibān-i Pākistān*, TṬP), who had started to study with Mawlānā Nūr Muḥammad Wazīr (killed 1431/2010), he in turn a student of the Deobandī scholar and long-term JUI president Muftī Maḥmūd (d. 1400/1980) at the *Dār al-ʿUlūm Wazīristān*, established in 1962.[53]

Reportedly, Nek Muḥammad, who is said to have stood out for his attitude of impatience and insubordination, left the school without completing his course of study;[54] other ventures into the field of education also remained incomplete. Instead, he established closer acquaintance with Muḥammad Gul, allegedly of the Kharoṭī tribe in Southern Afghanistan and a longstanding confidant of Mullā ʿUmar, who was running a recruitment operation out of the Zār-i Nūr refugee camp near Wānā. The years of the *Islamic Emirate of Afghanistan* saw the rise of Nek Muḥammad as a *Ṭālibān* military commander over increasingly larger contingents of troops at the Qarghah water reservoir of Kabul. During this time, he was openly exposed to almost all the leading representatives of international Islamic militancy that had assembled in the Emirate. In early 2002, when the US-led military operations in Afghanistan ended *Ṭālibān* rule, he finally organized the retreat of the international militants from Afghanistan to Pakistan's Federally and Provincially Administered Tribal Areas (FATA and PATA) and in so doing established himself as a leading authority in South Waziristan and beyond. This authority remained little contested until, on 18 June 2004, Nek Muḥammad was killed in the very missile attack that is said to have inaugurated Pakistan-sanctioned American drone operations in the area.

One further important dimension of the challenge posed to the *masharān* and the structures they represent lies in what can well be regarded a moderate empowerment of rural Pashtun women. Given the reported misogynic attitudes of the *Ṭālibān* on either side of the national border between Afghanistan and Pakistan, this may come as a surprise. Moreover, the

Ṭālibān affirmed the gender divide in Pashtun society as far as the role of females in the public spaces is concerned.[55] Yet, against the traditional deprivation of women even of basic education, TṬP activists stressed the religious duty of acquiring (mainly religious) knowledge for all believers regardless their sex. Thus, while the spatial segregation of women was well maintained, leading TṬP activists, here first and foremost Mullā Faẕl Ḥayāt ibn Biladār Khān, a.k.a. Mawlānā Faẕlallāh (b. 1394/1974), from Swat, utilized new media to impart education to females. Pashtun women in rural areas stated that they used to regularly listen to Faẕlallāh's radio broadcasts that began in 2006 and earned him the nickname 'Mullā Radio.' Indeed, Faẕlallāh, who would later become commander-in-chief of the TṬP, spoke out from an Islamic legal perspective against domestic violence, to which many women in the region were subjected. Consequently, many women stated that they initially felt quite empowered by the broadcasts, leading them to lend massive financial support to Faẕlallāh for the construction of a mosque and *madrasah* in his native Mām Ḋherī – Islamically renamed by him as 'Imām Ḋherī' – near Mīngorah in Swat (see Rafi 2016, 26; also, see Yousafzai 2014, 91–97). It was only after Faẕlallāh's broadcasts became more militant in the wake of the siege of Islamabad's *Red Mosque* (*Lāl Masjid*) in July 2007 that women would withdraw their material and spiritual support. The subsequent establishment of harsh TṬP rule in Swat, ended only by a massive intervention by Pakistani armed forces under the code-name 'Operation *Rāh-i Rast*' during much of 2009, was a major setback to women who were unmistakably put in their place. This was perhaps nowhere more explicitly expressed than when Faẕlallāh declared them ineligible to participate in political activities, such as voting, reportedly also announcing severe punishments for any who violated this decree, which he claimed was based on traditional custom (*dod*). Such curtailment of women's spheres of activity would soon expand to public education, eventually leading to the failed assassination attempt on young women's rights activist and Nobel laureate Malālah Yūsufzəy (b. 1418/1997) on 9 October 2012 (see Yousafzai 2014, 190–203; also Rafi 2016, 52, 57 and 61).

Despite the eventual relapse into misogynic patterns as soon as he assumed charge, Faẕlallāh, like Nek Muḥammad, can be viewed as an exemplary model for the young generation of religiously inspired activist Pashtun males, whose challenge to prevalent authority structures does not stop at the social, economic and political level, but targets also any religious authority, including even the Deobandī reformism in the wake of the efforts of Maḥmūd al-Ḥasan and his associates in the early decades of the twentieth century. Originating from families with very restricted economic means and low social status, the very fact of the rise of both Nek Muḥammad and Faẕlallāh to eminence in the region, oftentimes through militant means, indicates the failure of traditional socio-political stratification and tribal administration, insofar as their ascent to prominence can be interpreted as a deliberate affront to the *masharān*, that is, the *malik*s and *khān*s.[56]

In addition, Nek Muḥammad's success despite an incomplete religious education indicates a departure from the Deobandī tradition of learning, not least from the absolute obedience to the teaching authority enshrined in the legal procedure of *taqlīd-i shakhṣī*.[57] Instead, Nek Muḥammad pursued radical ideas of independent interpretation (*ijtihād*) that had trickled into the region mainly through radicalized Muslim activists from Arab countries. Usually considered a component specifically of legal decision-making, the notion of *ijtihād* in the circles of Nek Muḥammad and his like appears to have become almost entirely detached from this limitation and expanded in meaning to sanction self-confident independent decision-making in whatever domain, under the premise that all these decisions should be in correspondence with the requirements of the *sharīʿa*. Such views have been further strengthened through their enthusiastic reception by militant Muslim circles in Central Asia and the Caucasus region, many of whom have meanwhile declared their allegiance to the still somewhat thriving *Dawla Islāmiyya* (IS) under the leadership of Abū Bakr al-Baghdādī (b. 1391/1971).[58]

Historically, all the canonical legal orientations (*madhāhib fiqhiyya*) agreed that *ijtihād* was not to be practiced by everybody (see Hallaq 1984, 6–7). Even the most ardent advocates of *ijtihād*, like the celebrated Yemenite jurist and traditionarian Muḥammad ibn ʿAlī al-Shawkānī (d. 1250/1839), were opposed to what he called 'individual reasoning' (*ijtihād al-raʾy*), practiced by those who do not qualify as scholars (see Peters 1980, 138–140 and 142–143). Shawkānī's radical position against *taqlīd*, in turn, became the dominant viewpoint of the *Ahl-i Ḥadīs̱*,[59] a movement against whose views early Deobandīs, prominently among them Maḥmūd al-Ḥasan, had explicitly positioned themselves.[60] The stance of the *Ahl-i Ḥadīs̱*, in turn, moved them very close to the official interpretation of Islam in the Kingdom of Saudi Arabia, that is, that of the *Wahhābiyya*.[61] Here we come full circle, as radical manifestations of the Wahhābī interpretation of Islam constitute an important undercurrent in those contemporary militant Muslim circles to which Nek Muḥammad and those in his wake have developed a close affinity.

In fact, in the oftentimes quite heated debates on *sharīʿa*-related matters within the movement that, since the late 1930s, has prominently been referred to as the 'neo-Ḥanbaliyya' – that is, a radical theological and subsequently judicial reformulation that is traced back to Taqī al-Dīn ibn Taymiyya (d. 728/1328) and his master student Ibn Qayyim al-Jawziyya (d. 751/1931) in thirteenth century Damascus[62] – various Muslim theorists have argued for the permissibility of *ijtihād* by those who do not formally qualify as *ʿulamāʾ*. While they all still stress that profound religious knowledge is an inevitable precondition, they appear to have a rather ambiguous understanding of what would qualify as 'religious knowledge.'[63] The smallest common denominator would be familiarity with the Qur'an and the Prophetic *ḥadīth*; the proposed indicator here is in many cases the amount of memorized text from these two primary sources, for which a formal religious training under guidance is not necessarily required. Increasingly, however, this is supplemented with the ability to properly assess the respective actual circumstances to which a certain legal problem relates (*fiqh al-wāqiʿ*) (see Nedza 2016, 241–245).

While the debates over such rather technical legal matters seem rather irrelevant from a geopolitical perspective, this impression is somewhat deceptive. After all, such a discourse informs us of the conditions on the ground that are oftentimes overlooked in frameworks that consider large and abstract entities, such as states, as the principle actors. In fact, I argue here that what links such ostensibly remote debates to geopolitical issues is recent and constantly evolving access to communication technologies. Indeed, the control of these technologies turns out to be yet another opportunity for the younger generations of militant Muslim activists in the borderscape to establish their supremacy over the traditional elites. This – and here we encounter a decisive leap – it is not confined to the Pashtun context anymore, but appears to be a global trend in the current generational conflict that, moreover, seems to compute well with notions of 'youth (counter-) culture.' After all, in a world that has become ever more complex and technology-driven, an ability to properly assess the current situation – the *fiqh al-wāqiʿ* – presupposes the capacity to handle new electronic media and the corresponding technological tools.

The relationship between age and mastery of rapidly reinvigorating new technologies is at the core of the Sociology of Technology, a rather young field of sociological enquiry. However, so far most studies are focused on highly industrialized societies in Europe and North America, and new technologies – especially in the field of communications – are also seen as a support for the elderly, not in the first place as a means to delineate biological generations from each other.[64] At any rate, this very issue becomes even more virulent in rural and so-far rather low-tech societies, in which the geographical scope of unmediated communication was until recently fairly restricted. In Pakistan, for example, mobile telecommunication was not widespread before the introduction of the *Mobile Cellular Policy* of January 2004 and the *Broadband Policy* of December of the same year by the Pakistani *Ministry of Information Technology*; in Afghanistan, the situation was similar prior to the interim government of Ḥāmid Karzəy (b. 1957) taking office in Kabul in the summer of 2002. Before cellular telecommunications and portable internet devices became a regular feature almost everywhere on the globe, the former existed only in form of satellite phones, provided to *mujāhidīn* field commanders in combat with the Soviet army mainly by their Western military supporters-cum-advisors. Moreover, smartphones, which combine telephony and computing, did not reach a mass audience before the introduction of the GMS BlackBerry in 2003 and then, more emphatically, of the iPhone in 2007.

It is during these years that the communication behaviour of militant Islamists has significantly shifted from cheap print media to electronic publishing, thus strategically impacting geopolitical discourse. Its pinnacle so far has been the elaborate media work of the IS, with the *Markaz al-Ḥayāt li'l-I'lām*, or *al-Hayat Media Centre*, at its pivot, and the various and ever-growing number of so-called 'social media' at the disposal of IS activists. Other movements have attempted to establish a similar internet presence, but fall clearly short in comparison;[65] even its prototype, the *Mu'assasat al-Saḥāb li'l-Intāj al-'Ilāmī* of *al-Qā'ida*, established in 2001, pales in comparison. It is the imaginary of omnipresence of the IS that suggests superior authority in religious matters to such an extent that now more established patterns of authority formation in the borderscape between the contemporary nation-states Afghanistan and Pakistan are beginning to crumble. Thus, the authority of Deobandī scholars and their emphasis on religious learning was brushed aside by a young generation of Islamist activists who regarded courage and self-sacrifice in what they considered the defence of Islam as of higher value than bookish knowledge. In any way, this is not the end of the story. A so far final layer in the discursive formation around 'egalitarianism' in the Pashtun-inhabited borderscape emerged when a split occurred within the TṬP on the question whether or not they should now submit themselves to the authority of Abū Bakr al-Baghdādī in place of Mullā 'Umar or his successors. Here, then, the conflict is not anymore between old and young in the religious realm, but between radical activists of more or less equal age.

The Ultimate Layer: Challenges Among the Radicals

The long-standing factionalism within the TṬP became irreconcilably manifest when a group of TṬP activists under the leadership of Ḥāfiẓ Sa'īd Khān of the Orakzəy, who was killed in a bomb blast less than four months later, and 'Abd al-Ra'ūf Khādim Abū Ṭalḥah, who died two months earlier than that in an US airstrike, established the so-called *shūrá* for 'Khurasan,' following their alleged pledge of allegiance (*bay'a*) to al-Baghdādī (al-'Adnānī 2015). Their rationale for defection from the *Ṭālibān* followed a similar logic as that of the IMU in September 2014: Mullā Muḥammad 'Umar, to whom they had all pledged their allegiance at the outset, had neither been physically seen nor had he directly communicated for over a year, leading to the suspicion that he might in fact be dead and the *Ṭālibān* thus without a leader. In this regard the IMU ideologue Asadulloh Urganchiy, then based in the Fāryāb province of Northern Afghanistan,[66] has claimed that the maintenance of allegiance to Mullā ʿUmar, despite his physical absence, would be in contradiction to the *sharīʿa*.[67]

The toponym for the *shūrá* is of quite some interest and has recently given rise to numerous speculations regarding what it might signify. Some have argued that it refers to a Prophetic *ḥadīth* which foretells the advance of an army from Khurasan towards Jerusalem in the days of the Final Battles with the Dajjāl before the Judgement commences.[68] This view certainly carries some weight, bearing in mind the significance of this *ḥadīth* during the so-called 'Abbasid Revolution' in the late eighth century CE, and in turn the conscious embrace of such 'Abbasid symbolism by Abū Bakr al-Baghdādī.'[69] In this context, the establishment of a *shūrá* for Khurasan would clearly point towards the significance of the region for the establishment of the 'sound' caliphate of the 'chosen one from the House of the Prophet' (*al-riḍā min āl Muḥammad*) (see Crone 1989) and its focus of allegiance, which would be clearly towards the Arab Middle East, not to the region between (that is, Imāmī Shiite Iran), and of Afghanistan and Pakistan. There is, however, an alternative interpretation that ties the 'Khurasan *shūrá*' more into the local context: it is quite conceivable that the trope of 'Khurasan' was adopted in reminiscence of the claims of the leaders of the *Ṭarīqah-yi Muḥammadiyyah* in the 1820s to establish their sovereignty over a territory that encompasses the lands from Western Afghanistan to the Indus river in the East, and from the Āmūdaryā river and Kashmir in the North to the Arabian Sea in the South (see Gaborieau 2010, 189). This area coincided to quite an extent with the notion of 'Yāghistān' to which Sayyid Aḥmad of Rāʾe Baraylī referred in his letter to the *amīr* of Bukhara Ḥaydar Tūrah ibn Shāh Murād (r. 1800–26), in which he requested official recognition as *imām* for the region (see Gaborieau 1996, 273–277). Not surprisingly, the notion of 'Yāghistān' was appropriated again by the revolutionary Deobandīs who spread their message on behalf of the 'Shaykh al-Hind' Maḥmūd al-Ḥasan.

If the renegade *Ṭālibān* in fact had this context in mind when establishing a 'Khurasan *shūrá*' under the umbrella of the IS, then this strategic move has a much more pointed significance for the region: it would then seriously challenge the *sharīʿa*-conformity of all those in the region of the two nation-states Afghanistan and Pakistan who continued, despite his elusiveness, to submit themselves to Mullā Muḥammad ʿUmar. Similar to the challenges that the *Ṭālibān*, especially in their entanglement with various forces that did not originate in the region, had posed to the Deobandīs there, the 'Khurasan *shūrá*,' under the strong influence of the massive media presence of the IS, was now challenging the *Ṭālibān*'s religious and political authority. Unsurprisingly, the *Ṭālibān* reacted strongly to what they saw as sowing dissent within the community of upright believers: in an official address to Abū Bakr al-Baghdādī on 16 June 2015, the then deputy commander-in-chief (*nāʾib*) and chairman of the Central Council (*da rahbarī shūrá sarʾparast*)

Mullā Akhtar Muḥammad Manṣūr (killed 1437/2016) warned the IS leader that 'meddling in the affairs [of the *mujāhidīn*] creates division [*ikhtilāf*],' and that 'in order to defend its achievements [*mawqif*] the Islamic Emirate will be forced to react.' 'The multiplicity of views concerning *jihād*,' he stated 'is conducive [*maṣāliḥo*] neither for *jihād*, nor for the *mujāhidīn* or Islam.'[70] This official memorandum was preceded by al-Baghdādī's reported own attempts a few months earlier – almost coinciding with the establishment of the 'Khurasan *shūrá*' – when he labelled Mullā ʿUmar 'an idiot [*maʿtūh*] and ignorant warlord [*amīr ḥarb jāhil*]' who 'does not deserve any spiritual or political credibility [*ayy miṣdāqiyya rūḥiyya aw siyāsiyya*]' (Anonymous 2015).[71]

Already a month before the official memorandum issued by the *Islamic Emirate*, the TṬP activist Abū ʿUs̲mān Salārzəy published an almost 60-page refutation of al-Baghdādī's claims of caliphate both in Pashto and Arabic on the TṬP official website (Salārzaʾī 1436/2015).[72] In this treatise, Salārzəy presents twenty-two arguments against the validity of al-Baghdādī's caliphate; unlike the latter, he does not condescend to mere polemics, but bolsters his arguments by a recourse to a vast array of works from across the Islamic scholarly tradition. The backdrop of his discussion is the contentions over the caliphate between Muʿāwiya ibn Abī Sufyān and the Prophet's son-in-law ʿAlī ibn Abī Ṭālib during the first Islamic *fitna*, used as an analogy to the controversy between al-Baghdādī and the late Mullā Muḥammad ʿUmar.

His references are certainly remarkable here, as they appear rather eclectic at first sight, ranging from classical Arabic historiographies and works on *ḥadīth*, *fiqh* and *kalām*, to works of more contemporary Islamists of various regional backgrounds. Given the task that he has set himself, and the fact that al-Baghdādī clearly enjoys considerable support throughout the Muslim world, Salārzəy's references serve as an indication that his arguments can be sustained by a consensus (*ijmāʿ*) of the scholarly community across time, space and even dogmatic disparity. However, his most weighty references are those authors whose thought also forms the backbone of the religious universe of the IS, especially medieval Ḥanbalī scholars like Ibn Qudāma (d. 620/1223) and Ibn Taymiyya, and beacons of later critical *ḥadīth* scholarship, like the above mentioned al-Shawkānī and Ṣiddīq Ḥasan Khān Qannawjī (d. 1307/1890).[73] Moreover, with regard to Salārzəy's hermeneutics and how he positions himself as a scholar, he appears to be entirely detached from the *taqlīd shakhṣī* that characterizes the Deobandī approach, and therefore also that of the *akābīr* of those institutions that are usually regarded as 'producers' of the *Ṭālibān*. He confidently roams through the classical Islamic literature, but includes also luminous more contemporary political thinkers like Muḥammad Rashīd Riḍā (d. 1354/1935), *Ḥizb al-Taḥrīr* founder Muḥammad Taqī al-Dīn al-Nabhānī (d. 1398/1977), Sayyid Abū 'l-Aʿlá Mawdūdī (d. 1399/1979), and even the renegade Egyptian Muslim Brother Muḥammad ʿAmāra (b. 1350/1931) (see Salārzaʾī 1436/2015, 16, 23, 25, and 39).[74]

A further feature to note is that the Pashto version of the treatise contains additional materials, which apparently are directed less towards al-Baghdādī and the majority of his followers, but rather to a Pashto-speaking and -reading audience. The extra sections, containing numerous direct references to Prophetic *ḥadīth* on the issues at hand, as well as a *fatwá*-like section of questions and responses (see Salārzəy 2015/2015, 78–91), seem rather to serve an ulterior purpose: to establish Salārzəy as a learned authority against the monopoly held by the established *ʿulamāʾ* and the structures at their disposal. In a way, this could well be understood as complimentary to Nek Muḥammad's earlier challenge to learned authority as well as the dominance of the *masharān*. While the latter stood out rather by his fervour that was yet again reminiscent of the early Islamic *futuwwāt*, Abū ʿUs̱mān Salārzəy challenges the very same structures by indicating the redundancy of traditional Islamic learning in the Deobandī way; his refutation of al-Baghdādī is therefore aimed against him and his claims as well as at demonstrating the deep erudition of its author for the regional audience.

Concluding Thoughts

In this article, I have suggested an alternative understanding of the various militant movements subsumed under the label 'Ṭālibān.' By adopting a *long durée* perspective on processes of identity formation in the border region between today's Afghanistan and Pakistan, I also have identified a multi-layered discourse on 'egalitarianism' as the pivot of the genesis of the *Ṭālibān*. It seems entirely possible to understand this discourse by analytically separating the various temporal layers and by highlighting the various historically generated threads that run through it. In order to do so, I have not confined myself to the review of secondary works, but have first and foremost engaged primary literature produced within the border communities as well as those who claim full sovereignty over them. This reference to primary texts in the various relevant languages – Urdu, Arabic, Pashto and Persian – has in turn informed my critical stance towards some of the secondary literature.

The benefit of this approach is quite obvious: I have been able to demonstrate that the *Ṭālibān* on either side of the today's national border between Afghanistan and Pakistan did not emerge overnight, rather they can be reasonably conceptualized as the product of a long-term radicalizing discourse of 'egalitarianism' in the region, which has been evolving since the Mughal era.

I have demonstrated that the processes of ethnic self-affirmation, mainly enacted by socio-political elites, established the Mughals as the fundamentally 'other.' These processes, however, unfolded synchronically with subaltern articulations; these, in turn, not only positioned the 'own' against the 'alien,' but also threatened to challenge established patterns of social, economic and political organization within the 'own.' The celebrated poet and tribal leader Khūshḥāl Khān Khaṫṫak represents in an exemplary fashion the position of the elites at this point, while Bāyazīd Anṣārī, and the *Rawshāniyyah* movement that traces its roots to him, epitomize the subaltern and emphatically rural voice.

Each of the two perspectives is sustained by a recourse to distinct normative references. The resort to traditional tribal patterns, symbolized by the somewhat idealized *paxtūnwālī*, works only in an ethnically defined context of justification, and thus helps to reinforce the validity of established hierarchies within the 'own.' The employment of universalistic religious precepts shifted the pivot beyond the distinctly shaped region and argued within a hiero-historical framework for the greater reality of the divine plan for the salvation of humankind as a whole. From such a perspective, perceived social, economic and political inequalities within one's own community appear as a substitute for the 'alien,' indicating that in a sound society there would be no contradiction between ethnically defined and confined patterns of socio-political organization and the religiously grounded precept of fundamental equality of all human beings as God's creatures. Whenever both frameworks clash, it is the religious one that must take priority.

The universality of the Islamic message, including the notion of 'equity' (*inṣāf*) and its various related concepts such as 'justice' (*'adl*), had two important effects on the region: first, it tied the Muslim communities in the Pashtun-inhabited borderscape to a much larger and very diverse community of believers, thus causing a growing awareness of similar constellations in different regions. Second, it made the Muslims in this borderscape susceptible to egalitarian agitation from outside the region: the long-term effect of religiously inspired movements such as the *Ṭarīqah-yi Muḥammadiyyah* in the early nineteenth century and the Deobandī mission under the leadership of the 'Shaykh al-Hind' Maḥmūd al-Ḥasan around the First World War can well be attributed to this factor; the activism of the followers of the Īpī Faqīr meanwhile complemented these efforts from within the region.

The opening up of the Pashtun tribesmen to the influence of external Islamic forces in turn also caused a cross-examination of the traditional religious authorities in the borderscape, authorities which are usually centred around the local mosque, Sufi shrine or refuge (*khānaqāh*). Pashto folklore encompasses a lengthy tradition of satire on the 'Mullā,' and also on the transgressing Sufi *shaykh* (see Ahmed 1980, 166–168); building upon these were puritanical and pietistic conceptions of 'proper' religious devotion from the direction of the *Ṭarīqah-yi Muḥammadiyyah* and the Deobandīs, thus establishing over time their own monopoly of definition in the region over that of the indigenous religious elites.

The emergence and success of the *Ṭālibān*, besides significant geopolitical factors,[75] must be viewed in this very context. Riding on a wave of accelerated discourse over 'egalitarianism,' these young and religiously trained men would, perhaps more than anyone before them, challenge almost all prevalent societal structures, be they social, economic, political or religious: TṬP commander Fażlallāh's initial empowerment of rural Pashtun women through his radio broadcasts is a telling case in point. In a society where females are rigidly excluded from participation in public affairs and deprived of even basic education, where females are even framed as essentially corrupted and corrupting through their affinity with evil spirits, Fażlallāh's broadcasts brought at least very basic religious knowledge into the separated female quarters of the village households (see Grima 1992, 2004).

In this, the challenges they posed contained an important new momentum: now it was the generation of young rural Pashtun males, as yet uncorrupted by wealth or status, who established their moral framework as the yardstick for measuring the appropriateness of belief and practice. The ensuing generational conflict between *masharān* and *kasharān*, while predominantly directed against social, economic and political elites, did also not stop short of the new and very much Deobandī-inspired religious leadership in the region: devout fervour in militant action – construed as defence of Islam and its believers against any harm – became increasingly valued above bookish knowledge and non-violent pious community service. It is here that the medieval ideal of adolescent religious warriors who joined up in almost knightly associations (*futuwwāt*) is somewhat reinvigorated: the defence of Islam requires, besides deep piety, necessary bravery, physical strength and, last but not least, the ability to handle the latest weapons as well as communication technology.

Finally, the very discursive layer of 'egalitarianism' as an ethnic constituent that produced the *Ṭālibān* has created a stratum of young Pashtun men of mainly rural background whose self-confidence is bolstered to such an extent that they now even dare to challenge authority within the *Ṭālibān*. The fierce discussion over the enduring validity of allegiance to the then commander-in-chief Mullā Muḥammad ʿUmar in view of his prolonged physical absence, and the eventual defection of a group of TṬP activists to the IS under the leadership of Abū Bakr al-Baghdādī, is to be considered a vivid expression of this final and most radical development in the complex discourse on 'egalitarianism' that has become ever more radical over time.

The future implications of the latest developments portrayed here are difficult to assess at present. What seems clear, though, is that the oath of allegiance pledged to al-Baghdādī embeds religiously inspired militancy in the Pashtun-inhabited borderscape in a much wider geographical context, in which the Pak–Afghan borderland is reduced in significance once again to just one province among numerous others, thus almost resembling the situation in which it was just an outpost of the Mughal empire, where discursive self-affirmation as a distinct ethnicity that transcends smaller communal identities appeared less virulent for most of the time.

Notes

1. For first attempts to take *Ṭālibān* legal and theological epistemology serious, see Hartung (2015, 198–220); Hartung (forthcoming); also, if only cursorily, Halverson (2010, 115–125).
2. According to these authors, it helps 'to describe new geographies and socio-spatial identities that, as the result of negotiations between identity and territorial claims and counter-claims, challenge the modern geopolitical, territorialist imaginary,' and to 'express the spatial and conceptual complexity of the border as a space that is not static but fluid and shifting; established and at the same time continuously traversed by a number of bodies, discourses, practices, and relationships that highlight endless definitions and shifts in definition between inside and outside, citizens and foreigners, hosts and guests across state, regional, racial, and other symbolic boundaries.' (Brambilla 2015, 19). Yet, with this notion Brambilla substantially advances the concept of 'borderscape' against earlier contributions to this discussion, first and foremost Rajaram and Gundy-Warr (2007, ix–xl), they still relate the concept of 'borderscape' to established geo-political categories, prominently borders between states 'where the territorial resolutions of being and the law that props them up collapse [; …] a zone where the multiplicity and chaos of the universal and the discomfits and possibilities of the body intrude' (p. x).
3. Examples for this are manifold and include Warren (2000); Haroon (2007); Qadir (2015). All three studies are predominantly reliant on British colonial archives, while the latter two also utilize later (and thus rather secondary) works in Urdu.
4. Those platforms include prominently the journals *Geopolitics, Political Geography* and *Regional Studies*, as well as the *Journal of Borderland Studies*.
5. Contributions that demonstrate a degree of sensitivity to the historical genesis of egalitarianism in borderland communities are, for instance, Jolicœur and Labarre (2013, 21); Power and Mohan (2010, 471, 479 and 486); Prévélakis (2000, 173 and 183).
6. Foundational to this notion, see Braudel (1958, 729–731). The conception refers, in the words of Koselleck (2000, 12), to 'an extended duration which structurally underlies or precedes all individual histories' [my translation]. Koselleck, however, demands a somewhat clarificatory modification of Braudel's concept, as shall be discussed below.
7. Examples here are manifold. In Hartung (2017), for instance, I correlate the Pashtun setting with Alpine Tyrol and indicate remarkable parallels between the two. Another European case which could also well be tested in this regard is the Basque country in and around the Pyrenees.
8. The first of such attempts to be documented happened under the Mughal ruler Jahāngīr (r. 1605-27), who had his courtly minute-taker (*wāqiʿ-nawīs*) Niʿmatallāh ibn Kh^{W}ājah Ḥabīballāh Harawī (d. *c.* 1039/1630) devise an ethnogenesis of the 'Afghans' from the Semitic prophet Yaʿqūb. See Harawī (1960, 1: 10–28).
9. This is a conscious reference to a core component of the historical theory of Reinhard Koselleck with which he aimed at modifying the Braudelian concept of 'longue durée' (see above, note 8). In Koselleck (2000, 9 [trans. mine]), he defined 'layers of time'

(*Zeitschichten*) as follows: 'Informed by the geological model, layers of time [*Zeitschichten*] refer to several period levels [*Zeitebenen*] of variant duration and origin which nonetheless exist and operate simultaneously.'

10. None of the standard chronicles for the reign of Shāh Jahān, the *Bādishāh'nāmah* of ʿAbd al-Ḥāmid Lāhawrī (d. 1064/1654) and Muḥammad Amīn Qazwīnī (d. after 1042/1632) respectively and the *ʿAmal-i Ṣāliḥ* of Muḥammad Ṣāliḥ Kanbūh (d. *c.* 1085/1675), mention Khūshḥāl among the listed military ranks of the nobility. Much of the narrative on Khūshḥāl's earlier amicable relation with the Mughals seems to originate from Khān (1867, 389–390).
11. See, for example, Khaṫṫak (2001, 19), especially the famous line 'For this state of things, no other termination can be seen/than that the Mughals be annihilated, or the Pashtuns undone' (*balah hīč līd lah nah shay pah dā miyanź kx̌ī/yā mughal da mīnźah warak yā pax̌tūn khwār*).
12. Such works range from *On a Foreign Approach to Khushhal: A Critique of Caroe and Howell* by the celebrated Dost Muḥammad Khān 'Kāmil' Mohmand (d. 1981) (1968) to the recent *Khushal Khan: Life, Thoughts and Contemporary Pakhtuns* by Ghanī Khān Khaṫṫak (b. 1948) (2014).
13. It appears likely, however, that this event took place during Akbar's stay at the garrison of Aṫṫak on 15 Muḥarram 994/6 January 1586, that is immediately before the disastrous campaign of Zayn Khān Kokah (d. 1010/1601) and Rājah Bīrbal (killed 994/1586) against the Yūsufzəy of Swat. See Harawī (1911–1935, Vol. 2, 398–400); also, ʿAllāmī (1877-86, Vol. 3, 484–485). Khūshḥāl himself, however, claims even to be in the sixth generation of loyal servants to the Mughals. See Khaṫṫak (2014, 1,019) (*Swāt'nāmah*): 'We were the servants of the Mughals for six generations/having earned [so much] gold that we are peaceful generations' (*da mughal namak me wa-khwaṛ shpaǵ pīṛəy/mā da zar wa-pake roghe kaṛe pīṛəy*).
14. Khūshḥāl's *Dīwān* is full of scattered verses that allude to his self-perception as a respected local representative of the Mughal establishment. For examples, see Khaṫṫak (2014, 28: 'As I was in complete uprightness/in the service of the Mughals, no other Afghan [ever] was' (*lakah zə wum pah rāstəy pah drastəy kx̌ī/da mughal khidmat nah wuh bal afghān*).
15. Khaṫṫak (2014, 11): 'My own truth, I say, is that I have been faithful and loyal to the Mughals' (*kih lah khpalah ḥaqīqatah dar tah wāyim/zah źāyay yam da mughal namak ḥalāl*).
16. See Karghar (1385/2004, 38–40); Ikrām (1967, 43–44). Both works, however, are contemporary hagiographical accounts with a clear, visible political agenda; their reliability — especially in the absence of sustaining references — must therefore be questioned.
17. Apparently, about half of Bāyazīd's works remain to be published. A glimpse of his view on the fundamental doctrine of God's oneness (*tawḥīd*), however, can be gained from Karghar (1385/2004, 200–212); and Quddūsī (1966, 193–194).
18. This passage was copied verbatim by Harawī (1911-35, #).
19. 'kih hindūstānī būd bā-andak dānishī wa ḥālan bah pīr-i tārikī ishtihār yāftah.' Allegedly, the pejorative title goes back to the Pashto *Makhzan al-Islām* of the Chishtī-*shaykh* ʿAbd al-Karīm Akhūnd Darwezā of Buner (d. 1048/1638), completed in 1615, which has not been available to me.
20. More recently, Carl W. Ernst (University of North Carolina at Chapel Hill) has highlighted the many serious flaws of this translation as well as the fact that it transports numerous Orientalist stereotypes, which needs to be born in mind here. See The Dabistan and Orientalist views of Sufism. MUSA Lecture May 24, 2016. Accessed

August 11, 2016. www.soas.ac.uk/south-asia-institute/musa/events/24may2016-the-dabistan-and-orientalist-views-of-sufism.html.

21. See Qur'an 3 (Āl ʿImrān): 104 and 110; 7 (al-Aʿrāf): 157; 9 (al-Tawba): 67 and 71.
22. In this endeavour, Bāyazīd's efforts appear to coincide with the admonitions of the Mughal rulers by Shaykh Aḥmad Fārūqī Sirhindī (d. 1034/1627) at around the very same time.
23. The significance of this work was acknowledged even by the Mughal court chronicler ʿAbd al-Qādir Badāʾunī (d. 1024/1615) – otherwise known for his rather critical stance toward Akbar's religious proclivities – who described the *Khayr al-Bayān* as containing 'his [i.e., Bāyazīd's] heretical tenets' (*ʿaqāyid-i fāsidah*): Badāʾunī (2001). For a more recent analysis of this work, see Bariyāləy (2011).
24. See the discussion by the editor in the work by Anṣārī (n.d., 96–97), and Bāyazīd's own justification in all four languages, 132–133: 'Spake the Prophet – Peace be upon him: "Oh Bāyazīd! Write those letters, which can give form to any language, for human-kind's sake!" You are All-Knowing; I know only the letters of the Qur'an, oh Glorious One!'.
25. Indicative is the following passage in Anṣārī (n.d., 206): 'Some involve themselves in the work of farming, or in market-trade, or the herdsman's trade of cattle, or go as far as the servitude to kings, or other professions, for the accumulation of wealth, whether permissible or dubious, or [even] prohibited' (*źinī pah bahnah da karlī yā da bāzargānəy yā da powandi-kaləy da źanāwarāno yā pah tir kshī bandəy da bādshāhāno yā pah nor čār māl-gird way kih ḥalāl yā shubuhāt day yā ḥarām*).
26. A view that relates the *Rawshāniyyah* to the early Islamic *futuwwāt* is presented by Malik (1993, 46–47).
27. The *ḥadīth* is *Ṣaḥīḥ Muslim*, Kitāb al-birr wa'l-ṣilla wa'l-ādāb, bāb taḥrīm ẓulm al-muslim wa-khadhlihi wa-iḥtiqārihi wa-dammihi wa-ʿaraḍihi wa-mālih, no. 3 (2,438).
28. Rural counter-cultures have come into the focus of cultural Studies only in the last few decades, thus challenging hegemonic discourses of culture. Prominent examples in this field of study are Appalachia and the rural South of the United States of America. See, for instance, various of the contributions in Cloke and Little (1997).
29. While working on this paper, events were overturning: in July 2015, the so-called 'Quetta *shūrá*' – Leadership Council of the *Ṭālibān* – officially confirmed earlier media reports of the death of Mullā ʿUmar and announced the succession of Mullā Akhtar Muḥammad Manṣūr as elected leader of the movement, to whom, according to another official statement, numerous commanders and dignitaries have pledged their oath of allegiance. Not even a year later Manṣūr was killed in a US drone strike; the appointment of Mawlawī Haybatallāh Ākhūndzādah (b. 1380/1961) as new *amīr* also revealed serious frictions within the *Ṭālibān* leadership over the earlier appointment of Mullā Manṣūr as supreme leader. See, for example, Qazi (2015).
30. Under this label, I also very much subsume the eschatologies of various political ideologies, in which the realization of social and economic justice, the ultimate goal of 'Providence,' 'History' and the like, becomes equivalent to salvation.
31. On the Pashtun tribal leadership model in settled as well as nomadic settings, see Ahmed (1980, 141–149).
32. This is indicated, for example, by Dupree (1973, 128–131).
33. It needs to be emphasized, however, that similar processes of assimilating variant communities and peoples under the umbrella of an economically powerful nation were happening at around the same time in Europe; their apparent success there may have well stimulated the application of such strategies in the colonies. See, for example, Chibber (2013, 263–267).

34. Khūshḥāl himself had negative things to say about the *Rawshāniyyah*, even after he had severed his relations with the Mughals, as they seem to have not only challenged imperial authority, but also the regional authorities that Khūshḥāl himself had claimed to represent. See Khaṭṭak (2001, 1,032–1,033) (*Swāt'nāmah*), where he accused them of spreading 'discord' and 'corruption' – using the religiously charged terms 'fitnah' and fasād' here – and insinuated the necessity to integrate into the prevalent societal order.
35. See here the numerous histories of the institution at Deoband, prominent among them Rizwī (1992–1993, Vol. 2, 33).
36. For a more detailed account on the life and work of Maḥmūd al-Ḥasan, including his placement in the social fabric of the North Indian Muslim communities, which are stratified along the lines of 'nobles' (*ashrāf*) and 'inferiors' (*ajlāf*), see Hartung (2016a 349–353).
37. See Qur'an 2 (al-Baqara): 247, 8 (al-Anfāl): 28, 18 (al-Kahf): 47, 23 (al-Mu'minūn): 55f, 26 (al-Shu'arā'): 88f, 34 (Saba'): 37, 63 (al-Munāfiqūn): 9, 64 (al-Taghābun): 15, and 68 (al-Qalam): 14f. Also, see the comments of Maḥmūd al-Ḥasan and his student Shabbīr Aḥmad 'Us̱mānī on these verses in 'Us̱mānī (1428/2007, Vol. 1, 207 and 813, Vol. 2, 449, 647, and 751, and Vol. 3, 175, 701, 709, and 745).
38. This rhetoric is especially strong with regard to a distinct regional Islamic tradition, portrayed in essentialist fashion as an entirely spiritually oriented and peaceful Sufi-Islam, in the wake of military operations against Islamic militancy in the borderscape of today's nation-states Afghanistan and Pakistan. Conversely, all militant inclination is blamed on foreign actors, currently especially Arabs and Central Asians who would abuse the traditional Pashtun obligation of hospitality (*melmastiyā*, or *melmah palānah*) and sanctuary (*panāh*, or *nanawātəy*) and lead youngsters astray to radical interpretations of Islam that have no local antecedent.
39. See, for instance, Qur'an 3 (Āl 'Imrān), 110: 'You are the best community I have brought forth among humankind; you enjoin the commendable and prevent the reprehensible …' (*kuntum khayra ummatin ukhrijat li'l-nāsi ta'murūna bi'l-ma'rūfi wa-tanhawna 'an al-munkar …*). In the Arabic historiographical tradition meanwhile, the question of how to deal with the non-Muslims in conquered lands plays an exponentially large role.
40. Gaborieau's argument here is based on a reading of Shāh Ismā'īl's rather late Persian treatise *Manṣib-i Imāmat.*
41. On the concept of 'hiero-history,' as coined and elaborated throughout much of his life by the French philosopher and orientalist Henri Corbin (d. 1978), see Corbin (1965).
42. On the concrete case of the local ramifications of the *Ṭarīqah-yi Muḥammadiyyah* in the Pashtun-inhabited borderscape, see Qadir (2015, 106–128 and 162–173).
43. Qadir's exposition, however, is based mainly on the significantly later account of writer-activist Mihr (2008, Vol. 2, 93–105), and therefore requires further fortification from contemporaneous documents. It might be interesting to note that the Arab volunteers in the guerilla war against the Soviet occupation of Afghanistan between 1986 and 1989 upheld a similarly suspicious attitude towards their Pashtun hosts. See al-Shaybānī (2003).
44. 'Popular mobilization' shall here be understood in dissociation from the narrower concept of 'political mobilization' that is well established in Political Science (see, e.g. Cameron 1974). 'Popular mobilization' refers therefore to ostensibly similar phenomena that are, however, not embedded in the context of nation state and socio-economic class determined by a distinct political class consciousness.
45. Oddly, however, Bāyazīd's Mahdist inclinations are related here to Ismā'īlī gnostic thought, ostensibly only on the basis of some general similarities.

46. This distinction in the conception of 'charisma' was made by Max Weber in his *Sociology of Power*, from which Wallace's theory draws heavily. See Weber (1972).
47. See Madanī (n.d., Vol. 2, 162–163, 165–168, 177–180, 188–190 et passim) and Madanī (2001). Whether or not, however, the Ḥājjī Ṣāḥib Turangzəy's relationship with the *ṣāḥib* of Haḍḍah Sharīf near Jalalabad was as crucial as suggested by Haroon (2007, 83–90, 98–99 et passim), remains to be established by future research.
48. Warren's statements are predominantly based on colonial archives and therefore reflect a pronouncedly British perspective. To develop a more balanced view, these archives would of course need to be correlated with indigenous narratives.
49. In this regard, the potential confluence with left-wing ideologies is obvious, and it is therefore scarcely surprising that around the very same time we see Deobandī scholars from and in the Pashtun-inhabited borderscape, prominent among them yet another student of Maḥmūd al-Ḥasan, the one-time grand-mufti (*muftī-yi a'ẓam*) of the NWFP 'Abd al-Raḥīm Popalzəy (d. 1363/1944), flirting seriously with Marxism.
50. This is a paraphrase of the famous closing statement in the *Manifesto of the Communist Party* (1848) of Karl Marx and Friedrich Engels.
51. See Nūrī (1318h, 235–271). The tale has meanwhile made it into a PTV romantic drama series (2013), with the focus clearly shifted onto Gul Basharah as the tale's main protagonist; a Pashto novel by Waǵmah Sabā 'Āmir with the title *Ṭālib Jān* was published in 2014.
52. In this regard, one may recall the anti-educational framework of the Egyptian *Jamā'at al-Muslimīn*, better known as *al-Takfīr wa'l-Hijra* of the late 1970s, led by the former agricultural engineer Shukrī Muḥammad Muṣṭafá (executed 1978). With reference to the early Muslim community during the lifetime of the Prophet Muḥammad as the ultimate benchmark, Muṣṭafá emphasized the ambivalent nature of knowledge (*'ilm*), which can lead to dangerous idle speculation beyond the sphere of belief, and pleaded therefore for its radical limitation by linking illiteracy to intellectual innocence. See Muṣṭafá (1991, 122–124). A somewhat similar attitude in this regard exemplifies the North Nigerian militant *Jamā'at Ahl al-Sunna li'l-Da'wa wa'l-Jihād*, better known by its Hausa name *Boko Haram*. See Higazi (2013). The target of *Boko Haram*, however, is not any form of knowledge, but all that is associated with the Latin script, epitomized in the bound book (Hausa: *boko*) that is contrasted with the loose sheet (*waraq*) of the Arabic manuscript tradition. I am grateful to Amidu O. Sanni (Lagos State University) for clarifying to me *Boko Haram*'s conception of 'knowledge' during our meeting in Riyadh in September 2015.
53. See Khan (2004). On Nūr Muḥammad Wazīr, see Ḥaqqānī (2010, 12–15).
54. Khan (2004) cites an anonymous teacher at the *madrasah* in Wānā, who said that 'Nek [Muḥammad] never had an intellectual mind but some other traits of his personality became evident during his stay at the Darul Uloom. He showed himself to be a hard-headed boy, endowed with an impenetrable soul and an obstinate determination to carry out his will no matter how mindless it might be.'
55. On the seriously restricted access and subsequent exclusion of rural Pashtun women from education, as well as the Pashtun male imaginary of females as potentially in league with evil spirits that aim at corrupting male honor and dignity, see Grima (1992, 2004).
56. The first attempt at this interpretation has, as far as I am aware, been made by Abou-Zahab (2013, 57–59). Here, role of the Pakistani State in changing the status quo in the authority structures in the region has also been touched upon.
57. On the role of and rationale for *taqlīd-i shakhṣī*, i.e. the unconditional emulation of the legal opinions developed by specific teachers, in Deobandī legal thought and practice,

see Hartung (2015, 201–202) and Hartung (forthcoming). For a lengthy exposition of this legal procedure, see Deobandī (1990, 73–88).

58. A prominent case in point is the *Özbekiston Islomiy Harakatī* (IMU), initially led by Nek Muḥammad's associate Tohir Yöldosh (killed 1430/2009), whose current *amīr*, Usmon Ghoziy, declared the IMU to be part of IS in September 2014. Perhaps as a result, the IMU's former webpage http://jundurrahmon.biz/ was shut down some time in late 2014 and was replaced by the Uzbek IS website http://hilofatnews.com/. Accessed August 12, 2016.
59. For the historical links between Shawkānī and the *Ahl-i Ḥadīs̱*, see Hartung (2004, 224–228).
60. Outstanding in this regard is Maḥmūd al-Ḥasan's popular *Adillah-yi Kāmilah* (ca. 1875), in which he defended the Ḥanafī positions followed by the Deobandīs against the staunch refusal of any form of *taqlīd*.
61. Relations between Najdī scholars of Wahhābī orientation and the *Ahl-i Ḥadīs̱* in India date back to the early nineteenth century and are largely maintained until today. See Hartung (2004, 337–360).
62. See Laoust (1939), where the label is however reserved for the developments from Muḥammad ibn ʿAbd al-Wahhāb Najdī (d. 1206/1791); also Lav (2012). Critically, see Krawietz (2010); also Nedza (2016, 251–258).
63. See Nedza (2016, 258–303), where the respective views of leading theorists of militant Islamism from Egypt (Sayyid Imām al-Sharīf, a.k.a. Dr. Faḍl, b. 1369/1950) and Saudi Arabia (Nāṣir al-Fahd, b. 1388/1968; ʿAlī al-Khuḍayr, b. 1373/1954; Aḥmad ibn Ḥamūd al-Khālidī, b. 1389/1969) are meticulously analyzed and contrasted with one another.
64. For a recent example in this rather optimistically pursued debate, see Pelizäus-Hoffmeister (2013).
65. See, for instance, the above-mentioned websites of the IMU, or also the websites of the TṬP (https://umarmedia.wordpress.com/) and the *Islamic Emirate of Afghanistan* (http://alemara1.org/and www.shahamat.com/), all accessed on July 2, 2015.
66. On Urganchiy, no further information could be found. Several of his writings, however, appear prominently on the various and oftentimes only short-lived IMU websites.
67. See Anonymous (2014). The video was released around 13 July 2014, but is not accessible anymore because of its violation of YouTube Terms of Service. Urganchiy's argument appears to resonate at least with the fourth normative conditions for a proper Imamate made by medieval Shāfiʿī jurist al-Māwardī (1422/2002, 8): 'sound in limb, free of any deficiency which might prevent them from normal movement [*salāmat al-aʿḍāʾ min naqṣ yumniʿa ʿan istīfāʾ al-ḥarakat wa-surʿat al-nahūḍ*].' Interestingly, however, Māwardī is much more precise when discussing the eventual physical absence of a claimant to the Imamate, stating that the jurists are holding different views over this matter. The ultimate *defininiens* would be the excellence (*faḍīla*) of the claimant.
68. The most important *ḥadīth* in this regard is al-Tirmidhī, *al-Jāmiʿ al-Ṣaḥīḥ*, kitāb al-fitan, bāb mā jāʾ fi'l-nahy ʿan sabb al-rayyāḥ, no. 17: 'Black banners will come from Khurasan, nothing shall turn them back until they are planted in Jerusalem [*takhruju min Khurāsān rāyātun sūdun lā yarudduhā shayʾun ḥattá tunṣaba bi-ʾIliyāʾ*].' For an example of the advocacy of this interpretation as a rationale for the 'Khurasan *shūrá*,' see Basit (2016, 82–83).
69. In the 'Abbasid revolution,' however, this *ḥadīth* apparently did not play a legitimizing role. For the significance of Khurasan and the black colour of the flags, see Sharon (1983–1990, Vol. 1, 51–54, and Vol. 2, 83–86). Abū Bakr al-Baghdādī has not explicitly claimed his caliphate to be the continuation of that of the ʿAbbasids that came to its

end with the Ottoman sack of Mamluk Cairo in 1517. However, the symbols he employs to enact his caliphal authority are too strongly reminiscent of those of the ʿAbbasids to be dismissed as mere coincidence.

70. http://alemara1.org/?p=17042 (Pashto text). The text has also been published on the official website of the *Islamic Emirate* in Arabic (www.shahamat-arabic.com/archives/2652), Urdu (www.shahamat-urdu.com/?p=1148) and Dari (www.shahamat-farsi.com/?p=2385). All four sites have been accessed on July 8, 2014. Interestingly, the terminology used in these translations differs somewhat from that of the original.
71. The original statement of al-Baghdādī, issued allegedly on January 29, 2015, could not be located and its veracity remains therefore to be proven.
72. About a year later, an Urdu translation of the text appeared in the same place. Honesty demands an acknowledgement that, because of linguistic limitations, I had to work mainly with the Arabic and Urdu texts, while using the Pashto one mainly for cross-checking on the terminology.
73. The works referred to by Salārzəy are the *Mughnī* of Ibn Qudāma (39), Shawkānī's *Nayl al-Awṭār* (49) and Ṣiddīq Ḥasan Khān's *al-Rawḍa al-Nadiyya Sharḥ al-Durar al-Bahiyya* (39). Of Ibn Taymiyya's works, the most frequently cited one is his *Minhāj al-Sunna al-Nabawwiyya fī Naqṣ Kalām al-Shīʿa al-Qadariyya* (11–13, 20, 30, 34–36 and 56); other of his titles are *Shubuhāt ḥawla al-Ṣaḥāba* (p. 10), *al-Khilāfa wa'l-Mulk* (22) and his famous *Fatāwá al-Kubrá* (p. 39).
74. For a more detailed analysis of Salārzəy's treatise within the current leadership disputes between the *IS* and *al-Qāʿida*, see Hartung (2016b).
75. Here belongs, first and foremost, the Communist *coup d'état* in Afghanistan and the subsequent Soviet invasion of the country in late December 1979, which, among other events, resulted in a great variety of substantial developments that irreversibly impacted upon the region as a whole.

Acknowledgments

Because of the subject matter of this paper and, related to this, the particular properties of the materials used, the format of this paper evidently differs to a great extent from that of the other contributions to this volume. I am most grateful to the editors for having been sensitive to discipline-specific formal particularities and, subsequently, allowing for this exception, even at the expense of formal consistency throughout the entire volume. All transliteration follows by and large the academic standard conventions for each relevant language; an 'h' struck out (ħ) indicates aspiration of the preceding consonant.

Furthermore, I would like to thank the editors of this special issue, as well as the editor-in-chief of *Geopolitics* and the anonymous referees for their repeated time and effort in helping me making my argument more stringent and, moreover, digestible for an audience less familiar with the history of the region in focus. Finally, I thank James Caron for his always stimulating companionship over the years.

References

Abou-Zahab, M. 2013. Kashars against Mashars: Jihad and social change in the FATA. In *Beyond Swat: History, society and economy along the Afghanistan-Pakistan frontier*, ed. B. D. Hopkins and M. Marsden, 51–60. London, Hurst/New York: Oxford University Press.

al-ʿAdnānī, A. M., 2015. Qul: Mūtū bi-ghayẓikum! *Muʾassasat al-furqān li'l-intāj al-iʿlāmī*, January 26. Accessed July 2, 2015, mins. 3′42″-5′07″. www.youtube.com/watch?v=pq61kGOa8AQ.

ʿAllāmī, A. 1877-86. *Akbar'nāmah*, 3 vols. ed. M. ʿAbd al-Raḥīm. Calcutta: Baptist mīshan press.

Ahmed, A. S. 1980. *Pukhtun economy and society: Traditional structures and economic development in a tribal society*. London and New York: Routledge.

Anonymous. 1877. *K. Dabistān-i maẕāhib*, 305. Lucknow: Maṭbaʿ Munshī Nawal Kishor.

Anonymous. 2014. *Shom TV*. http://hilofatnews.com/Video_v6902.html.

Anonymous. 2015. al-Baghdādī: Al-Mullā ʿUmar ... "maʿtūh". *al-Waṭan al-ʿArabī*, January 30. Accessed July 9, 2015. www.alwatanalarabi.com/article/61111/%D8%A7%D9%84%D8%A8%D8%BA%D8%AF%D8%A7%D8%AF%D9%8A%D8%A7%D9%84%D9%85%D9%84%D8%A7%D8%B9%D9%85%D8%B1%D9%85%D8%B9%D8%AA%D9%88%D9%87.

Anṣārī, B. n.d. *Khayr al-bayān*, ed. M. ʿA. Qāsimī. Chaman: Pashto adabī ṫolānah.

Arneson, R. 2013. Egalitarianism. In *The Stanford encyclopedia of philosophy*, ed. E. N. Zalta. Accessed July 27, 2015. http://plato.stanford.edu/entries/egalitarianism/.

Badāʾunī, ʿA. 2001. *Muntakhab al-Tawārīkh, 3 vols.* ed. M. A. ʿAlī. Tehran: Anjumān-i āṯār wa mafākhir-i farhangī.

Bariyāləy, ʿA. 2011. *Da Bāyazīd Rawx̌ān Khayr al-Bayān aw da muḥaqqīno da x̌eṛāno jāj*. Koṫah: Mullā Ẓarīf Akhūnd Kākaṛ faʾunḋex̌an.

Basit, A. 2016. Is the Islamic state of Iraq and Sham (ISIS) a security threat to Afghanistan and Pakistan? In *The dynamics of change in the Pakistan-Afghanistan region: Politics on borderland*, ed. S. S. Raza, 75–90. Peshawar: al-Qalam.

Brambilla, C. 2015. Exploring the critical potential of the borderscapes concept. *Geopolitics* 20:14–34. doi:10.1080/14650045.2014.884561.

Braudel, F. 1958. Histoire et Sciences sociales: La longue durée. *Annales ESC* 13(4):725–53.

Cameron, D. R. 1974. Towards a theory of political mobilization. *The Journal of Politics* 36 (1):138–71. doi:10.2307/2129113.

Caron, J. 2012. Taliban, real and imagined. In *Under the drones: Modern lives in the Afghanistan–Pakistan borderlands*, ed. S. Bashir and R. D. Crews, 60–82. Cambridge, MA and London: Harvard University Press.

Caron, J. 2016. Sufism and liberation across the Indo-Afghan border, 1880-1928. *South Asian History and Culture* 7(2):135–54. doi:10.1080/19472498.2016.1201567.

Chatterjee, P. 1993. *The nation and its fragments: Colonial and postcolonial histories*. Princeton, NJ: Princeton University Press.

Chibber, V. 2013. *Postcolonial theory and the specter of capital*. London and New York: Verso.

Cloke, P., and J. Little, eds. 1997. *Contested countryside cultures: Otherness, marginalisation and rurality*. London and New York: Routledge.

Corbin, H. 1965. La Configuration du Temple de la Ka'ba comme secret de la vie spirituelle d'après l'œuvre de Qâzî Sa'îd Qommî (1103/1691). *Eranos Jahrbuch* 35:79–166.

Crone, P. 1989. On the meaning of the ʿAbbāsid Call to *al-Riḍā*. In *The Islamic World: From classical to modern times. Essays in honor of Bernard Lewis*, ed. C. E. Bosworth, et al., 95–111. Princeton, NJ: The Darwin Press.

Deobandī, M. Ḥ. 1990. *Adillah-yi kāmilah, yaʿnī ghayr-muqallidoṇ ke das suʾālāt awr unke taḥqīqī jawābāt*. Karachi: Qadīmī kitāb'khānah.

Dupree, L. 1973. *Afghanistan*. Princeton, NJ: Princeton University Press.

Edwards, D. B. 2002. *Before Taliban: Genealogies of the Afghan Jihad*. Berkeley, CA: University of California Press.

Eilenberg, M. 2012. *At the edges of states: Dynamics of state formation in the Indonesian Borderlands*. Leiden: KITVL Press.

Gaborieau, M. 1996. l'Asie centrale dans l'horizon de l'Inde au début du XXe siècle: à propos d'un lettre de Sayyid Ahmad Barelwî à l'emir de Boukhara. *Cahiers De l'Asie Centrale* 1-2:265-82.

Gaborieau, M. 2010. *Le Mahdi incompris: Sayyid Ahmad Barelwî (1786-1831) et le millénarism en Inde*. Paris: CNRS Éditions. 215-68.

Glatzer, B. 1996. Schwert und Verantwortung: Pashtunische Männlichkeitsideale. In *Krieg und Kampf: Die Gewalt in unseren Köpfen*, ed. E. Orywal, A. Rao, and M. Bollig, 107-20. Berlin: Reimer.

Grima, B. 1992. *The performance of emotions among Paxtun Women: "The misfortunes which have Befallen me"*. Austin, TX: University of Texas Press.

Grima, B. 2004. *Secrets from the field: An ethnographer's notes from Northwest Pakistan*. Bloomington, IN: AuthorHouse [sic].

Gustozzi, A. 2007. *Koran, Kalashnikov and laptop: The Neo-Taliban insurgency in Afghanistan*. London, Hurst/New York: Columbia University Press.

Hallaq, W. B. 1984. Was the gate of Ijtihad closed? *International Journal of Middle East Studies* 16(1):3-41. doi:10.1017/S0020743800027598.

Halverson, J. R. 2010. *The Muslim brotherhood, Ash'arism, and political Sunnism*. New York: Palgrave Macmillan.

Ḥaqqānī, N. 2010. Shajarah-yi nasab-i ḥaẕrat Mawlānā Nūr-i Muḥammad Ṣāḥib-i shahīd. *Ṣadā-yi Wazīristān* 1(5):12-15.

Harawī, N. 1960. *Tārīkh-i Khān-i Jahānī wa makhzān-i afghānī*, 2 vols., ed. S. M. Imām al-Dīn. Dacca: Asiatic Society of Pakistan.

Harawī, N. A. 1911-35. *Ṭabaqāt-i akbarī*, 3 vols., ed. B. De and M. H. Ḥusayn. Calcutta: Maṭba' baptist mīshan.

Haroon, S. 2007. *Frontiers of faith: Islam in the Indo-Afghan borderland*. London, Hurst/ New York: Columbia University Press.

Hartung, J.-P. 2004. *Viele Wege und ein Ziel: Leben und Wirken von Sayyid Abū l-Ḥasan Ḥasanī Nadwī (1914-1999)*. Würzburg: Ergon.

Hartung, J.-P. 2015. Legal discourses on faith in the Pak-Afghan borderlands. In *Conference proceedings: Dynamics of change in the Pak-Afghan borderland: The interplay of past legacies, present realities and future scenarios: Third international conference, 25-26 June, 2014*, ed. S. Aman and M. Ayub Jan, 198-220. Peshawar: Printman.

Hartung, J.-P. 2016a. The praiseworthiness of divine beauty: The "Shaykh al-Hind" Maḥmūd al-Ḥasan, social justice, and Deobandiyyat. *South Asian History and Culture* 7(4):346-369. doi:10.1080/19472498.2016.1223719.

Hartung, J.-P. 2016b. Between a rock and a hard place: The *Ṭālibān*, Afghan self-determination and the challenges of transnational jihadism. *Die Welt des Islams* 56(2):125-52. doi:10.1163/15700607-00562p01.

Hartung, J.-P. 2017. Frontiers – pieties – resistance. In *Dynamics of change in the Pak-Afghan borderland: Politics on borderland*, ed. S. Aman and M. Zubair, 39-54. Peshawar: al-Qalam.

Hartung, J.-P. forthcoming. The *Ṭālibān* legal discourse on violence. In *Legitimate and illegitimate violence in modern Islamic thought*, ed. R. Gleave and M. Baig. Edinburgh: Edinburgh University Press.

Higazi, A. 2013. Les origines et la transformation de l'insurrection de Boko Haram dans le Nord du Nigeria. In *Crises et chuchotements au Sahel*, ed. V. Bonnecase, 137-64. Paris: Éd. Karthala.

Ikrām, S. M. 1967. *Rūd-i kaws̱ar: Islāmī Hind wa Pākistān ke maẕhabī awr 'Ilmī Tārīkh 'ahd-i mughaliyyah se pahle*. Delhi: Matiyā maḥall.

Jolicœur, P., and F. Labarre. 2013. The breakup of Georgia: Fragmentation or settlement fringe? *Journal of Borderland Studies* 30(1):19-36. doi:10.1080/08865655.2015.1012730.

Karghar, M. A. 1385/2004. *Pah Ḥālnāmah ke da Bāyazīd Rawx̌ān ʿarifānī aw falsafī čeṛah.* Kabul: Da Afghānistān da ʿulūmī akādiməy.

Khān, M. Ḥ. 1867. *Ḥayāt-i afghānī.* Lahore: Matbaʿ-i kūh-i nūr.

Khan, M. I. 2004. Profile of Nek Mohammad. *Dawn,* June 19. Accessed July 1, 2015. www.webcitation.org/query?url=http%3A%2F%2Fwww.dawn.com%2F2004%2F06%2F19%2Flatest.htm&date=2009-05-16.

Khaṫṫak, G. K. 2014. *Khushal Khan: Life, thoughts and contemporary Pakhtuns.* Rawalpindi: Faiz-ul-Islam Printing Press.

Khaṫṫak, K. K. 2001. *Armaghān-i Khūshḥāl,* 2nd ed., ed. M. S. R. 'Rasā'. Peshawar: Yūniwarsitī būk ejensī.

Koselleck, R. 2000. *Zeitschichten: Studien zur Historik.* Frankfurt a.M.: Suhrkamp.

Krawietz, B. 2010. Transgressive creativity in the making: Ibn Qayyim al-Ǧawziyyah's reframing within Ḥanbalī legal methodology. *Oriente Moderno* 40(1):47–66.

Laoust, H. 1939. *Essai sur les doctrines sociales et politiques de Taki-d-Din Ahmad b. Taimîya, cononiste hanbalite, né à Harrān en 661/1262, mort à Damas en 728/1328.* Cairo: l'Institut français d'archéologie orientale.

Lav, D. 2012. *Radical Islam and the revival of medieval theology.* Cambridge and New York: Cambridge University Press.

Madanī, Ḥ. A. 2001. *Safarnāmah-yi asīr-i Mālṫā.* Lahore: Ṭayyib pablisharz.

Madanī, Ḥ. A. n.d. *Naqsh-i ḥayāt: Khūd-niwisht-i sawāniḥ,* 2 vols. Karachi: Dār al-ishāʿat.

Malik, J. 1993. 16th century Mahdism: The Rawšaniya [*sic*] movement among Pakhtun Tribes. In *Islam and Indian regions,* 2 vols, ed. A. L. Dallapiccola and S. Zingel-Avé Lallemant, vol. 1, 31–59. Stuttgart: Steiner.

al-Māwardī, A. ʿA., (d. 450/1058). 1422/2002. *K. al-Aḥkām al-sulṭāniyya.* Beirut: Dār al-fikr, 6.

Mihr, G. R. 2008. *Taḥrīk-i Sayyid Aḥmad-i Shahīd,* 4 vols. Mumbai: Maktabat al-ḥaqq.

Mohmand, D. M. 1968. *On a foreign approach to Khushhal: A critique of Caroe and Howell.* Peshawar: Maktabah-i-Shaheen.

Muṣṭafá, S. A. 1991. Wathīqat al-khilāfa: Asās al-fikrī li-jamāʿat al-takfīr wa'l-hijra. In *al-Nabī al-musallaḥ,* 2 vols, ed. R. S. Aḥmad, vol. 2, 115–60. London: Riad el-Rayyes Books.

Nedza, J. 2016. *Der Staat als Feind: Die Rolle des* takfīr *im militanten salafistischen Diskurs.* Ph.D. diss., Ruhr-University Bochum.

Nichols, R. 2001. *Settling the frontier: Land, law, and society in the Peshawar Valley, 1500-1900.* Karachi: Oxford University Press.

Nūrī, M. G. ed. 1318h. *Millī hindārah.* Kabul: Da pax̌to ṫolane da nashriyāto ʿumūmī lambar.

Pelizäus-Hoffmeister, H. 2013. *Zur Bedeutung von Technik im Alltag Älterer: Theorie und Empirie aus soziologischer Perspektive.* Wiesbaden: Springer.

Peters, R. 1980. *Ijtihād* and *Taqlīd* in 18th and 19th Century Islam. *Die Welt des Islams* 20:131–45.

Power, M., and G. Mohan. 2010. Towards a critical geopolitics of China's engagement with African development. *Geopolitics* 15(3):462–95. doi:10.1080/14650040903501021.

Prévélakis, G. 2000. The hellenic diaspora and the Greek state: A spatial approach. *Geopolitics* 5(2):171–85. doi:10.1080/14650040008407685.

Qadir, A. 2015. *Sayyid Ahmad Barailvi: His movement and legacy from the Pukhtun Perspective.* New Delhi, Thousand Oaks, CA and London: Sage.

Qazi, S. 2015. Taliban leaders dispute appointment of Mullah Mansoor. *Al Jazeera Online.* Accessed August 16, 2016. www.aljazeera.com/news/2015/07/taliban-leaders-dispute-appointment-mullah-mansoor-150731151533576.html.

Quddūsī, I. 1966. *Tazkirah-yi ṣūfiyyā-yi Sarḥadd.* Lahore: Markazī urdū barḋ. 193–94.

Rafi, G. 2016. *The Taliban crisis in Pakistan: Implications for the social fabric of the Pukhtuns of Swat.* M.phil. diss., University of Peshawar.

Rajaram, P. K., and C. Gundy-Warr. 2007. Introduction. In *Borderscapes: Hidden geographies and politics at territory's edge*, ed. P. K.Rajaram and C. Gundy-Warr, ix–xl. Minneapolis, MN and London: University of Minnesota Press.

Rashid, A. 2008. *Taliban: Militant Islam, oil and fundamentalism*, revised ed. London and New York: I. B. Tauris.

Rawls, J. 1999. *A theory of justice, Revised ed.* Cambridge, MA: Belknap Press.

Rawls, J. 2001. *Justice as fairness – A reassessment.* ed. E. Kelly. Cambridge, MA: Belknap Press.

Rizwī, S. M. 1992–1993. *Tārīkh-i Dār al-ʿulūm Deoband*, 2 vols. Deoband: Idārah-yi ihtimām-i Dār al-ʿulūm.

Salārzaʾī, A. ʿU. 2015/2015. *Mawqif Ḥarakat Ṭālibān al-Bākistāniyya ʿan khilāfat al-Shaykh al-Baghdādī.* n.p.: Idārah ʿUmar barā-yi nashr wa ishāʿat. Accessed July 2, 2015. https://umarmedia.files.wordpress.com/2015/05/d985d988d982d981d8add8b1d983d8a9d8b7d8a7d984d8a8d8a7d986d8a7d984d8a8d8a7d983d8b3d8aad8a7d986d98ad8a9-click-here-to-download1.pdf.

Salārzəy, A. ʿU. 2015/2015. *Da Shaykh Abū Bakr al-Baghdādī – ḥifẓahu allāh – da iʿlān kṛe shwəy khilāfat pah ḥawāle sarah da Taḥrīk Ṭālibān Pākistān sharʿī mawqif*, 78–91. n.p.: Idārah ʿUmar barā-yi nashr wa ishāʿat. Accessed July 2, 2015. https://umarmedia.files.wordpress.com/2015/05/d985d988d982d981d8add8b1d983d8a9d8b7d8a7d984d8a8d8a7d986d8a7d984d8a8d8a7d983d8b3d8aad8a7d986d98ad8a9-click-here-to-download1.pdf.

Schetter, C., and J. Klußmann,eds. 2011. *Der Taliban-Komplex: Zwischen Aufstandsbewegung und Militäreinsatz.* Frankfurt/M.: Campus.

Sharon, M. 1983–1990. *Black banners from the East: The establishment of the ʿAbbāsid State*, 2 vols. Jerusalem: The Max Schloessinger Memorial Fund.

al-Shaybānī, M. 2003. Afghānistān … ḥaqīqat al-jihād wa-wāqiʿ al-irhāb. *al-Riyāḍ*, December 30, 1.

Shea, D., and A. Troyer. 1843. *The Dabistan, or school of manners, translated from the original Persian, with notes and illustrations.* Paris: Oriental Translation Fund of Great Britain and Ireland. cxlvi.

Taeschner, F. 1979. *Zünfte und Bruderschaften im Islam: Texte zur Geschichte der Futuwwa.* Zurich: Artemis.

Tapper, N. 1991. *Bartered brides: Politics, gender and marriage in an Afghan tribal society.* Cambridge: Cambridge University Press.

ʿUsmānī, S. A. 1428/2007. *Tafsīr-i ʿUsmānī*, 3 vols., ed. Muḥammad Walī-yi Rāzī. Karachi: Dār al-ishāʿat.

Wallace, A. F. C. 1956. Revivalist movements. *American Anthropologist* 58(2):264–81. doi:10.1525/aa.1956.58.2.02a00040.

Warren, A. 2000. *Waziristan, the Faqir of Ipi, and the Indian Army: The North West Frontier [sic] Revolt of 1936-37.* Oxford: Oxford University Press.

Weber, M. 1972. *Wirtschaft und Gesellschaft. Grundriß der verstehenden Soziologie*, 5th ed. Tübingen: J. C. B. Mohr.

Yousafzai, M. [sic], with C. Lamb. 2014. *I am Malala: The girl who stood up for education and was shot by the Taliban.* London: Phoenix.

Zaeef, A. S. 2010. *My life with the Taliban*, ed. A. Strick van Linschoten and F. Kuehn. London, Hurst/New York: Columbia University Press.

Legal Sovereignty on the Border: Aliens, Identity and Violence on the Northwestern Frontier of Pakistan

Syed Sami Raza

ABSTRACT

In the summer of 2011, two incidents of coldblooded violence took place at the hands of law enforcement agencies (LEAs) in Pakistan. One incident involved the killing of a group of foreigners/aliens traveling across the Pakistan–Afghanistan border, and the other involved the killing of a citizen in an area under curfew in the metropolitan city of Karachi. On one hand, the Supreme Court of Pakistan took a *Suo Moto* action in the case of the latter incident, while remaining silent on the former. On the other, the Pakistani government, instead of reviewing the powers of LEAs, increased them by passing new security laws in the following years. In this article, I focus on these two incidents of violence to question how/why aliens are treated differently from citizens in the Pakistan's criminal justice system. I trace the legal genealogy of that differential treatment and highlight the different stages of its growth. I also throw light on the way lethal force was used on the victims to show the drawbacks in the operational side of law enforcement. Finally, I engage critical theory to understand the nature of this violence, which now resides in the structure of the legal regime of security.

Introduction

A few years ago, in an essay engaging critical geography, I explored the tendency or preoccupation among the geo-politicians and military geo-strategists of the War on Terror with 'unveiling' the supposedly obscure battleground of the northwestern borderland of Pakistan.[1] I pointed out how the preoccupation with unveiling the borderland led to the deployment of new military technology, cartographic practices and cultural quantitative analysis on the basis of visual data, which while giving a strategic advantage over the adversary took the obscurity of the borderland to another level—the digital–technological level. More importantly, I argued that geo-politicians and military geo-strategists were indirectly engaged in building an imaginative geopolitical representation of the borderland. In order to critically analyse their endeavours, I engaged Michael J. Shapiro's concept of a violent cartography. The concept explains how geo-political and geostrategic representations of a given space were/are basically 'historically developed, socially embedded interpretations of identity and space' and hence are 'based on models of identity-difference'.[2] In the light of this concept, I highlighted the implications of employing geopolitical cartographic practices based on an identity-difference framing. Here, in the present essay, I want to further extend my analysis to security practices that involve the use of lethal force sanctioned by law, which create a legal regime of security derogatory to human rights on the borderland. In other words, I pursue the concept of violent cartography, along with certain other concepts—especially structural violence and necrobiography—to present a critical analysis of the *legally embedded* interpretations of identity and place on the border.

Two recent incidents of coldblooded killings at the hands of the law enforcement agencies (LEAs) of Pakistan present the context for this essay. These incidents took place in the summer of 2011—the first incident involved a killing of a group of aliens/foreigners who were traveling across the border from Afghanistan into Pakistan, and the second involved the killing of a young man (a Pakistani citizen) who happened to be in an area under curfew and who was suspected of theft in a local park in the metropolitan city of Karachi. Although these incidents took place one after the other, within a period of less than a month, the attention and responses they received from the government, and especially the superior judiciary, were quite different. While the latter incident (Karachi killing of a citizen) moved the Supreme Court to take a *Suo Moto* action and to replace the heads of LEAs in charge, the former incident (Kharotabad killings of foreigners) went almost overlooked, subsequently passing into oblivion. The judicial ambivalence towards the Kharotabad incident raises the question as to what was so different in the two incidents, especially from the point of view of the law or (formal) justice that gave them such a differential response?

However, before we begin to seek an answer to that question, I deem it useful to narrate the details of the two incidents. This narration is crucial for the second half of the essay in which I engage in a critical analysis of these events of violence. On May 17, 2011, a group of five foreign travellers set out on the journey, in a hired cab, across the Pakistan–Afghanistan border and headed towards the city of Quetta in the province of Baluchistan. They crossed a couple of check-posts from the border to the outskirts of the city. Here, outside the city when they reached a check post in Kharotabad, a small town, and disembarked from their cab for a routine check-up, the Frontier Corps (FC) personnel opened fire on them. Three of them died on the spot, while two women fall on ground injured. They laid there for more than half an hour while the officers in command deliberated on their fate. Meanwhile, a few media men arrived at the spot. The FC personnel sent an armoured vehicle down to the injured women to see if they were armed with suicide jackets. The vehicle returned without finding anything conclusive. After their brief deliberation, the FC personnel decided to kill the wounded women. A second fusillade was discharged and the wounded women were killed despite their calls for mercy. Interestingly, a local media man recorded this second half of the incident including the fusillade of fire on video camera. The recording soon hit local news networks and social media and generated a public outcry for an inquiry. Soon it also turned out after the postmortem that the victims were neither Chechens nor were they armed as initially claimed by the LEAs. As the public pressure for accountability increased, the government promised to carry out an inquiry. After many delays, the Pakistani government put together an 'internal inquiry committee' under the Anti-Terrorism Act, 1997, to investigate the killings. However, at the end of the investigation, neither the report of the committee was made public in its full original version nor was a trial registered.

In less than a month, on 8 June 2011, a young man was shot dead by the Rangers, a para-military force deployed to aiding the police in the metropolitan city of Karachi. A private TV channel crew, which coincidentally happened to be nearby, recorded this incident on camera. The video recording was shown on local news channels, and it went viral on social media. In the video recording, the victim is shown being roughly handled by a group of five Rangers personnel. Then, one of the personnel shoots the victim twice in the leg. The victim falls to the ground crying in pain and begging to be taken to a hospital. However, the Rangers personnel disregard his imploring and let him bleed to death. The erstwhile Chief Justice of the Pakistani Supreme Court Iftikhar Chaudary took a *Suo Moto* action ordering the registration of a case of murder against the Rangers personnel involved. He also advised the government to remove the incumbent Director General of Rangers and the Inspector General of police to ensure that a fair investigation in the case could take place. The case proceeded in an antiterrorism court, which ensured speedy criminal procedure and decided within a couple of months to award heavy punishments to the personnel involved.

The point that I want to emphasize in these incidents is that they received diametrically different responses from the Supreme Court. Although both incidents involved coldblooded violence and were equally reproachable, what differentiated them in the eyes of the criminal justice system was the difference of personal legal identity. It should be noticed that in the former incident, foreigners or non-citizens were involved while in the latter incident, a citizen was involved. In the former incident, the court doesn't intervene to order the registration of a case, while in the latter, not only the court orders to register a case under the antiterrorism law against the Rangers personnel but it also ensures the speedy procedure in the trial. In this essay, I emphasize on this differential response to highlight the tendency to discrimination in the criminal justice system of Pakistan inasmuch as its operation rests on the political condition of personal identity rather than the ethical and empathic conditions of human rights law. In other words, the system makes distinctions in personal legal identity of individuals in matters as basic as the right to life. Furthermore, I argue that the practice of making these identity-difference distinctions in the personal legal status of individuals does not just victimize aliens/non-citizens but also at times citizens are victimized. In the course of my analysis, I highlight that the practice of making identity-difference distinction is associated with the border, both historically and conceptually. The border is its potent source of initiation and enforcement. The practice of making identity-difference distinction is normally condoned through a persistent security discourse and it gradually begins to take roots in law. The border creates an ontological crisis of identity in everyday encounters of individuals with LEAs. In this line of argument, I question the relationship of the border with the violence of law enforcement. My exploration in the essay is divided into two parts. The first part traces the practice of making identity-difference distinction in security administration and law to highlight the legal structures of violence; and the second part explores the applied side of this practice—that is, the events of violence.

Legal Sovereignty on the Border

Legally Embedded Identity-Difference Model

When viewed from the perspective an 'empathic vision,' to borrow Jill Bennett's phrase,[3] the two incidents of violence occasion the need for critical self-reflection, especially on the part of lawmakers, to assess the growing powers of LEAs vis-à-vis the state of human rights—specifically the right to life. However, the local political stage, remarkably charged with a pervasive security discourse that is predicated on the ostensible existence of an existential threat to state security, spares no room for a debate that takes as its object ethical, human rights deliberations. Thus, in the years that followed the incidents, the government went on to introduce more security laws and greater powers for LEAs. The government thought it had strong reasons for so doing. First, the Haqqani network of the Taliban, based along the border in North Waziristan, had increased its suicide bombing campaign inside the country. Second, the Army, engaged in operations along the border and elsewhere in the country, had been levelling complaints against the criminal justice procedure, which often let go apprehended terrorists for want of substantive evidence or other procedural requirements. Third, as a consequence of their frustration with the criminal justice procedure, the Army through its intelligence agencies resorted to extrajudicial detentions of suspected terrorists and carried out secret investigations. The extrajudicial detentions, however, led to the much vexed issue of 'missing persons,' which towards the end of 2012 generated serious tension between the judiciary and the intelligence agencies. It is in this fraught political environment and with a self-conscious effort to address extrajudicial practices that the newly elected government of Nawaz Shareef (May 2013) decided to amend the Anti-Terrorism Act, 1997 (Act XX of 2013) and to issue an ordinance called the Protection of Pakistan Ordinance (PPO) 2013.[4] Later in June 2014 after the Haqqani Taliban attacked the Karachi Airport, and after the Army's subsequent operation against them, the government passed the PPO into an Act—the Protection of Pakistan Act (PPA) 2014. It is interesting to note that the government hoped to address the problem of the extrajudicial practices of LEAs only by giving more powers to them. Thus, the government indirectly empowered them to engage in almost the same extrajudicial practices, but now by legal means.

Before I shed light on these security laws, I want to spend a few lines on the methodological purpose and approach in the essay. My approach is informed by Michel Foucault's insight that the law is a complex site of enunciation of specific governmental programmes. It is through the law that these programmes are couched in normative and positive codes of conduct and avoid practical and political difficulties in their implementation. When these laws come into force, Foucault writes, 'They crystallize into institutions, they inform individual behavior, and they act as grids for perception and evaluation of things'.[5] It is this grid of perception and evaluation of *things*—in our case, identity—that interests me, especially because it opens the way to understanding and conceptualizing the applied side (i.e. the possibility of violence) of security laws. Since as Julia Kristeva writes, 'it is precisely with respect to laws that a foreigner exists,'[6] we need to focus on security laws and the grid of perception and evaluation that they create.

The latest security laws, as mentioned above, contain provisions that inscribe and embed the identity-difference distinction making and the use of lethal force. For instance, the primary subject in the PPA, 2014, is the category of the enemy alien. This category for the first time was defined in the PPO 2013, even though it was present in the Article 10(9) of the current Constitution. The definition of the category of enemy alien in PPO 2013 was worded in simple terms: an enemy alien is a person (a) who failed to establish his/her Pakistani citizenship and (b) he/she is found engaged in any of the offences of waging war, insurrection and/or depredation. This definition of enemy alien is however redefined and made complex in the PPA 2014, as it is indirectly defined through another category—that of the militant.

In the Protection of Pakistan (Amendment) Ordinance (PPAO) 2014, introduced six months before the PPA, 2014, the government also introduced a new category of the 'combatant enemy'. Although the government did not give reasons for introducing this new category, it can be surmised that the scope of the earlier category of the enemy alien was perhaps not broad enough to serve the security purposes of the state. The definition of the category of the combatant enemy in PPAO, 2014, comprises at least two main dimensions—identity of the individual and involvement in offences. First, a combatant enemy could be just 'any person,' unlike the enemy alien who had to be an alien. Second, such person should be involved in (a) raising of arms or waging war, or in aiding and abetting the same, (b) threatening of the security and integrity of the state, (c) committing or threatening to commit a Scheduled Offence and/or (d) involved in depredation. The category of combatant enemy is substituted with the category of militant in the PPA 2014, while the definition of the former category is retained from PPAO 2014 to define the latter category in PPA 2014. The definition is however broken down into five clauses and some new phrases are added to it. For instance, in clause (c) of section 2(f), two new phrases—'advocating' and 'encouraging'—are added to define the act of engagement in an offence. Apart from that, a new offence of 'violent struggle' is introduced. These new phrases and the offence of violent struggle have neither been defined in the act or any previous security laws, nor debated in the case law. Hence, it remains to be seen how the superior courts define and fix the meaning of these new additions. With these additions, nevertheless, the scope of the law to deal with security threats from both aliens and citizens has already widened even beyond the scope of the Anti-Terrorism Act, 1997.

In PPA 2014, with the introduction of the category of the militant, the category of the enemy alien is also redefined. Now, an enemy alien is not simply an alien person, but a militant, who happens to be an alien. In other words, he/she is a militant 'whose identity is not ascertainable as a Pakistani' or who has been deprived of his/her naturalized citizenship. Obviously, this is a nuanced change in the definition from the active tense (in PPO 2013, where it was said that an enemy alien is 'a person who fails to establish his citizenship') to the passive tense (in the PPA). However, this change does not suggest that the burden of proof has been brought back on the shoulders of the state. It rather points to an enhanced power of the state over the individual by giving the state the power to determine the individual's identity, to pronounce him/her an alien and potentially a militant. Theoretically, this power is akin to the sovereign power to determine in a state of exception case whether an exception exists and to make a decision on it.[7] It should also be noted that the category of the militant stands at a point midway between the categories of citizen and alien. In fact, it transforms both: if a citizen commits a scheduled offence, he/she becomes a militant and if an alien commits a scheduled offence, he/she becomes a militant of an enemy alien type. This legal strategic category of the militant challenges another theoretical insight in critical legal studies that separates a political decision (to exclude an alien) from a sovereign decision (to exclude a citizen).[8] Inasmuch as the sovereign can create middle categories like the militant as in the case of PPA 2014, we notice that the political and the sovereign decision collapse into a legal black hole.

It is worth pointing that The Protection of Pakistan laws provide for a double burden of proof—one relating to proving (national) identity and the other to proving non-involvement in a scheduled offence. The first type of burden of proof requires an individual to prove his/her identity as a citizen of Pakistan or of another country, or to prove that he or she has a different international legal status. The second type of burden of proof requires the individual to produce evidence to dispel the criminal charge made against him/her by a LEA. Another controversial aspect of the Protection of Pakistan laws relates to the use of lethal force sanctioned in them. The LEAs under Section 3 of PPA (2014) and PPO (2013) can open fire to kill an individual suspected of being an enemy alien or militant. This power to fire to kill was earlier provided under the Anti-Terrorism Act 1997, although later, some restrictions were placed on it by the superior courts. In a number of cases, the courts ruled that if law enforcement personnel are not fired upon or if they overpower a terrorist, the use of lethal force against him/her is illegal.[9] On the other hand, it is interesting to note that the power to use lethal force is not provided in the Foreigners Act 1946, which has been a law dealing with aliens for a long time. I shall return to this Act in a moment.

Furthermore, the Protection of Pakistan laws, like the earlier ATA 1997, afford unfettered search and arrest powers to LEAs. In Section 3 of PPA, 2014, the section that provides for the use of force, it is provided that LEAs can arrest a suspect and search any building or premises without warrant. Such arrests and searches can be made if there is reasonable suspicion or credible information that a person has committed or is about to commit a Scheduled Offence. It should be noted that the phrase 'about to commit' is coterminous with the scope of another phrase 'preparation to commit'. These phrases are quite broad in their legal scope/construction, and as I have elsewhere shown, they were first developed against rebellion and treason cases as long ago as the mid-nineteenth century in colonial times.[10] Now, they are being used in cases of the 'protection' of the state.

For providing speedy justice, the Protection of Pakistan laws and the ATA 1997 provide for setting up special courts. Both PPO 2013 and PPA 2014 provide the government the discretion to set up 'as many' special courts as it deems appropriate. Moreover, the government can set up special courts in high security prisons, which can be built under this act. In order to carry out speedy and effective prosecution, the Protection of Pakistan Laws also provide for establishing an independent Prosecuting Agency. Moreover, they provide for 'joint trials' of the accused—that is the government can transfer from any other court any case against an accused to a special court to be tried alongside the case already being heard.

Lastly, the Protection of Pakistan laws provide for a greater increased punishment than the ones provided in the Criminal Code. The PPO 2013, for instance, provided that a maximum of 10 years of imprisonment along with fines and confiscation of property could be awarded for a Scheduled

Offence. The PPA 2014 increased the ceiling to 20 years. Moreover, both laws provide that if the punishment in the panel code for a scheduled offence is higher than the one given in these laws, then the court can consider the higher punishment as well. And, a special Court can also deprive a person of his naturalized citizenship. It is interesting to notice that the punishment of confiscation of property from a citizen is symbolic of the crime of treason. Such confiscations were provided in colonial times to punish offences against the state. The provenance of this punishment of confiscation of property came from the treason laws of Britain.[11]

A Historically Embedded Identity Difference Model

In order to understand what the identity-difference distinction making in the Protection of Pakistan laws encompasses, therefore, we need to dig deeper into the layers of history and illuminate the various stages of its development and embedding. The genealogy of the identity-difference distinction making, as per this study, goes as far back as the initial stages of the British state-making in colonial India in the mid-nineteenth century. As I have pointed out elsewhere, this state-making began with penal laws and a penal code, rather than with constitutional law and defined rights and duties for the subjects.[12] In the wake of a burgeoning state making project in India, the British colonial administration deemed it essential to draw defined borders and harness the endemic trans-regional mobility of the people. On the northwestern frontier, apart from the reason of state making, the geostrategic imperatives of the Great Game and other British sponsored state-making projects in Afghanistan led the administration to consider a well-defined and securitized border. Hence, the border that was drawn at the turn of the century, which is often counted as a milestone political achievement of the colonial administration, was but a result of the contemporary geopolitics of war and state making in the region.

It is important to note that the British colonial administration took its first practical step towards this geo-political act of drawing and securitizing the colonial border in the realm of penal law. The administration passed a series of laws to check the free movement of people, especially those migrant peoples who valued their territorial identity (as often indicated by their territorially based surnames), and who refused to identify themselves with any specific territorial state or government. According to some recent studies, 'Mobility has been a key feature of life on the Frontier, with its inhabitants employing movement as strategy of survival and response to political pressure, as well as economic opportunism'.[13] On the other hand, Chris Bayly explains how the British administration was averse to free movement in the region:

> Nomads and wanderers were seen as disorderly elements—carriers of roguery and dissidence. This stereotype was often applied to traveling groups as

> harmless as ironsmiths and potters who linked up areas of production and consumption. It is not difficult to see how attitudes like this derived from experience of the great increase in social control which had taken place in contemporary England.[14]

In contemporary England, the government had introduced laws restricting the free movement ('vagrancy') of disorderly elements, including poor wandering people ('paupers') and aliens with criminal records, or aliens without the means of subsistence. Similar laws were then introduced in colonial India in the form of Act XXXIII of 1857, Act I of 1861 and Act III (Foreigners Act) of 1864. The legal harnessing of free trans-regional movement was the logical result of the contemporary political vision in England (and for that matter in the West in general) that the modern state was essentially a territorial state with defined territory, population and law of the land. In his seminal work, *The Status of Refugees in International Law*, Atle Grahl-Madsen, for instance, writes that it was the nineteenth century that witnessed the birth of the nationality law in Europe. In several countries, nationality laws came with other laws relating to aliens (the Aliens Acts)[15] much as if their 'correlative other'.[16] Both these types of laws—nationality acts and aliens acts—Nevzat Soguk further points out, carried relevance for 'the crafting of the sovereign territorial state'. In other words, they constituted 'yet another field of statist activity clearly linked to the name of the alien'.[17]

In a recent play on the negotiations of the Durand Line, Ron Hutchinson illuminates this British territorial vision for the modern state by juxtaposing it with its opposite vision entertained on the northwestern frontier of colonial India. In this play, the British representative Sir Mortimer Durand debates with King Abdur Rehman over the need for drawing a border between colonial India and Afghanistan. His primary argument underpins the contemporary British vision for a state to be territorially defined. On the other hand, Rehman is not only hesitant to negotiate a border but is also averse to the very idea of the border. Durand therefore tries to convince him by pointing to the geopolitical benefits of the border for the project of state making in Afghanistan. A part of the dialogue merits quoting here at length:

> Rehman: Is there not a case for leaving the exact borders undefined for now?
>
> Durand: (*Even more perplexed*) A thing has to be defined – Good God, that's what this whole century has been about. A disease, a law of science, an international border – they need defining; progress flows from the act of it.
>
> Rehman: But to define a country? Where there have been only tribes?....
>
> You want order—this is how to get its opposite.
>
> Durand: My head spins....

He brandishes the map, passionate—

There is no government without a map. You can put it on a wall, stick pins in it, point at it, make policy about it, if you have a go to war over it see what you've won and what you've lost. It is the abstract of decision, it is fact unvarnished. Absent it, there's nothing there, the world has no shape and that which has no shape has no meaning.

Rehman: If it leads to greater problems than it pretends to cure?
Durand: We'll fix those in turn.
Rehman: If it leads to endless war?
Durand: Then we'll fight it.[18]

Durand's adamant advocacy of a territorially defined state reflected the contemporary political vision of the colonial administration, which was centred on 'fact,' 'order,' 'shape' and 'progress'. In geopolitical terms, the vision entailed controlling the tribes, mapping the topography and harnessing the free movement on the frontier to give it some semblance of 'order' and 'shape,' and thereby, potentially register a modern/colonial 'fact'. In this way, it can be argued that the vision reflected the 'birth of biopolitics' on the frontier.[19] While Rehman might have agreed to Durand's proposal for a defined border, however, the former's interest in acquiring the mountainous region conflicted with the Forward Policy of the Raj, which was designed to expand the colonial sphere of political influence and control in the mountainous region. What this policy and the territorial vision immediately afforded the colonial administration was the increased control of the state over, and vis-à-vis, the individual's long-standing practice, if not right, of free movement. While the colonial administration was negotiating border with the Amir of Afghanistan, the control of free movement on the border was already in place in the legal realm (e.g. The Foreigners Act 1846). The administration had also developed politico-moral predicates of justification (which in a way also reflected the colonial political morality) for controlling the border. These politico-moral justifications were poverty or the lack of means of subsistence, lack of professional skills, mental soundness, criminality and/or simply foreignness/alienage of individuals involved in transregional movement.

Thus, in the Foreigners Act, 1864, the colonial administration introduced a number of substantive and procedural controls on free movement. The aim, which was quite telling, was to 'preventing foreigners from residing, sojourning, and passing through or traveling in British India without *consent* of the Government' (emphasis added). Here, it can be noticed that because both local subjects and foreigners were already subject to Penal Code 1860, which addressed crimes, it can be surmised that the political aim of the Act was not simply to check crimes committed by itinerant groups and wanderers but also to harness free movement across the region. In this line of policy then the colonial administration often placed emphasis on the principle of nativity to the land and loyalty to the Crown (Indian Council Act, 1861). Although both these principles were derived from the contemporary British political vision, they however lacked legitimate local political roots. Nevertheless, the administration went on to introduce them and thereby differentiated and discriminated between foreigners and natives. The Act clearly stipulated that difference by providing that anyone who was not a natural born subject of Her Majesty or a native of British India would thus be considered a foreigner. Although this new definition provided for an Indian subjectivity that was quite broad, it practically excluded those living in princely states, autonomous or tribal territories and border territories. Moreover, the Act placed the burden of proof of identity—whether or not an individual was a foreigner—on the individual. This provision was directly borrowed from British laws relating to aliens in England and it inverted the principle of presumption of innocence—innocent until proven guilty.[20] From the very early laws on the subject of aliens in England, it should be noted that the principle of presumption of innocence was never extended to aliens. This exclusion of aliens from fundamental legal principles of justice has since been at the base of the discriminatory legal regime (now globally in force), which privileges subjects/citizens over aliens/foreigners. In the wake of the War on Terror in Pakistan, the burden of proof on aliens has doubled as they are not only required to prove their identity but also their non-involvement in the alleged offence.

In order to check free movement after a foreigner had entered British India, the Foreigners Act provided that he/she should be placed under police surveillance as long as the requirement of peace and security demanded it. Apart from police surveillance, the Act also gave powers to the government to place foreigners in 'safe custody,' which could extend for an indefinite time, and their release depended on the 'conditions of peace and security'. Thus, we see that the use of state authority over aliens was institutionalized long ago, and it kept on growing.

The critical legal significance of the Foreigners Act, 1864, it can be argued, is not limited to how the colonial administration inscribed the substance and procedure for exercising control over the free movement in the penal laws. Rather, the significance goes beyond that inasmuch as it is related to the foundational aspect of defining personal legal identity on the basis of the fledgling Western political principle of 'difference'—the difference between subjects and foreigners, nativity and foreignness, local and foreign birth, and loyalty and treason. In this way, the Act gave effect to the oppositional binaries, which in turn related to the border and to the characteristic of foreignness as their permanent point of reference, and therefore that of personal legal identity as well. In other words, these oppositional binaries, as well as the personal legal identity that is based on them, surface and take their roots in the law because there existed a (geostrategic will to) border. Thus, a point can be made that legal subjecthood in colonial India began with imagining and defining its outside, i.e. with imagining the border and defining border law.

Over the next half century, the colonial administration engaged in drawing a complex and legally embedded border cartography of the northwestern frontier. The geopolitical exigency of the Great Game combined with an outward deference for the social customs of local tribal people led the colonial administration to introduce a series of criminal regulations called the Frontier Crimes Regulation (FCR) 1872, 1876, 1887 and 1901, and the Criminal Tribes Act, 1871, especially to border the frontier. With these regulations, the mountainous strip of the northwestern frontier was virtually transformed into a legal grey zone, with an external international border separating British India from Afghanistan and an internal border separating the tribal mountainous belt from the settled districts of British India. Inside this legal grey zone, the colonial administration further inscribed two zones: *Ilaqa ghair* (Area Foreign/Other) and *Ilaqa Sarkar* (Area Administration). In this mountainous strip, apart from controlling certain other strategically important tracts, the colonial administration took control of and securitized mountainous passes, roads and forts—collectively these constituted the *Ilaqa Sarkar* and the rest the lawless *Ilaqa ghair*. It is also worth noting that from the letter and spirit of the FCRs, the legal subjectivity of tribal people living in the mountain belt immensely suffered such that they were recognized neither as Indian subjects nor as foreigners, but as somewhere between these two categories. With the creation of this complex legal grey zone, having two controlled borders, the free movement of the people (including the tribal peoples) eventually came under the effective surveillance, if not full-fledged control, of the colonial administration.

Apart from the Foreigners Act, 1864, the Civil Procedure of 1908 presents another crucial marker of the identity-difference model in colonial legal history. At the beginning of twentieth century, before the outbreak of World War I, we find the terms 'alien enemy' and 'alien friends' which were provided for the first time in the Civil Procedure. In colonial India, the term 'foreigner' was in legal use, rather than the term alien, which was in common use in England and the United States. The Civil Procedure provided that even alien enemies could register and maintain civil suits in colonial courts. This provision meant that alien enemies had some legal persona and rights in the eyes of law at the beginning of the twentieth century. It is in this still liberal posture of law that Lord McNair in his contemporary seminal work on the legal effects of war indicated that in the British Empire, before World War I, there was not much difference between the legal status of subjects and aliens.[21] However, this observation should not be construed to mean that there was no legal distinction between subjects and aliens, or that the Empire did not want one, but that the drastic change in the legal standing of aliens that at once came along with World

War I made the previous distinction look negligible. By the time World War I ended, we notice that the category of 'enemy friend' phases out: in the United States, a century-long debate on immigration involving the concepts of enemy friend versus enemy alien comes to an end and in colonial India, the term 'alien friend' is not used again in any penal or civil law.[22] With these developments, the possibility of engaging in a liberal debate on human rights is negatively affected as one valuable concept drops out of the formal lexicon of the debate. In England, the government introduces the Defence of the Realm Act and the Defence of the Realm Regulations, 1914–1919, which places strict checks on the free movement of aliens. In colonial India, the Defence of India Act and Defence of India Regulations, 1915–1919, are passed, which impose similar checks on the free movement of foreigners. The Foreigners Act, 1864, is also then strictly enforced for the registration of foreigners, their police surveillance and safe custody. On the other hand, the British government transfers a large number of European enemy aliens to India and detains them in makeshift camps. Towards the end of the war, the Government of India Act, 1919, transfers the power to deal with foreigners and enemy aliens to the central government. To enhance this power further the government introduces the Passport Act in 1920. With this Act, the discretionary power of the government to check free movement of both subjects in and out of the country tremendously increases. The Act becomes the first colonial political instrument to formally and effectively separate the legal identities of foreigners and subjects. Furthermore, at the end of World War I, three Imperial Conferences (1918, 1921, 1923) are held, which accepted the discretion of the state to allow or expel an alien from its territories. It is also worth mentioning that in January 1920, the colonial government of India decides to completely bar the entry of enemy aliens for a period of 5 years.

The identity-difference distinction making, especially in the form of the subject-foreigner binary, is further embedded in the next round of security laws passed in the wake of World War II. The Registration of Foreigners Act, 1939, for instance, makes it mandatory for all foreigners to report both their arrivals and departures, as well as carry their legal proof of identity with them at all times. Then, under Defence of India Rules, 1939, a foreigner could be stopped from both entering and leaving the country. The government could also order foreigners to submit to procuring their photographs, thumb impressions and specimens of handwriting. Moreover, they could be kept under safe custody or moved to any prescribed detention camp. At the end of the war, a new Foreigners Act, 1946, is passed, which incorporates a number of provisions from these regulations and the previous Foreigners Act, for instance, police surveillance, medical tests, prohibition from associating with certain groups or activities and safe custody. One of the additions the new Act makes, however, is the provision that if the identity of a foreigner could not be known or is difficult to ascertain, then the government would have the discretion to decide on his/her identity. This provision is reflective of a similar provision and discretion therein available to the government in the latest Protection of Pakistan laws. Here, I also want to point to the Enemy Agents Ordinance, 1943, to note that the local root of the term 'enemy' in the concept of 'enemy alien' goes back to this ordinance. The ordinance came with provisions for special courts and speedy criminal procedures. The present concept of enemy alien in the Protection of Pakistan laws takes the term 'enemy,' as well as the special courts and procedure, from this ordinance, and the term 'alien' from the Foreigners Act. In its undefined form, the category of enemy alien is also later provided in Article 10 of the Constitution (1973).

In this Article 10, the Constitution guarantees safeguards against arbitrary arrest and detention, except in cases of preventive detention. While the Constitution allows for indefinite preventive detention of a citizen, if he/she is declared as an enemy agent, there are some formal procedural protections afforded to them in the form of a Review Board consisting of judges from the superior judiciary to periodically evaluate the case. However, if an individual is an alien and is reported to be involved in an offence against the security of the state, he/she is considered as an 'enemy alien' and does not have any protection against arbitrary arrest and detention under the Article 10(9). It is interesting to notice that in 2014, the Supreme Court ruled in the case of 'missing persons' that although Pakistan is not signatory to the International Convention for the Protection of All Persons from Enforced Disappearance (2006), the convention could still be applied 'to achieve the ends of justice' for the citizens who are missing.[23] While the court addressed the question of enforced disappearance of citizens, it remains to be seen whether the court would support a similar claim for aliens.

Legal Sovereignty on the Border

Identity-Difference Model and the Event of Violence

In the above genealogical account, I highlighted three crucial stages in the geopolitical and legal history of bordering the northwestern frontier of colonial India/Pakistan. In the first stage, during the mid-nineteenth century, the colonial administration harnessed free trans-regional movement, which was widespread at the time. The colonial administration did this by envisioning a territorial state model for India—a model that was and still is the leading political conception of the state. With the territorial state model, there arose the need for drawing well-defined, fixed and protected borders for colonial India. Moreover, the model also indirectly impinged on the subject's personal identity, which began to be redefined on the basis of territorial belonging/bordering. Hence, free movement was not only harnessed but it was made to seem as a practice in conflict with one of the foundational principles of the modern territorial state—territorial belonging and sedentary life. In the second stage, from the middle to the turn of the nineteenth century, before the cartographic border could be negotiated and drawn, the colonial administration erected a legal border by passing a series of laws and crime regulations. The legal border was drawn primarily on the terrain of personal legal identity: subjects were distinguished from foreigners, and their rights and duties began to have a new legal base—territorial belonging and loyalty. Third, towards the turn of the nineteenth century, as the cartographic border was drawn, together with the legal border (the FCRs), it resulted in a complex border with internal and external borderlines. Inside this complex border, the colonial administration chose to suspend the operation of law and courts (by providing FCRs). The administration ensured that all mountainous passes and strategic peaks and plains were guarded and controlled. Subsequently, these cartographic and legal borders outlive colonialism and exist to the present day. They are further strengthened by the provision of more powers to LEAs under the antiterrorism and the Protection of Pakistan laws. In 2016, the government began to fence the border along the Khyber Pass.

In this genealogical account, my essential purpose was to highlight the legal dimension of the border to tease out the law's relationship with violence. In ways that resonate with Shapiro's concept of violent cartography, which I engaged in the beginning of the essay, the well-known sociologist, Johan Galtung, introduced the concept of structural violence. According to Galtung, there are different forms of violence, which can however be characterized into two broad forms: direct violence and structural violence. Galtung writes:

> Whereas in the first case [direct violence] these consequences can be traced to concrete persons or actors, in the second case [structural violence] this is no longer meaningful. There may not be any person who directly harms another person in the structure. The violence is built into the structure and shows up as unequal power and consequently unequal life chances.[24]

The two events of violence—the Kharotabad and Karachi killings—with which I began the essay, are examples of direct violence, while the laws that I highlighted above in the genealogical account are examples of structural violence. The two types of violence are related in such a way that the former is not possible without the latter—the Kharotabad and Karachi killings would not have been possible without the deeper, embedded structure of violence in laws.

The two forms of violence—structural and direct—although distinct are not, however, independent of each other. In a recent take on Galtung's work, James Tyner and Joshua Inwood point out that the two forms of violence can be conceptualized as distinct from each other, but making such a distinction should not elide the responsibility for action. Hence, they suggest that violence should be carefully considered in its spatial and temporal contexts, especially with the aim of showing who carries out violence, why and how it is carried out.[25] In our context, which is a reading of events of violence in securitized spaces, we also notice the transformations between direct and structural violence. We notice that structural violence not only provides structural support for direct violence (or at times translates into direct violence) but it also helps the latter to elide responsibility. The support is afforded through a structure created by provisions of burden of proof, indemnity in the use of force, administrative discretion to warrant detention, the defence of necessity, general administrative rules and training manuals and the unwritten security discourse. Borrowing Agamben's concept of the security *dispositif*, I want to name the support structure of structural violence, the legal-administrative *dispositif* of violence. In the Kharotabad incident, we come to clearly see the legal-administrative *dispositif* of violence at play. For instance, once the killing took place, the LEAs tried to cover it up through different tactics. The doctor who carried out the autopsies and provided evidence was stopped from doing so. The local government resisted carrying out an 'internal' investigation under the Anti-terrorism Act 1997, and once that was done, the findings were not published in the name of state security. Moreover, in the eyes of criminal law, the victims, because they were aliens, had no legal standing to seek trial and justice. The support for these tactics was available in security laws and administration, which create, as Judith Butler puts it, the conditions for normalization of the state of exception through the governmentality of bureaucracy.[26]

Let us turn to the operational side of direct violence in securitized spaces and the question of responsibility. In other words, how does the event of direct violence take place, and how is it subsequently justified or covered up, as in the Kharotabad and Karachi killings? I want to argue that a crucial aspect to note in most cases of direct violence is the temporality of the *modus operandi*. Obviously, the speed is meant to avoid exposure, and thereby to increase the chances of eliding responsibility and hiding behind the legal-administrative *dispositif* of violence. Accordingly, most cases of direct violence in securitized spaces (even though these spaces are often equipped with CCTV cameras) go unrecorded or else are shielded by the legal-administrative *dispositif* of structural violence. However, thanks to camera technology in mobile phones and the uploading of videos to social media, some cases of direct violence do get recorded, allowing us to see and analyse the method of violence engaged.

There is no denying the fact that oftentimes LEAs, faced with security situations, have to make quick decisions on potential cases of terrorism. It is also understandable that the power to the use lethal force is sanctioned by law. Moreover, we also know that in bureaucracy and public administration, the power to make such decisions based on legal provisions is recognized as an exercise of administrative discretion. However, we need to notice, as Mark B. Salter points out, that the power to exercise administrative discretion is 'a decision that is not grounded in fact, but solely in the power to decide'.[27] Therefore, there is a need to generate a more nuanced understanding of how this rapid operating method in direct violence works. To explain this, I want to engage a conceptual insight from Michael J. Shapiro. Writing in the context of precipitous discharge of violence by combat drones (UAVs) on suspected terrorists/targets, Shapiro says that the personnel in charge prepare a certain 'necro-biography' of the targeted persons. A necro-biography, he says, is a 'murder justifying biographical speculation, which rapidly turn what is arbitrary into what is regarded as 'obvious''.[28] From this insight, I argue that in other cases of violence in securitized spaces, where armed personnel discharge violence on targeted persons, the process involves making quick biographical speculations as well, which thereby determines whether or not targeted persons are *obvious* terrorists. For instance, in the case of the Kharotabad killings, we notice that the personnel draw quick biographical speculations about the aliens, assuming and later labelling them as Chechen terrorists. We know well that in the security discourse in Pakistan—and elsewhere in the world for that matter—Chechens may easily pass for terrorists, especially when found in securitized spaces or troubled borders. On the other hand, in the Karachi killing, the young man had roamed around in an area under curfew and was speculated to be a persona non-granta. In both events, the personnel relied on quick biographical speculations and resorted to the use of lethal force, rather than arresting and detaining the victims, which they could easily have done.

In this context of quick decision-making, I want to point to an insight by Salter that the decision involving the determination of the identity of an individual precedes any legal claim or right. He writes, 'At the actual place of the border, the determination of status precedes the grant of 'leave to enter''. He further writes that an 'administrative, discretionary decision' to that effect lies at 'the exceptional threshold of law'.[29] This threshold is in fact the thinly veiled border between law and political fact, where direct violence finds its appropriate place. In the Foreigners Act 1946 (Article 8), we find a clear provision for the determination of nationality. The Act provides that in cases of difficulty in determination due to lack of or shortcomings in legal identity documents or oral testimony, the government will have discretion to declare the nationality of the person to which he/she seems 'most closely connected' or to which he/she has been 'last so connected'. The Act further provides that the government's discretion cannot be challenged in a court of law. Under the Act, the government can practically detain a person for an indefinite period of time until his/her identity is determined. The recent antiterrorism and the Protection of Pakistan laws go a step forward in adding to the criminal side of the process of determination of identity. For instance, the PPA 2014 provides that if a person's identity is 'unascertainable as Pakistani,' and if he/she is found to be involved in a prescribed offence against the state, then LEAs can arrest, detain and/or use force against him. These laws relate the determination of identity to perceived involvement in an offence and/or to even the mere physical presence in the locality of the offence and hence make individuals vulnerable. On the other hand, these laws make the use of force contingent upon the good faith judgement of the personnel about identity. In this way, the *obvious* identity is connected directly to judgement and execution by short-circuiting the entire criminal procedure of justice.

Just as law enforcement personnel engage in administrative discretion while determining the identity of individuals, there is no guarantee that they will always make a correct decision. This problematic aspect is caused by what Shapiro calls 'the fogging effect'.[30] In other words, due to the generalized nature of training in the art of distinguishing terrorists from the common people and/or the lack of sufficient information and understanding of the situation, social culture and appearances of individuals, the security eye of LEAs might cast a blurred gaze. Shapiro engages the Lacanian concept of 'the gaze' or 'the cultural screen' to explain the possibility of (mis-)recognition. He writes that (mis-) recognition is created because 'what is perceived is what is filtered through the gaze or 'the cultural screen' that is the condition of possibility for subjectivity'.[31] I have earlier pointed to a similar concept by Foucault of the 'grids of perception and evaluation'. The legal dimension of this gaze/grid is what I am calling the legal-administrative *dispositif*. Engaging Kant's First Critique, Shapiro further explains that an individual's consciousness is related to objects not merely in representational fashion but also in productive fashion. Our consciousness, he writes, often produces—not just identifies or represents—security threats. On the border, which remains in a permanent encounter with its alterity (for instance, the acknowledgement in the discourse of the War on Terror that the enemy has no face or identity—a faceless war[32]), this productive relationship of consciousness in creating the enemy or misrecognition in creating the enemy is clearly possible and understandable.

The conscious role of border security is to hold the threshold between law and anarchy.[33] Accordingly, the border not only represents the inside (of the state) but also its outside, its alterity.[34] In its corporeal form, the border's alterity is embodied and reflected by the ontological figure of the alien/foreigner. The alien is the embodied corporeal site of the state of exception. In descriptive terms, an alien who arrives at a border risks exposing himself/herself (because of his appearance, disposition and culture) to the burden of that country's security laws, and the executive discretion of their LEAs. In case of the Kharotabad victims, because they represented the border's alterity, which was in a way further screened through their Chechen appearance/labelling (at least for those who fell in the first round of firing), they exposed themselves to the burden of Pakistan's security laws and its LEAs' discretionary powers—to the legal-administrative *dispositif* of violence.

Although Shapiro's concepts of necro-biography and the fogging effect help to conceptualize the direct violence perpetrated in the two incidents, I argue that the Kharotabad incident is more complex and therefore needs an exercise in further conceptualization. In this incident, we see that violence is discharged on the victims not only due to quick murder-justifying biographical speculation but also because of their ethnic profiling. The assumed Chechen ethnicity of the victims provided safe warrant to the personnel to discharge violence. This type of violence, which involves murder-justifying ethnic profiling, we may name, for lack of a better term, 'necro-ethnography'. A necro-ethnography is a form of racial or ethnic profiling in securitized spaces, which warrants LEAs to make sovereign decisions on the life and death of individuals (belonging to or labelled as belonging to certain already maligned ethnic groups in security discourse). The concept aims to expose the structure of ethnic/racial and sectarian violence built in security discourse, which warrants taking sovereign decisions on the right to life of individuals. Generally, it tends to understand the relationship between the (perceived) ethnic/racial identity of individuals and the state's legal-administrative *dispositif* of violence.

An alternative way of conceptualizing and making sense of the Kharotabad killings is possible through N. A. Wonders' concept of the choreography of the border on bodies. Writing in the light of the idea of the performativity of identity, which was articulated in detail by Judith Butler, Wonders conceptualizes the violent border–body relationship as an 'elaborate dance' between state agents and mobile individuals.[35] Wonders argues that

> although states attempt to choreograph national borders, often in response to global pressures, these state policies have little meaning until they are 'performed' by state agents or by border crossers … Border agents and state bureaucrats play a critical role in determining where, how, and on whose body a border will be performed.[36]

In this line of thought, when human losses on or due to borders are taken into account in today's securitized world, it can be argued that, on a territorial border, there often exists a corporeal border or performative stage of corporeal bodies of rightless, mobile individuals on which the choreography of violence is played.

Conclusion

To question the relationship between the border and law enforcement violence is to highlight what is at stake in the growing legal regime of security, both theoretically and practically. Part of this legal regime rests on a security discourse that conceives the figure of the alien/foreigner as an agent of uncertainty and danger, and who hence is subject to state intervention. The alien embodies otherness, alterity and the border; but at the same time, the alien is the correlative of order, citizenship and the centre. The figure of the alien is located and recognized through the 'grids of perception and evaluation' and is sacrificed at the altar of peace and order.

The relationship between the border and law enforcement violence originates in and/or is prompted by the state's security discourse. The border is a cartographic extension of the logic of law enforcement—to mark and maintain the threshold between inside and outside, identity and difference, and order and anarchy. Just as violence (or direct violence) is discharged to maintain the border, this logic of law enforcement is choreographed on bodies. On the other hand, the responsibility for (direct) violence is eluded with the shield of structural violence—the administrative legal provisions that warrant the good faith acts of LEAs. Moreover, as we see in the case of the Kharotabad killings, the structural violence is so effectively rationalized and deeply regimented that the courts find it beyond the point to intervene and make amends. What is at stake here in the relationship between the border and the law enforcement violence then is the basic right to life of every individual.

Juxtaposing the two incidents of violence in this essay is not meant to merely critique the legal regime of security and conceptualize the operation of violence. Rather, the purpose has been to expose the structure of violence both in the law and law enforcement. For this purpose, I have shed light on the latest security laws, the Protection of Pakistan laws and how they create the possibility of enacting violence against non-citizens. Moreover, the purpose has been to remind the superior courts in Pakistan that their silence on the rights of alien/non-citizens results in the increase of the powers of LEAs on the one hand, and on the other, it leaves the public debate (and case law) on human rights (understood as different from fundamental rights of citizens) uninformed of legal opinion and vision of the judiciary. I have tried to make the point that reforming the legal regime of security in the country is not possible without exposing and attending to those provisions in the security and panel laws that derogate against basic human rights.

Notes

1. Syed Sami Raza, 'The North West Frontier of Pakistan: Preoccupation with "Unveiling" the Battlefield and the Continuing Violent Cartographies', in Samson Opondo and Michael J. Shapiro (eds.), *The New Violent Cartography: Geo-Analysis after the Aesthetic Turn* (New York: Routledge 2012) pp. 173–94.
2. Michael J. Shapiro, *Violent Cartographies: Mapping Cultures of War* (Minneapolis: University of Minnesota Press 1997) p. ix; Michael J. Shapiro, *Cinematic Geopolitics* (New York: Routledge 2009) p. 18.
3. Jill Bennett, *Empathic Vision: Affect, Trauma, and Contemporary Art* (Stanford: Stanford University Press 2005).
4. On anti-terrorism laws in Pakistan, see Charles H. Kennedy, 'The Creation and Development of Pakistan's Anti-Terrorism Regime, 1997–2002', in Satu P. Limaye, Mohan Malik, and Robert G. Wirsing (eds.), *Religious Radicalism and Security in South Asia* (Honolulu: Asia-Pacific Center for Security Studies 2004); Raza (note 1).

5. Michel Foucault, 'Why the Prison', in Graham Burchell, Colin Gordon, and Peter Miller (eds.), *The Foucault Effect: Studies in Governmentality* (London: Harvester Wheatsheaf 1991) p. 79.
6. Julia Kristeva, *Strangers to Ourselves* (New York: Columbia University Press 1991) p. 96.
7. Carl Schmitt, *Political Theology: Four Chapters on the Concept of Sovereignty*, trans. George Schwab (Chicago: University of Chicago Press 2005).
8. Mark B. Salter, 'When the Exception Becomes the Rule: Borders, Sovereignty, and Citizenship', *Citizenship Studies* 12/4 (2008) p. 372.
9. *Mehram Ali v. Federation of Pakistan*, PLD SC 111 (2000); *Suo Motu Case No. 10 of 2011*, PLD SC 997 (2011).
10. See Raza (note 1).
11. Ibid.
12. Ibid.
13. Magnus Marsden and Benjamin D. Hopkins, *Fragments of the Afghan Frontier* (Karachi: Oxford University Press 2013) p. 2; Also see Robert Nichols, *A History of Pushtun Migration 1775–2006* (Karachi: Oxford University Press 2008).
14. Chris A. Bayly, *Rulers, Townsmen and Bazaars: North Indian Society in the Age of British Expansion, 1770–1870* (London: Cambridge University Press 1983) p. 219.
15. Atle Grahl-Madsen, *The Status of Refugees in International Law* (Leyden: A.W. Sijthoff 1966) pp. 11, 95, 319–20.
16. Rogers Brubaker, *Citizenship and Nationhood in France and Germany* (Cambridge: Harvard University Press 1992) p. 37.
17. Nevzat Soguk, *States and Strangers: Refugees and Displacements of Statecraft* (Minneapolis: University of Minnesota Press 1999) pp. 97–98.
18. Ron Hutchinson, 'Durand's Line', in Nicolas Kent (ed.), *The Great Game: Afghanistan* (London: Oberon Books Ltd 2010) pp. 45–46.
19. I borrow this phrase and the idea behind it from Foucault. See Michel Foucault, *Security, Territory, Population: Lectures at the Collège de France 1977–1978* (New York: St Martins Press 2009); Michel Foucault, *The Birth of Biopolitics: Lectures at the Collège de France, 1978–1979* (New York: Picador 2010).
20. The requirement of burden of proof on the individual in the criminal procedure was and is the first step of (determining) culpability.
21. C.B.E. Lord McNair and A.D. Watts, *The Legal Effects of War* (Cambridge: Cambridge University Press 1966).
22. Syed Sami Raza, 'A Preliminary Note on the Genealogy of the Concept of Enemy Alien in Pakistan', *Pakistan Journal of Criminology* 7/2 (2015) pp. 43–54.
23. *Human Rights Case No. 29388-K of 2013*, PLD SC 305 (2014).
24. Johan Galtung, 'Violence, Peace, and Peace Research', *Journal of Peace Research* 6/3 (1969) pp. 170–71.
25. James Tyner and Joshua Inwood, 'Violence as Fetish: Geography, Marxism, and Dialectics', *Progress in Human Geography* 38 (2014) pp. 771–85.
26. Judith Butler, *Precarious Life: The Power of Mourning and Violence* (London: Verso 2004).
27. Salter (note 8) p. 370.
28. Michael J. Shapiro, *Politics and Time* (Cambridge: Polity Press 2016) p. 123.
29. Salter (note 8) p. 368.
30. Shapiro, *Cinematic Geopolitics* (note 2) p. 64.
31. Ibid., p. 65.

32. Syed Sami Raza, 'Critical Reflections on the Reality of Drone Warfare: Thinking with Jean Baudrillard', *IPRI Journal* 16/1 (2016) pp. 1–21.
33. M. B. Salter drawing on R.B.J. Walker, for instance, writes, 'The only "ethic" of which governs the border is the Machiavellian "virtue" of society'; Salter (note 8) p. 372.
34. Thomas Nail, *Theory of the Border* (New York: Oxford University Press 2016).
35. Nancy A. Wonders, 'Global Flows, Semi-Permeable Borders, and New Channels of Inequality: Border Crossers and Border Performativity', in S. Pickering and L. Weber (eds.), *Borders, Mobility and Technologies of Control* (Amsterdam: Springer 2006) p. 64.
36. Ibid., p. 66.

Security is a 'Mental Game': The Psychology of Bordering Checkposts in Pakistan

Maximilian Lohnert

ABSTRACT
This article explores how checkposts, as a practice of everyday bordering, shape individuals' feelings of 'ontological security' in the Pakistani cities of Peshawar, Islamabad and Lahore in a sample of Pakistani middle- and upper-class citizens. In this article, checkposts are treated as urban manifestations of the Afghanistan-Pakistan border, being erected by the Pakistani state in the attempt to reinforce the border in the context of the war on terror. In contrast to the tendency in much of the political science literature to analyse 'security' in relation to states and militaries, this article interrogates individuals' personal experiences of security by drawing on Giddens' notion of 'ontological security'. This exemplifies a shift away from quantitative accounts of what it means to 'be secure' towards a qualitative account of what it means to 'feel secure'. The research analyses a series of semi-structured interviews conducted with psychologists, humanitarian workers and peace educators in Pakistan in 2014. Linking my participants' narratives to an account of 'ontological security', I argue that bordering at checkposts diminishes feelings of security, even among citizens who seem not to be the prime suspects and target of checkposts.

Introduction

> I am a faithful loyal citizen of this country, and if I am stopped somewhere [...], I need to show my identity card. And that's why not only the notion of trust is affected between the law enforcement agencies, the state and the people. It also gives you the impression that you live in a state which is a security state rather than a social state. You have to prove that you are not a terrorist or criminal.
>
> \- Mustafa

Since the founding of Pakistan on the 14th of August 1947, 'national security' has been the state's key policy framework and the academic community's favoured framework with which to analyse Pakistan's domestic and international politics.[1] The emphasis on national security has brought with it a close attention to the concept of borders, and analyses surrounding 'borders' have mainly focused on Pakistan's state borders with India and Afghanistan, as well as China and Iran.[2] In her article in the *Special Issue* of this journal, Alimia describes how the international border between Afghanistan and Pakistan has over the years shifted from a 'soft' to a 'hard' border.[3] She explains that during the Soviet invasion of Afghanistan in 1979, the border was considered 'soft', as Pakistan welcomed millions of Afghani *mujahideen* with US backing in their allied war against communism. However, as the Soviets withdrew from Afghanistan in 1989, and since the onset of the war on terror (WOT) post-9/11, the Pakistani state under General Pervez Musharaf distanced itself, at least publicly, from the Afghan regime, which was suspected of sheltering the 9/11 attackers. With the impetus for tighter control at border crossings triggered by the shifting geopolitics of the region, the Pakistani state has attempted to reinforce the Afghanistan-Pakistan border and encouraged Afghans to leave the country through various assisted voluntary repatriation schemes, as well as employing enumeration and surveillance strategies. This article looks at one such surveillance strategy as a practice of everyday bordering: checkposts.

I met Mustafa[4], a peace-educator in his mid-40s, for lunch at the Kabul riverside in Nowshera. In our interview, he described how passing through checkposts in city centres serve not only as constant reminders of a possible threat, but also require the citizen to demonstrate each time that they are, themselves, not the threat. In Pakistan, checkposts and road blockages have come to populate Pakistan's urban centres in the context of the WOT, the military actions in the Federally Administered Tribal Areas (FATA) and Afghanistan as well as increased terrorist attacks within Pakistan. They are generally erected by the law enforcement agencies (police personnel) or paramilitary forces – the Frontier Corps in the western provinces of Balochistan and Khyber Pakhtunkhwa and the Rangers in the eastern provinces of Sindh and Punjab. The first signs of a checkpost within a city are usually spotted from several hundred meters away as the traffic suddenly starts to jam, and speed bumps and other traffic calming devices become visible. Most checkposts feature armed policemen strategically placed around fences, supported by stacked sandbags and armoured vehicles. There are usually officials checking the bypassing cars, motorbikes and pedestrians. While some cars are waved through, others are asked to halt their vehicles and provide their identity cards. They may be interrogated about their departing and arrival destinations. There is a tendency not to stop women drivers or families, and motorbikes are stopped more regularly than cars, especially if the passenger is male and travelling on his own. Over the years, there have been many shootings at checkposts, where suspected militants have been killed by security personnel at checkposts. One key example is the

2011 Kharotabad Incident, where four Russians and one Tajik citizen were gunned down on false police reports that there were suicide bombers – an incident covered by Raza's article in this issue.[5]

There are diverging views about 'for whom' and 'for what' checkposts in Pakistan are erected. In particular, in light of internal bombings in the urban centres of Pakistan, checkposts are, from an official perspective, considered and justified to be a means to install security for society.[6] By drawing particular attention to differing identification cards of Pakistanis and Afghans, Alimia argues that checkposts specifically target Afghans, who are perceived as 'mobile embodiments of the frontier – and indeed the wrong side of the frontier'.[7] However, she also notes that the state's rhetoric, which continually conflates 'Afghans' and 'Pashtuns', serves to justify the military operations in Pashtun-dominated areas in the Afghanistan-Pakistan borderland (such as the *Zarb-e-Azb* operation in FATA). According to her, checkposts are therefore not only 'about security and protection of the city and residents from bombings' but also a means through which the state engages in humiliation strategies, specifically targeting Pakistan's Afghan population and Pashtuns. This suggests that checkposts provide a means for the Pakistani state to shift the international border with Afghanistan inward. Checkposts have therefore become characteristic of bordering processes *within* the Pakistani state's territory. Checkposts bring the question which originates from the Afghanistan-Pakistan borderland – who is an intruder to the Pakistani state and a subversive political actor? – into Pakistan's domestic territory.

Building on Alimia's work, this article interrogates the flip side of the so-called protective security measure of checkposts: *insecurity*. It considers that bordering practices, including the crossing of checkposts, are practices of difference which both represent and produce identity, distinguishing between citizens and non-citizens in an inclusion/exclusion dynamic.[8] While Alimia's work analyses how Afghans and Pashtuns are excluded during the checkpost encounter from the nation–state through humiliation strategies, this article analyses the experience of Pakistani citizens and holders of national identity cards, who – theoretically – are 'embraced' into the state during the checkpost encounter. This form of embrace could establish a sense of shared national identity, leading to the feeling of protection and ultimately security. This article interrogates the extent to which this is the case, using a sample of middle- and upper-class Pakistani citizens. My own concern is not so much the question of for whom (or *against* whom) checkposts have been installed, nor the variety of checkposts in Pakistan or checkposts at the border crossings of Afghanistan and Pakistan and FATA. Instead, and in order to counter the trend of restricting analyses of security to national security and of studying borders in in Pakistan in strictly territorial and state-centric terms, I analyse individual experiences of bordering at checkposts in urban centres by reconceptualising the concept of *'human security'* in terms of a 'feeling of security'. To that end, this article analyses *how* such checkposts are experienced by citizens. It conceptualises this experience by drawing on Giddens' notion of 'ontological security', which he defines as the 'confidence that most human beings have in the continuity of their self-identity and in the constancy of the surrounding social and material environments'.[9] For the purpose of this article, an individual's feeling of security consists of three main building blocks: a) the predictability of the future, b) a sense of 'basic trust' in everyday life, and c) the construction of a *coherent* self-narrative that provides meaning and order to our lives overall.

This article is based on 14 semi-structured interviews conducted in the Pakistani cities of Islamabad, Lahore, Nowshera and Bara Gali in 2014. To get participants for the study, I followed a purposive sampling approach. Since I was interested in the relationship between the 'violent' state of Pakistani politics and the reported increase in people looking for and requiring mental health assistance since the early 2000s, I approached psychiatrists, psychotherapists, humanitarian activists and peace educators: participants I considered directly 'relevant to the [mental health] research questions [...] being posed'.[10] Through a 'snowball'-sampling technique, whereby the initially sampled participants 'propose other participants',[11] I interviewed 'colleagues of colleagues' and 'friends of friends', resulting in a sample that comprises people who are similarly positioned in Pakistan's social spectrum: within an educated urban-based Pakistani middle and upper class. All of my participants were fluent English-speakers (the language, all interviews were conducted in) and employed in official job sectors. All attended university, some of them abroad, and many were still active researchers. Nine were female, five male, and their ethnicity was Punjabi, Pashtun or mixed (although the role of ethnicity was not explicitly mentioned and discussed in many of the interviews). Hence, at no point did I intend to generate a representative data set for Pakistani society as a whole. Rather, the goal was to establish conceptual categories which correspond with the individual *bordering* experiences of the participants in this study. That is, the categories of 'security' used in this article have been directed by the data gathered from my respondents. When I asked my participants whether state security and checkposts help to overcome certain fears about terrorism and other insecurities in everyday life, their responses suggest that they conceive of 'security' and 'insecurity' as highly personal, emotional and everyday, that is, that 'security' is not only dependent on material forms of security, but also rather: 'feelings of security'. It is this understanding of security which prompts the first enquiry of this article: a conceptualisation of individuals' feelings of security in the context of Pakistan and political science. Overall, this article argues that even for Pakistani middle- and upper-class citizens, who are not the prime suspect and target of bordering practices, checkposts do not prevent but rather reinforce feelings of everyday insecurity.

Shifting the Referent of Security in Pakistan

Security lies at the heart of the discipline of international relations. Building on the Hobbesian notion of the insecurity in the state of nature – the war of all against all – the liberal paradigm traditionally defines security by the lack of a 'global securing subject or sovereign'.[12] For realists, security is quantifiable by calculating and comparing (material) military capabilities. Hence, traditionally, the main unit for realist security studies is the state and its territorial integrity. The key intention of the 'Copenhagen School', pioneered by the work of Barry Buzan and Ole Wæver, was to establish 'a new framework for analysis' for the study of security (1998).[13] By drawing on John L. Austins work on 'Speech Act Theory' (1962),[14] Wæver conceptualises 'security' as a speech act, arguing that 'security is not of interest as a sign that refers to something more real; the utterance *itself* is the act'.[15] 'Securitisation', thus, describes a *process*, whereby *labelling* a 'referent object' a security issue, casts it as an 'existential anxiety' and removes it from the normal procedures of politics.[16] Whereas the Copenhagen school moved away from an analysis of security in 'material' terms towards the social construction of security threats, they remained committed to a 'methodological collectivism' in which security was associated with the group as a unit such as the 'nation' or 'society'.[17] In the case of Pakistan, 'prolonged military rule and the country's peculiar geo-political situation [especially its relationship to India] have led to the adoption of a security paradigm that has always driven policies and practices in all fields of national life'.[18] The Pakistan Armed Forces are regularly listed among the ten biggest armies in the world (ranked by man power), with more than one million men in their security forces retaining control of 'foreign policy, national security and the nuclear arsenal'.[19] Yet, throughout Pakistan, conceptions of 'security' are generally linked to the 'nation' and the 'state' and those of 'borders' to its state borders with India, Afghanistan, China and Iran.

At the beginning of the 1990s, mainly as a response to the changing nature of conflict from inter- to intra-state conflicts, the concept of 'human security' became prominent through the 1994 Human Development Report from the United Nations Development Programme. The report argued that security 'has been related more to nation-states than to [the] people [...] who sought security in their daily lives'.[20] The report listed seven distinct categories of human insecurity – health, food, economic, personal, community, political and environmental – and was directed towards achieving individuals' 'freedom from fear' and 'freedom from want'.[21] More generally, the UN report resulted from the recognition that the security of individuals and communities did not necessarily 'follow from the security of the state in which they are citizens'.[22] In fact, the concept of human security made space for the recognition that individuals' human security may not only be threatened by 'external aggression, but also by factors within a country, including security forces'.[23] In the sparse literature of human security in Pakistan, Suleri argues that human security has been compromised in the country's quest for national security.[24] The paradigm shift away from national and state security towards human security was also witnessed in interdisciplinary border research, where increasingly a focus is put on 'decentralised society's (human) security concern'.[25] It is in this vein, as Joseph and Rothfuss note, that borders are no longer primarily preoccupied with how to guard 'against external threats to state territory [but rather with] securing everyday life', that is, borders have become a 'means by which the state territorialises fear and securitises spaces'.[26]

A Case for the Psychological Dimension of Security

Despite the analytical insights gained from shifting the focus of security studies from states to people, the concept of human security has analytical shortcomings. It has recently come under attack for silencing difference due to its reliance on a liberal notion of selfhood.[27] Traditionally, the emphasis on how global actors and forces such as humanitarian interventions or development aid are rolled out in the name of human security relies on a liberal notion of selfhood in quest of worldly salvation. In doing so, the human security paradigm has not only been largely 'impervious to specific to historical specificity, locality or place'[28] but also failed to take into account how that subject of human security is constantly reconfigured. This article aims to take account of this critique by focusing on individualised experiences of security at checkposts and aims to root the understanding of security within the specific geographic and social context in which the study takes place. There is another impetus to critique and re-conceptualise the understanding of human security: the concept of 'human security' was born out of development, humanitarian and global policy circles and is often defined as a list comprising several distinct (and apparently objective) aspects of security such as 'health' or 'home'. Since it is 'often easier to measure the absence of a qualitative good to its presence', many studies of human security tend to identify negative indicators[29] of human security – threats to human security – instead of human security itself.[30] For example, instead of analysing what a 'sense of home' really is, Leaning and Arie define it by identifying the 'threat' to a 'sense of home', namely 'social dislocation', which is more easily measurable.[31] This urge to quantify has not only been prevalent in research on human security, but also in psychological studies which aim to measure the level of depression or anxiety among population-based samples in

Pakistan.[32] In their systematic review of 20 quantitative studies on anxiety and depressive disorders in different population samples in Pakistan, Mirza and Jenkins found out that the 'mean overall prevalence of anxiety and depressive disorders' in Pakistan lies at 34%.[33] They note that they found 'little qualitative work',[34] underlining the need for qualitative approaches to the study of insecurity, anxiety and depression – indeed, an account of what those terms might actually mean in Pakistan.

This relates to the question of whether security is conceptualised as being objective or subjective, a crucial point of contention throughout the history of the term's use. Both the Cold-War conception of security, where security was viewed as the 'probability of states posing a threat or being able to deter enemies on the basis of their material capabilities',[35] and the human security paradigm which attempts to quantify what it means to 'be secure' by quantifying its absence, have relied on *objective* accounts of security. In her review of what the 'human-security' literature has contributed to the wider arena of security studies, Wibben turns to Krause and Williams who identified the two general trends in security studies: 'a *broadening* – "to include a wider range of potential threats" – and *deepening* – by "moving either down to the level of the individual or human security or up to the level of national or global security."'[36] The concept of human security has contributed greatly to these two trends. However, in primarily adding new dangers and referent objects to traditional security studies, the human security literature has failed to interrogate more precisely what 'security' means. This is why Wibben calls for an '*opening* of the agenda' of security, which includes challenging the underlying ontological and epistemological assumptions of traditional conceptions of security studies.[37]

Calls for shifting the emphasis towards a psychological and experiential dimension of security come from feminist security studies (FSS) and critical border studies (CBS). FSS has put a consistent impetus to account for individuals' emotions in the study of security. The classic feminist claim in security studies that 'the personal is international and the international is personal'[38] has always brought with it an emphasis on the personal and hence subjective dimension of security. In her recent article, Sjoberg argues for the benefits of extending feminist security studies to all investigations of security, and more particularly, for a 'recentering' of security studies to experiences and senses.[39] This includes accounting for 'experience *as* knowledge' – an approach this study endorses by drawing on participants' experiences of security during checkpost encounters.[40] Furthermore, this article takes up key concerns of CBS, particularly as formulated by Parkers and Vaughan-Williams' attempt to broaden and deepen the 'Lines in the Sand' agenda.[41] CBS urges analyses to move away from strictly territorial conceptions of borders to a notion of *bordering practices*, drawing attention to the fluid character of borders which are always in the making. This shifts the focus away from analysing controlling territory towards controlling mobility and emphasises the 'everyday' in how mobility is controlled and borders are experienced. CBS scholars furthermore adopt the 'lens of *performance* through which bordering practices are produced and reproduced', making space to analyse how borders are interlinked with identity-making ('producing') activities.[42] Taken together, the outlined critique of human security, and the calls of FSS and CBS, provides distinct but mutually helpful perspectives on the need to move to a different framework and vocabulary for conceptualising security. It is in this vein that this article's analysis can have particular value: in correcting the slant in the understanding of security by considering a psychological dimension. In doing so, this articles directly follows Stritzel and Vuori's call to bring back the dimension of the 'mind' to the study of security[43] by, instead of relying on materialist and objectivist accounts of security, constructing an understanding of the 'subjective and mental dimensions' of security.

Reconceptualising Human Security as Ontological Security

The psychological dimension of security has been queried by sociological studies that focus on how fear,[44] the assessment of risk[45] or anxiety[46] arises in the context of late-modernity and globalisation. Giddens most clearly elaborates on the relationship between security and identity in late-modernity, emphasising what Sweetman describes as 'the way in which individual identities can no longer be assumed, but have to be actively constructed from a range of available options'.[47] In this context, individuals struggle to uphold 'ontological security',[48] which Giddens defines as individuals' confidence in the 'continuity of their self-identity and in the constancy of the surrounding social and material environments'.[49] 'Ontological security' entered the discipline of politics through the doorway of international relations theory. Its first proponent, Mitzen, argued that, besides physical security, states also drive towards achieving 'ontological security', conceptualised as the security of a state's self/identity.[50] A recent Special Issue of the journal *Cooperation and Conflict* reviews the contribution 'ontological security' has made to the study of IR. According to Croft and Vaugham-Williams, there are two strands of how ontological security has been applied to IR.[51] The first strand[52] (primarily represented by the work of Mitzen[53] and Zarakol[54]) has moved Giddens' notion of ontological security from an individual to a statist ontology, with an emphasis as to how routine practices of states help to uphold a stable state identity. A second line of work, primarily represented by the work of Kinnvall[55] and Huysman[56], exists rather at the margins of IR and focuses more closely on the role of anxiety/dread in the conceptualisation of ontological security. This scholarship also draws on applications of ontological security from social science fields outside of IR, where the concept is, as envisioned by Giddens, applied to the individual. In their clear focus on the role of anxiety necessitating the construction of ontological security at the level of the individual, these authors stand more clearly in the tradition of Giddens' conceptualisation of ontological security. Yet, Croft and Vaugham-Williams argue that the first strand has been taken up more successfully by IR, partly because of the disciplines own ontological insecurity of being focused on the study of states and their relations to one another[57]. However, since this current article's focus is on individuals' ontological security, it follows more clearly the 'second strand' and takes Giddens' definition of ontological security (including the psychological scholarship he builds upon) as the starting point of its interrogation of individuals' ontological security. Ontological security investigates why states or individuals 'experience insecurity and existential anxiety and explores the emotional responses to these feelings'[58] and is therefore highly suited to investigate the psychological and emotional responses to bordering checkposts.

There has been little application of the concept of 'ontological security' at the level of the individual and to the human security paradigm, which is primarily concerned with physical human needs.[59] Revising the concept of human security by drawing on Giddens' concept of 'ontological security' exemplifies a shift away from an analysis which defines human security (or the lack thereof) by quantitatively identifying threats to it – as for example Leaning and Arie's attempt to identify 'home' (an aspect of human security) by measuring 'social dislocation' as its negative indicator. Instead, analysing human security as 'ontological security' is a move towards (qualitatively) illuminating the psychological processes involved in the construction of a 'feeling of security'. Overall, this is a shift away from an account of what it means to 'be secure' towards what it means to 'feel secure'. For example, in Pakistan, places of worship are a major site of terrorist attacks. Despite this, people continue to go because praying in one's (local or traditional) place of worship is important for sustaining the continuity of one's personal environment and self-identity as envisioned by Giddens. Thus, despite the fact that places of worship are likely to be highly *insecure* in quantitative terms (i.e. the number of killings), they are crucial for upholding people's feelings of security. Whereas Giddens puts forward his analysis in the context of discontinuities introduced by late modernity, the concept of 'ontological security' is also helpful for a study set in a conflict-ridden society. This is particularly true in the context of Pakistan, where matters of 'security' are not only abstract considerations but also materialised through the threat of terrorism in everyday life. In this setting, the possibility of upholding one's feeling of security has become more difficult – particularly in everyday settings where checkposts interrupt the constancy of the environment and appear to suggest that everyone is potentially dangerous. Despite its focus on applying the concept of 'ontological security' to my participants' bordering experiences, this article stays within the human security paradigm since the latter recognises that individuals' human security may not only be threatened by 'external aggression, but also by factors within a country, including security forces'.[60] Considering that checkposts are an encounter between security forces and individual citizens, they illuminate a distinction between state and human security – as envisioned by the human security paradigm. This allows this article to answers its key question: to what extent do checkposts, as a form of state security, influence human security – conceptualised as ontological security – among a sample of middle- and upper-class Pakistani citizens?

Bordering Checkposts and the Three Pillars of the 'Feeling of Security'

With the aim of clarifying the concept and analysis, as well as capturing different nuances of this study's participants' experiences of bordering checkposts, this article divides 'ontological security' into three interrelated pillars: unpredictability of the future, basic trust and coherent self-narratives. Each of these pillars will now be discussed in turn and integrated with the empirical findings.

(Un)Predictability of the Future

The work of the German philosopher Heidegger[61] provides a useful starting point for interrogating the relationship between future uncertainty, conceptualised as 'unpredictability', and ontological security, conceptualised as the construction/maintenance of a coherent stable identity. As the title of his magnum opus 'Being and Time' suggests, Heidegger focuses on the temporal aspect of being in his 'interpretation of *time* as the possible horizon of any understanding of being'.[62] According to Berenskoetter, Heidegger's argument is built on the insight that 'being takes place in a time-span between birth and death and so, because until it is dead, there is always something the Self is not-yet, being is always incomplete'.[63] 'Being-in-the-world' is not static, but rather a continuous 'process of *coming into being*'[64] and 'moving *towards* death'.[65] Since we cannot possibly know what 'death' is like, it is not fear but anxiety[66], 'coming out of the unknowability of the future, which is [according to Heidegger] the foundational sentiment [...] of the human condition'.[67] As a result, understanding the future is not only a key to grasping our own existence,[68] but also a major 'anxiety-controlling mechanisms'.[69] Giddens argues that 'colonising' the future is one of the means to achieve 'ontological security'.[70] Since routines 'hold the promise to exist indefinitely',[71] they, in a very practical sense, become a 'crucial bulwark against threatening anxieties' throughout life.[72]

In almost all interviews, this study's participants alluded to the fact that both the anticipation of dangers and the presence of checkposts interrupt their sense of 'everyday' life, where routines would be established and upheld without interruption. Mahnoor, a young English teacher and peace educationist from Peshawar, argued that 'people can no longer separate conflict from everyday life'. She recalled how in

> 2008 and 2012 it was normal, very normal: we came out of our university, we saw the blast, and we saw the smoking gear. We stood for half an hour, and then, we got inside and started our work. [...] That became a part of our life.

Underlying the inseparability of conflict and everyday life is what Noor called the 'Pakistan scenario', which she described as the 'uncertainty of everyday life'. She argued that Pakistanis are in a permanent state of 'not being sure what's happening', thus preventing Giddens' notion of a colonisation of the future. Mustafa narrated a story which exemplifies how far the images and vocabulary of conflict have entered everyday imaginings. He described how many children no longer play 'robber and police', but 'Taliban and police'. According to him, the Taliban are usually the more popular role in this game since they are simply more powerful:

> The children [who play the Taliban] throw dust in the air as an explosion and then capture the police. Then, they take them to the leader who will deliver a speech: "Oh, these are non-believers. These should be killed."

Mustafa himself recognised that 'this type of game already shows how much trauma there is in society where children have no other game to play'.

My field trip to Pakistan collided with the 'Azadi march', the anti-government protests organised by Imran Khan's *Pakistan Tehreek-e-Insaf* and Muhammad Tahir-ul-Qadri's *Pakistan Awami Tehreek* between August and December 2014. During the months-long sit-ins in front of the parliament in Islamabad, checkposts were installed throughout the city as 'security measures'. For weeks, my participants and many others I encountered during fieldwork waited every morning for a word from their bosses and supervisors informing them whether their workplace would be open or closed due to the day's 'checkpost-situation'. This interruption to their everyday routines caused great frustration. Many of my interviewees recalled the widespread frustration associated with checkposts and road blockages. Shahid emphasised that 'checkposts cause stress, because generally people have not factored in that it takes longer to get to work. [...] Sometimes there are long queues, so there is irritation'. Similarly, Zainab believed that 'these containers and road blockages are unnecessary. They are nonsense. It takes you three hours to get to work'.

Routines are one means for an individual to 'establish a sense of temporal continuity'[73] and thereby to make sense of the future. I found that it was not only the inseparability of conflict and everyday life which caused frustration, but particularly checkposts and road blockages which additionally undermine the sustenance of routines, thereby reducing an individual's ability to colonise the future.

Basic Trust in Everyday Life

After the 'predictability of the future', basic trust' as conceptualised by Erikson[74] is the second pillar of ontological security. Erikson argued that an individual's sense of 'basic trust' is acquired in the interaction with the primary caretaker during early childhood.[75] Basic trust also extends to things which are absent and is initially acquired by the child's insight that the primary caretaker who is out of sight will return.[76] It is this 'emotional acceptance of *absence*'[77] which underpins Giddens' definition of trust as 'confidence in the reliability of a person or system'.[78] Since basic trust is a sense of 'invulnerability' which blocks off negative possibilities in favour of a 'generalised attitude of hope',[79] it explains why individuals are not constantly feeling insecure in the face of the countless dangers they could potentially confront in everyday life. It allows Giddens to conceptualise trust as a 'protective cocoon', a 'screening-off device' constantly ruling out possible (negative) future events.[80] Goffman argues that trust in the public realm is sustained by what he describes as the state of 'normal appearances', wherein individuals feel 'safe and sound to continue on with the activity at hand with only peripheral attention given to checking up on the stability of the environment'.[81] This state of 'normal appearances' provides 'us with feelings of safety, certainty and familiarity'[82] as well as predictability. In effect, recalling Giddens, 'normal appearances' and 'basic trust' help us to colonise the future.

Multiple participants alluded to the fact that checkposts interrupt this state of 'normal appearances'. It is through checkposts that 'danger becomes physically real,' Shafaq said. 'If you see a new barrier somewhere, then you feel bad'. This line of reasoning was confirmed by Mustafa, who argued that checkposts are

> there because the state is not able to resolve the issue. [They remind you that] you are living somewhere, where anything could happen. I am here talking to you, but I have constant fear about my child in school and that my wife will reach home safely.

This is why, according to Mustafa, checkposts, instead of increasing security, are 'doing the opposite. They are causing the feeling of insecurity within the general population'. Since in their attempt to install security, checkposts may *decrease* the feeling of security, I argue that there is a paradoxical psychological dynamic underlying the process of securitisation. The literature on 'securitisation' focuses on the political consequences of labelling an issue or territory a 'security issue' – removing it 'from the realm of normal day-to-day politics [and] casting it as an 'existential threat' calling for and justifying extreme measures'.[83] But, moving away from this shift to 'extreme measures' within the work of the state itself, I want to emphasise the psychological consequences of the securitisation and bordering process. Sarah described security as a 'double-edged sword'. She recalled the irony that even a person's own private security guards do not necessarily increase the person's feelings of security since people 'pick up on the presence of guns', diminishing the expected feeling of security. Furthermore, in her work as a child therapist, Sarah experienced that increasing number of parents

> now decide that the children should sleep in the parents' bed. In some way, the parents are causing the child anxiety by doing this.

The parents who want their child to be sleeping in their bed trigger a feeling of insecurity in the same way as security guards, simply by turning one's attention to the presence of a 'security issue'. This helps explain how the securitisation of a particular area through a bordering practice at checkposts interrupts what Goffman describes as 'normal appearances'.[84] Hence, the utterance of 'security' has not only political (i.e. justifying extreme measures), but also psychological consequences: it creates the feeling of insecurity. In our interview, Anam captured the psychological dimension of 'security' by saying that

> It's always a mental game – right?! Nobody in the world can claim that you are secure. It's a mental game. Anything can happen to anyone at any point in life.

This section has shown that the presence of checkposts interrupt what Goffman described as the 'state of normal appearances'.[85] It undermines an individual's 'protective cocoon' of trust which usually helps in ruling out possible negative (future) events.[86] As a consequence, the negative possibilities exemplified in Mustafa's concern about his wife and child come to the fore of consciousness.

Coherent Self-Narratives

The third pillar of the 'feeling of security' builds on Giddens' conceptualisation of identity as the '*self as reflexively understood by the person* in terms of her or his *own narrative*'.[87] The idea that identity is based on the 'consistent feeing of biographical continuity where the individual is able to sustain a narrative about the self[88] has found resonance in the field of narrative psychology. McAdams, one of the field's seminal figures, argues that people 'reconstruct the personal past, perceive the present and anticipate the future in terms of an internalised and [...] integrative narrative of self'.[89] Underlying this is the idea that individuals' self-narratives are fundamental in 'constructing order and making sense of our lives'.[90] Since without a 'narrative structure, our lives can seem fragmented and devoid of meaning',[91] the self-narrative's degree of coherence is related to psychological well-being.[92] Coherent self-narratives provide 'answers to fundamental existential questions'[93] – for example, the question of 'Who am I?' could be answered by 'I am a loyal Pakistani citizen' – and in this, they are essential for attaining ontological security. IR scholars have added another dimension to this notion of narrative security, namely that the sense of self needs to be 'affirmed by others'.[94] Rumelili draws attention to the fact that 'ontological security requires differentiation and in that sense presupposes an other'.[95] This relationship can be a 'negative relationship of enmity as well as a positive one of friendship and amity'.[96]

Some of the participants experienced the interaction with policemen at checkposts as a form of protection. When asked about her experiences at checkposts, Shafaq replied that 'even policemen are so nice. They are also from *us* and from *our* community' (my emphasis). She even goes so far to argue that if one is considering the situation at checkposts 'in a way that this person [the policemen] is asked to do his job [...], if you understand it from a human point of view, you may not see it as a barrier'. Mahnoor was eager to highlight the 'effectiveness' of checkposts. 'Checkposts do make us feel secure in a way, because it has reduced all this violence and bombings in Peshawar', she said. Despite the fact that checkposts may cause

> frustration in the morning when people are going to office or school, [...] people think that they are there for *us*. We should support them [policemen at checkposts]. They are working for *us*' (my emphasis).

The bordering process during the checkpost encounter confirms her self-narrative, wherein she and the policemen are on one side (forming a 'cohesive order'), and the terrorist – the *other* – on the other side. Since the coherency of her personal narrative is sustained and because she feels protected by the policemen, her feeling of security is enhanced by the presence of checkposts. This corresponds to Rumelili's argument that self-narratives can be sustained by 'positive' others such as friendship, amity or, as in this case, a fellow loyal citizen.[97] Both her and Shafaq's view correspond with the official discourse which states that checkposts are installed 'to survey, police and deter subversive political actors, i.e. potential bombers', in the WOT and thereby to protect the city and its citizens.[98] In these cases, checkposts as a bordering practice embrace the participants as citizens and a bounded identity of being a Pakistani citizen gets confirmed.

In contrast to Shafaq's and Mahnoor's perspective on the self-other dynamic at checkposts, who are 'embraced' into state during the checkpost encounter, some of the participants felt themselves 'othered' during the bordering process at checkposts. They experience the checkpost encounter as a personal accusation and feel not embraced but excluded from the state. When asked about his experience at checkposts, Shahid angrily said

> Why should they think I'm a terrorist? They tell me that they're stopping me to protect me, but I don't buy this that easy.

In a similar vein, Mustafa described his bordering experience at checkposts in the following way:

> If I am going to my routine work, if I am a faithful loyal citizen of this country, and if I am stopped somewhere and somebody is asking for my identity – in my eight months in the US, no one was asking for my identity –but here, when I go to Peshawar, three, four times I need to show my identity card. And that's why not only the notion of trust is affected between the law enforcement agencies, the state and the people. It also gives you the impression that you live in a state which is a security state rather than a social state. You have to prove that you are not a terrorist or criminal.

Mustafa considers himself to be a 'loyal' Pakistani citizen. At the checkpost, however, he feels 'othered', having to defend himself from not being perceived as a terrorist, that is, to be on the opposing side of the Pakistani state in the WOT. This interaction stands in opposition to his self-understanding. The checkpost encounter fractures the coherency of his self-narrative, thereby reducing his feeling of 'narrative' security.

Building upon my data, I want to draw attention to an often overlooked quality of security: that security and insecurity can by no means be understood as a dichotomy. Sjoberg draws attention to the fact that 'those feelings are not stable constants existing on one side or the other of an imagined secure/insecure dichotomy; they are floating parts of security assemblages – collected, gathered, but not necessarily coherent'.[99] Let us remind ourselves of my participant Shafaq's accounts. Reflecting on how checkposts interrupt routines, she told me that it is through checkposts that 'danger becomes physically real. If you see a new barrier somewhere, then you feel bad'. Through this statement, she lays open her feeling of insecurity in the face of checkposts. Later on in our interview, however, she was eager to highlight that 'even police men are so nice [...] and from our community', arguing that 'in a way that this person [the policemen] is asked to do his job [...], if you understand it from a human point of view, you may not see it as a barrier'. Her 'narrative security' is therefore upheld. Shafaq's example shows that she is insecure about some dimension of checkposts, while feeling secure about others. This shows that security and insecurity are not necessarily dichotomous values and feelings, but can coexist.

This section has shown that an individual's *perception* of 'for whom' and 'for what' checkposts are installed, influences whether the checkpost encounter is experienced as a form of personal protection or surveillance. It has shown how the questions born from the Afghanistan-Pakistan borderland regarding who is a subversive political actor affects this study's middle- and upper-class Pakistani citizens passing checkposts in Pakistan's urban centres. The conveyed suspicion is often contrary to their self-understandings as respectable Pakistani citizens, and the implicit accusation of potential disloyalty diminishes their sense of 'narrative' security.

Disentangling Checkposts from 'Security'

From the perspective of Shahid and Mustafa, who both felt themselves othered during the checkpost encounter, the following question arises: If checkposts are not for their protection, for whom are checkposts actually installed? Farooq, another psychologist from a university in Islamabad, argued the following:

> Checkposts do not increase any sense of security, because public opinion is different. All these security measures, checkposts every kilometre, they are not for public security – they are for high-profile people. The public is only facing trouble. I have to go to my workplace two hours earlier due to ten checkposts. Our politicians are concerned about themselves, not the public.

Abdul similarly argued that 'only few people need this kind of security. [...] Most people are frustrated [by the presence of checkposts], and they don't see it as protection'. Farooq's and Abdul's perspectives confirm Suleri's assertion that in Pakistan human security is compromised for state (officials') security.[100]

While Farooq and Abdul expressed the idea that checkposts simply protect high-profile people, several of my participants argued that in some cases checkposts are a means to an end for the government. This view is underpinned by the idea that 'governments are able to rule by capitalising on citizens' fear'.[101] Referring to the Azadi march, which during my field research was widely called the 'Islamabad drama', Ayesha made the following observation:

> If you look at it more objectively, so-called security measures are also efforts to block protests that are anti-government. When the government had their own rally two days ago here in Lahore, there were no containers. There was nothing blocking them. It is not security so much, but a hassle they want to create for the anti-government slogans that these people are chanting.

I happened to encounter this pro-government rally myself, travelling in a rickshaw from Model Town to the Old Town of Lahore. Hundreds of Nawaz Sharif's followers were driving in cars overloaded with people chanting pro-government slogans, as well as motorbikes with *Pakistan Muslim League* flags on their side. The jubilant atmosphere of these protests was reinforced by the complete absence of police forces. The contrast to the anti-government protests in Islamabad was striking. Building on my discussion of the psychological consequences of the securitisation process, it can be argued that the presence of checkposts surrounding the anti-government demonstrations in Islamabad is vital for creating an atmosphere of insecurity. Since, following Beck, it is the '*perception* of threatening risks [which] determines thoughts and actions',[102] all my local acquaintances advised me not go to the area of the anti-government demonstrations. Similar to arguments posed by Beck, Shafaq argued that 'more than the actual threat, it is a perceived threat that we are at risk'. In such a way, playing with the population's perception of risk through securitising an area and thereby furthering individuals' feelings of insecurity is a *means* for the Pakistani government to block off anti-government protests. These observations confirm the recent trend that borders are 'increasingly becoming mechanisms to control mobility rather than territory'[103] and a 'means by which the state territorialises fear and securitises spaces'.[104]

The variety of perceptions regarding the function of checkposts indicate that 'security' itself can never be taken for granted, nor be seen as being either 'good' or 'bad'. Rather, security is very much a 'floating' signifier, a term that can be filled and instrumentalised with a variety of political content.[105] Bearing this in mind, I have followed Wibben's advice to 'tackle the politics of security [...] head on'[106] and interrogated my participants' accounts of what they believe that checkposts are *really* for. The variety of conceptions of what the Pakistani state intends to achieve through checkposts, ranging from protecting its citizens or only high-profile politicians, controlling citizens' mobility, humiliating or surveilling them, to some extent disentangled checkposts from the state's notion that 'security' measures are about protection of the general public. This underlines that the Pakistani state's accounts of 'security' (measures) cannot be taken for granted but must rather be dissected and analysed within specific contexts.

The Limits of Human Security as Ontological Security and the Resilient Self

So far, this article has employed an account of 'ontological security' and shown that for this study's participants, checkpoints often seem to undermine it. Such an analysis presupposed the possibility of 'security' – a notion worth questioning in its own right. Drawing on the theories of Beck and

Giddens, Chandler establishes a post-liberal account of human security, arguing that 'security' is not something which can be achieved by either a securing state or individual. He argues that the forces of globalisation, and globalised threats such as terrorism, have undermined the possibility of establishing security with the notion of 'the human as a knowing instrumental agent or an actor capable of shaping the external environment in order to secure itself'.[107] Instead, what this post-liberal account of human security works towards is the establishment of resilience, which Chandler defines as the 'capacity to positively or successfully adapt to external problems or threats'.[108] Similarly, Browning and Joenniemi critique recent applications of 'ontological security' for their emphasis on the need for identity-related stability, where change is perceived as anxiety-inducing and potentially harmful.[109] By linking their account of 'ontological security' more closely with a notion of reflexivity, they argue that 'ontological security is not just a question of stability but also adaptability, that is, openness towards and the ability to cope with change'.[110] Many of this study's participants, while emphasising the powerlessness and insecurities they experience in the face of checkposts and insecurities in everyday life, also highlighted their capacity to be resilient in the face of hazards. Hence, in contrast to previous sections which have shown how checkposts undermine individuals' feelings of security, this section – employing notions of security as adaptability – gives space to explore my participants' efforts to stay resilient in the face of the everyday insecurities (including checkposts) they encounter in their everyday lives.

For example, Salma argued that

> it is not all that bleak in that sense. There are many who have developed new ways of releasing their stress. We have really explored our own resilience of how to still stay sane in this chaos. […] People joke about what is going on.

For her, the Azadi March, the months-long anti-government protest organised in the summer of 2014 by Imran Khan's *Pakistan Tehreek-e-Insaf* and Muhammad Tahir-ul-Qadri's political party *Pakistan Awami Tehreek*, was an

> expression of resilience. People still have hopes […] they are voicing their concerns. Their strategy might be wrong, but they agree on the concern and the issue. This is hopeful to me: there is a resilient self [besides the] distressed self.

Referring to the rupture of checkpoints in everyday life, Benish recalled that this

> became part of our life. People told "us you know you will be late, so get out earlier of your house." We are resilient.

Similarly, Salma recalled how during the Azadi March demonstrations 'the shops were closed. Initially, we were hold up in the house, but then everybody just got out and started doing their stuff'.

While it is important to recognise the 'resilient self' of Pakistanis, I follow Gayer's analysis that Pakistanis have 'adjusted their everyday life, as best as they could, to the virtual or actual threat of political, ethnic and criminal violence. Rather than coping *with* crisis, they have learned to cope *in* crisis'.[111] Reflecting on how people cope with insecurities in everyday life, Salma argued that 'compartmentalisation' is one form of coping *in* crisis:

> people have become emotionally numb to these things. [...] Unless they are directly effected, people's lives go on. [..] If you look at what is going on everywhere in the country – people compartmentalise what's going on because if you think about it all the time, it is so overwhelming, it takes you over and consumes you.

These accounts give some credibility to the notion of human security as resilience. At this point, however, it is once more crucial to emphasise this study's sample of upper- and middle-class Pakistani. The very fact that they themselves brought resilience as a conceptual tool into the discussion of our interviews shows the familiarity with humanitarian discourses. This is probably symptomatic of their privileged status in society, and the fact that they have the resources and capacities to maintain resilience in the face of everyday hazards.

Conclusion

This article has explored multiple meanings of 'security' in the context of Pakistan – a question, which, despite the broadening and deepening of security studies, has received too little analytical engagement. Through a reconceptualisation of human security as ontological security, this article has been able to interrogate its participants' feeling of security at the moment of bordering checkposts. In doing so, it has shown that state security, as manifested in the presence of checkposts, does not foster but undermine this study's participants' feelings of security. This shows that checkposts, while being an attempt to reinforce the Pakistan-Afghanistan border and therefore primarily targeted at Afghans, has also psychological consequences for Pakistani middle- and upper-class citizens. Instead of being embraced into the state at the moment of bordering, checkpoints have diminished the feeling of security for the middle- and upper-class Pakistanis of this study in three ways: by undermining their ability to colonise their future, by rupturing their sense of basic trust in everyday life, and – crucially – by othering their self-narrative of being loyal Pakistani citizens. This finding complements Alimia's findings in the Special Issue of this journal, investigating the experience of the border for Afghans. She argues that Afghans spend so much time undergoing bordering practices that the border effectively 'becomes a part of them and [their] understandings of self'.[112] Her analysis is similar to Khalidi's and Rumelili's analysis of Palestinians' experiences at Israeli checkposts, where whatever 'happens to the Palestinians at these crossing points brings home to them how much they share in common as people,[113] and therefore, Israeli checkposts are a 'source of ontological security for Palestinians'.[114] In this case, as envisioned by Zarakol, Palestinians' sense of self is affirmed by (in this case, negative) others.[115] Since, as in contrast to Afghans (and to a lesser extent also Pashtuns) who already hold a minority position with respect to the Punjabi-dominated Pakistani state elite, checkposts in urban centres of Pakistan *other* Pakistani citizens themselves and thereby do not affirm but question my participants' sense of self.

While this article's emphasis lay on showing how checkposts undermine individuals' feelings of security, the end of the article – in line with the recent recognition of the impossibility of complete security and a notion of security as adaptability/resilience – showed how many of this study's participants emphasised the need to be resilient in the current climate of insecurity in Pakistan. Crucially, feelings of security in relation to checkposts but also other everyday hazards are likely to play out differently depending on how an individual is situated in Pakistan's social structure. For example, one aspect of the feeling of security as conceptualised in this article includes the ability to colonise the future and uphold routines. In addition to checkposts, everyday life in Pakistan is also interrupted by power outages and water shortages. Being adaptable in the face of such hazards requires economic capital. Hence, upholding routines and colonising the future are likely to be more difficult for a daily labourer as compared to the middle- and upper-class citizens included in this study – including upholding routines in the face of everyday security threats and checkposts. Furthermore, economic capital is often connected to other kinds of capital, including cultural capital, which became apparent in this study's participants' familiarity with the humanitarian discourse of resilience. Hence, not only the experience of in/security, but also how it is articulated, is likely to differ for people who occupy different positions in Pakistan's social structure. Hence, the undermining and upholding feelings of security in the face of everyday insecurities and checkposts require further investigation with a bigger and more diverse sample size than the current study.

The analytical distinction between quantitative and qualitative accounts of security made the opposition between checkposts – as a form of state security – and those of my participants (i.e. their 'feelings of security') possible in the first place. While checkposts may be counted as a sign for security in quantitative terms (i.e. where the number of security personal or guns add up to security), this understanding of security does not map onto this study's participants' feelings of security. The human security paradigm often ignores the difference between material and psychological security, and as a consequence, the relationship between these two distinct concepts. The analysis of the paradoxical dynamics underlying securitisation has shown that checkposts, simply by drawing attention to the existence of a security issue, can trigger the feeling of insecurity among my participants. This draws attention to the fact that security and insecurity are intimately bound up with one another, since, as Stritzel and Vulori put it: 'As security arguments contain a threat, they, in effect, reproduce insecurities'.[116] Overall, this article highlights the indispensability of a qualitative analysis of bordering experiences and (human) security, as in-depth interviews and ethnographic research hold the possibility of shedding light upon people's experiences of 'feeling secure' as juxtaposed to mainstream political perceptions of 'being secure'. This article has taken up FSS's call to focus on the emotional aspects of security, as well as CBS's call to draw attention to the experiences of border crossing. This psychological angle has allowed this article to lay bare contractions and oppositions within the 'understanding' of security in contemporary Pakistani society, produced alternative readings of the 'checkpost' and its crossings, and has highlighted the need to take seriously the mental worlds of individuals in the understanding of security.

Acknowledgments

I want to sincerely thank Dr. Matthew Nelson, Dr. Felix Berenskoetter, Dr. Sami Raza and the anonymous reviewers for their feedback to earlier versions of this manuscript.

Notes

1. E. Sridharan, 'International Relations Theory and the India-Pakistan Conflict', *India Review* 4/2 (2007) pp. 103–24.
2. Ibid.; P. Das, 'Issues in the Management of the India-Pakistan International Border', *Strategic Analysis* 38/3 (2014) pp. 307–24; G. Perkovich and T. Dalton, *Not War, Not Peace?: Motivating Pakistan to Prevent Cross-Border Terrorism* (New Delhi: Oxford University Press 2016).
3. S. Alimia, 'Performing the Border: Afghan Refugees, Identity Cards, and the Expulsion from Pakistan', *Geopolitics*.
4. All the study's participants' names are pseudonyms.
5. S. Raza, 'Legal Sovereignty on the Border: Aliens, Identity, and Violence in the Northwestern Frontier of Pakistan', *Geopolitics*.
6. S. Alimia, *The Quest for Humanity in a Dehumanised State: Afghan Refugees and Devalued Citizens in Urban Pakistan, 1979–2012* (PhD-thesis submitted at the Department of Politics and International Studies, School of Oriental and African Studies) (2013) p. 277.
7. Ibid., pp. 307–8.
8. A. M. Bouzas, 'Mixed Legacies in Contested Borderlands: Skardu and the Kashmir Dispute', *Geopolitics* 17/4 (2012) pp. 867–86.

9. A. Giddens, *Modernity and Self-Identify: Self and Society in Late Modernity* (Cambridge: Polity Press 1991) p. 92.
10. A. Bryman, *Social Research Methods* (Oxford: Oxford University Press 2012) p. 414.
11. Ibid., p. 424.
12. D. Chandler, 'Rethinking the Subject of Human Security', in M. K. Pasha (ed.), *Globalization, Difference, and Human Security* (New York: Routledge 2013).
13. B. Buzan et al., *Security: A New Framework for Analysis* (London: Lynne Rienner Publishers 1998).
14. J. L. Austin, *How to Do things with Words* (Oxford: Clarendon Press 1962).
15. O. Wæver, 'Securitisation and Desecuritisation', in R. D. Lipschutz (ed.), *On Security* (New York: Columbia University Press 1995) p. 35.
16. J. Huysmans, 'What's in an Act? On Security Speech Acts and Little Security Nothings', *Security Dialogue* 42/4–5 (2011) p. 372.
17. C. Peoples and N. Vaughan-Williams, *Critical Security Studies: An Introduction* (London and New York: Routledge 2010) p. 82.
18. A. Q. Suleri, 'Insecurity Breeds Insecurity', in A. M. Weiss and S. G. Khattak (eds.), *Development Challenges Confronting Pakistan* (Virginia: Stylus Publishing 2013) p. 57.
19. A. Rashid, *Pakistan On the Brink* (New York: Penguin Group 2012) p. 27.
20. United National Development Programme (UNDP), *New Dimensions of Human Security* (New York: Oxford University Press 1994) p. 22.
21. J. Leaning and S. Arie, *Human Security: A Framework for Assessment in Conflict and Transition*, Thinking Complex Emergency Response and Transition Initiative - Crisis and Transition Tool Kit (2000) p. 8.
22. P. Bilgin, 'Individual and Societal Dimensions of Security', *International Studies Review* 5/2 (2003) p. 213.
23. R. Thakur, 'A Political Worldview', *Security Dialogue* 35 (2004) p. 347.
24. A. Q. Suleri (note 18) p. 57.
25. Y. Joseph and R. Rothfuss, 'Symbolic Border and the Securitization of Identity Markers in Nigeria's Ethno-Religiously Segregated City of Jos', in R. Jones and C. Johnson (eds.), *Placing the Border in Everyday Life* (Farnham: Ashgate Publishing Limited 2014) p. 167.
26. Ibid., p. 171.
27. M. K. Pasha, *Globalization, Differences, and Human Security* (Oxon: Routledge 2013).
28. Ibid., p. 28.
29. Stritzel and Vuori have drawn attention to the etymology of the English word 'security' which derived from the 'Roman word *securus*, where *se* means "without" and *cura* means "worry", "care", "concern" or "anxiety."' Hence, security has also, traditionally, always been defined in negative terms, as *not being insecure;* H. Stritzel and J. Vuori, 'Security', in F. Berenskoetter et al. (eds.), *Concepts in World Politics* (London: Sage Publications 2016) p. 45.
30. J. Leaning and S. Arie (note 21) p. 35.
31. Ibid., p. 24.
32. N. Husain et al. 'Social Factors Associated with Chronic Depression Among a Population-based Sample of Women in Rural Pakistan', *Social Psychiatry and Psychiatric Epidemiology* 39 (2004) pp. 618–24; R. Kidwai,'Demographic Factors, Social Problems and Material Amenities as Predictors of Psychological Distress: A Cross-sectional Study in Karachi, Pakistan', *Social Psychiatry and Psychiatric Epidemiology* 49/1 (2014) pp. 27–9.
33. I. Mirza and R. Jenkins, 'Risk Factors, Prevalence, and Treatment of Anxiety and Depressive Disorders in Pakistan: Systematic Review', *BMJ* 328/7443 (2004) p. 794.

34. Ibid., p. 795.
35. H. Stritzel and J. Vuori (note 29) p. 44.
36. A.T.R. Wibben, 'Human Security: Toward an Opening', *Security Dialogue* 39/4 (2008) p. 455.
37. Ibid., p. 456.
38. C. Enloe, *Bananas, Beaches and Bases: Making Feminist Sense of International Politics* (Oakland: University of California Press 1990)
39. L. Sjoberg, 'Centering Security Studies Around Felt, Gendered Insecurities', *Journal of Global Security Studies* 1/1 (2016) pp. 51–63.
40. Ibid., p. 60.
41. N. Parker and N. Vaughan-Williams, *Critical Border Studies - Broadening and Deepening of the 'Lines in the Sand'-Agenda* (Oxon: Routledge 2014).
42. Ibid., p. 3.
43. H. Stritzel and J. Vuori (note 29) p. 45.
44. Z. Bauman, *Liquid Fear* (Cambridge: Polity Press 2006).
45. U. Beck, *Risk Society: Towards a New Modernity* (London: Sage 1992).
46. A. Giddens (note 9).
47. P. Sweetman,'Twenty-first Century Dis-ease? Habitus Reflexivity or the Reflexive Habitus', *The Sociological Review* 51/4 (2003) p. 530.
48. Giddens borrows the concept from R.D.Laing, a psychoanalyst, R.D. Laing, *The Divided Self* (Harmondsworth: Penguin 1965).
49. A. Giddens (note 9) p. 92.
50. J. Mitzen, 'Ontological Security in World Politics: State Identity and the Security Dilemma', *European Journal of International Relations* 12/3 (2006) pp. 341–70.
51. S. Croft and N. Vaughan-Williams, 'Fit for purpose? Fitting Ontological Security Studies 'into' the Discipline of International Relations: Towards a Vernacular Turn', *Cooperation and Conflict* 52/1 (2017) pp. 12–30.
52. J. Mitzen (note 50) pp. 341–70.
53. Ibid.
54. A. Zarakol, 'Ontological (In)Security and State Denial of Historical Crimes: Turkey and Japan', *International Relations* 24/1 (2010) pp. 3–23.
55. C. Kinvall, 'Globalization and Religious Nationalism: Self, Identity, and the Search for Ontological Security', *Political Psychology* 25/5 (2004) p. 741–67.
56. J. Huysmans (note 16).
57. S. Croft and N. Vaughan-Williams (note 51).
58. C. Kinvall and J. Mitzen, 'An Introduction to the Special Issue: Ontological Securities in World Politics', *Cooperation and Conflict* 52/1 (2017) pp. 3–11.
59. B. Rumelili, 'Identity and Desecuritisation: The Pitfalls of Conflating Ontological and Physical security', *Journal of International Relations and Development* 18/1 (2015) pp. 52–74.
60. R. Thakur, 'A Political Worldview', *Security Dialogue* 35/3 (2004) pp. 347.
61. M. Heidegger, *Being and Time* (Oxford: Blackwell 1962 [1927]).
62. Ibid., p. 1.
63. F. Berenskoetter, 'Parameters of a National Biography', *European Journal of International Relations* 20/1 (2014) p. 268.
64. Ibid., p.7.
65. F. Berenskoetter, *From Friends to Strangers: A Theory of Interstate Security Cooperation Applied to German-American Relations, 1945–1995* (PhD thesis submitted to the Department of International Relations of the London School of Economics and Political Science 2008) p. 99.

66. Building on Freud, Giddens notes that whereas 'fear is a response to a specific threat', anxiety 'disregards the object'; A. Giddens (note 19), p. 43.
67. F. Berenskoetter (note 65) p. 100.
68. B. W. Davis, *Martin Heidegger: Key Concepts* (Durham: Acumen 2009) p. 70.
69. A. Giddens, *The Constitution of Society: Outline of the Theory of Structuration* (Cambridge: Polity Press 1984) p. 50.
70. A. Giddens (note 9) p. 114.
71. F. Berenskoetter (note 65) p. 105.
72. A. Giddens (note 9) p. 39.
73. F. Berenskoetter (note 65) p. 105.
74. E. Erikson, *Childhood and Society* (London: W.W. Norton & Co 1951).
75. Ibid., p. 94.
76. Ibid., p. 222.
77. A. Giddens (note 9) p. 38.
78. Ibid., p. 34.
79. Ibid., p. 41.
80. Ibid., pp. 40–1.
81. E. Goffman, *Relations in Public* (London: Penguin 1971) p. 239.
82. B. A. Misztal, 'Normality and Trust in Goffman's Theory of Interaction Order', *Sociological Theory* 19/3 (2001) p. 312.
83. M.C. Williams, 'Modernity, Identity and Security: A Comment on the "Copenhagen Controversy"', *Review of International Studies* 24/3 (1998) p. 435.
84. E. Goffman (note 81) p. 239.
85. E. Goffman (note 81) p. 239.
86. A. Giddens (note 9) p. 40.
87. A. Giddens (note 9) p. 53.
88. C. Kinvall (note 55) p. 746.
89. D. P. McAdams, 'The Psychology of Life Stories', *Review of General Psychology* 5/2 (2001) p. 101.
90. C. P. Casanave, *Writing Games: Multicultural Case Studies of Academic Literary Practices in Higher Education* (London: Routledge 2002) p. 262.
91. Ibid., p. 262.
92. D. P. McAdams and D.R. Baerger, Life Story Coherence and its Relation to Psychological Well- Being', *Narrative Inquiry* 9/1 (1999) p. 75.
93. A. Giddens (note 9) p. 47.
94. A. Zarakol (note 54) p. 6.
95. B. Rumelili (note 59) p. 54.
96. Ibid., p. 57.
97. Ibid., p. 57.
98. S. Alimia (note 6) p. 277.
99. L. Sjoberg (note 39) p. 57.
100. A. Q. Suleri (note 18) p. 59.
101. E. Zureik et al., *Surveillance and Control in Israel/Palestine* (New York: Routledge 2011) p. 11.
102. U. Beck, 'Risk Society Revisited: Theory, Politics and Research Programmes', in U. Beck and B. Adam et al. (ed.), *Risk Society and Beyond: Critical Issues for Social Theory* (London: Sage Publications 2000) p. 213.
103. A. Cooper, C. Perkins, and C. Rumford, 'The Vernacularization of Borders', in R. Jones and C. Johnson, *Placing the Border in Everyday Life* (Farnham: Ashgate Publishing Limited) p. 18.

104. Y. Joseph and R. Rothfus (note 25) p. 171.
105. H. Stritzel and J. Vuoriy (note 29) p. 43.
106. A. T. R. Wibben (note 36) p. 460.
107. D. Chandler, 'Rethinking the Subject of Human Security', in M. K. Pasha (ed.), *Globalisation, Difference, and Human Security* (Oxon: Routledge 2013) pp. 45–6.
108. Ibid., p. 47.
109. C. S. Browning and P. Joenniemi, 'Ontological Security, Self-Articulation and the Securitisation of Identity', *Cooperation and Conflict* 52/1 pp. 31–47.
110. Ibid., p. 32.
111. L. Gayer, *Karachi: Ordered Disorder and the Struggle for the City* (Uttar Pradesh: Harper Collins Publishers India Ltd. 2014) p. 241.
112. S. Alimia (note 3).
113. R. Khalidi, *Palestinian Identity: The Construction of Modern National Consciousness* (New York: Columbia University Press 1997) p. 1.
114. B. Rumelili (ed.), *Conflict Resolution and Ontological Security* (New York: Routledge 2015) p. 2.
115. A. Zarakol (note 53).
116. H. Stritzel and J. Vuori (note 29) p. 46.

Performing the Afghanistan–Pakistan Border Through Refugee ID Cards

Sanaa Alimia

ABSTRACT

This paper explores the relationship between surveillance, refugee ID cards, population control, and the making of the Afghanistan-Pakistan border in the 2000s and 2010s. The paper uncovers how, in the security-dominated Pakistani state, during the Soviet-Afghan War it was politically expedient to host a large Afghan refugee population in the country and make use of a flexible Afghanistan-Pakistan border, but in the "Global War on Terror" this no longer applies. As geopolitical circumstances change, this paper explores how ID cards for Afghan refugees are tools of surveillance that facilitate refuge and the legal/documentary, social, and physical exclusion of the non-citizen refugee. These forms of exclusion allow the Pakistani state to "perform" the Afghanistan-Pakistan border into effect. The border is not simply located at the territorial frontier but is in process and comes into being through the control over the mobility of citizen and non-citizen populations and forms of social exclusion that are enacted through surveillance and documentation.

Introduction

> They are not doing this [the Afghan identity (ID) card] for us; they want to know how many of us there are. They are keeping an account of us and monitoring us ... You know there was a time last year [2009–2010] when people were constantly being arrested. One elder had to go and get 150 people released who were arrested in one go. At another point 40 people were taken. Since we have this card, that's it... freedom over. As soon as we started to be identified as Afghan with this [card], problems started for us.
>
> Interview with Habibullah, Karachi.

Habibullah is an Afghan Uzbek who moved to Karachi from Baghlan, Afghanistan in 1987 when he was a young boy. Now approximately 40-years-old, he has lived most of his life in an informal low-income housing area in the city working as a daily labourer. I interviewed him after he had spent a few days trying to get residents of the area released from a local police station. Most

Color versions of one or more of the figures in the article can be found online at www.tandfonline.com/fgeo.

residents are of various Afghan ethnic backgrounds (Tajik, Turkmen, Uzbek and Pashtun) and either moved to the city during the Soviet-Afghan War (1979–1988), were born in the city or migrated from Afghanistan in the 1990s and 2000s during the Afghan civil war and rise of the Afghan Taliban. During the months in which I interviewed Habibullah, residents were frequently being arrested after being profiled for being Afghan. This was assumed to be visible through physiognomy, Urdu accent and dress, and was subsequently proven by the possession of an Afghan refugee ID card. Residents were only released after paying local police officers a bribe in cash. The Afghan ID card was introduced to improve the management of an over two million-strong Afghan population in Pakistan and to uphold principles of refuge as outlined by the United Nations (UN) to which Pakistan is in *de facto* agreement with. Yet the card has also inadvertently led to an increase in lived insecurities for Afghans in everyday life. In addition, the card is the lynchpin of assisted voluntary repatriation (AVR) programmes managed by Pakistan and the United Nations High Commission for Refugees (UNHCR) with the cooperation of Afghanistan.

This paper explores the relationship among surveillance, ID cards, population control and the making of the Afghanistan–Pakistan border in the 2000s and 2010s. The paper uncovers how, in the security-dominated Pakistani state, during the Soviet-Afghan War it was politically expedient to host a large Afghan refugee population in the country and make use of a flexible Afghanistan–Pakistan border, but in the "Global War on Terror" (GWOT) this no longer applies. As geopolitical circumstances change, this paper explores how ID cards for Afghan refugees are a tool of surveillance that facilitates refuge *and* the legal/documentary, social and physical exclusion of the non-citizen refugee. The Afghan ID card does not simply "embrace" (Torpey 2000) individuals *into* the state and civic political life, which has tended to be the argument put forward by scholarship on modern surveillance that is predominantly centered, first, on the Western liberal/democratic state and, second, on the citizen. Instead, the ID card and its database identify and register Afghans in order to provide relief and more powerfully, in the current moment, control their mobility with the intent of physically excluding them from the country via AVR programmes. In addition, in everyday life the card itself is a form of "media" and a "material artefact" (Tawil-Souri 2011) that communicates information to the everyday state that enables more accurate discrimination and profiling of Afghans. These forms of exclusion allow the Pakistani state to "perform" (Salter 2011, 66–67) the Afghanistan–Pakistan border into effect. The border is not simply located at the territorial frontier but is *in process* and comes into being through documents, the control over the mobility of citizen and non-citizen populations, and by enacting everyday forms of social exclusion. The border exists through acts (performances) that are repeated on a daily basis, some of which create sentiments of exclusion (harassment and violence) and others that change facts on the ground (population transfers).

This paper uses a historical narrative approach to unpack the relationship among surveillance, ID cards and border performativity. The paper draws from fieldwork conducted during 2010–2011 and 2013–2016. The fieldwork used a mixed-methods approach, which included ethnographic observations in ID card registration centers and checkpoints. It also included semi-structured interviews with Afghan refugees and undocumented migrants from low-/middle-income households, government officials, UNHCR representatives and human rights lawyers. Finally, it included the collection of judicial and magistrates' rulings, private lawyers' reports, NGO legal aid reports, policy documents and different types of ID cards and documentation. Pakistan is administratively divided into four federal provinces, Khyber Pakhtunkhwa (KP), Punjab, Sindh and Balochistan. Each province is explained as possessing a demographic majority of one ethnic group that has led to Pakistan being described as possessing an "ethno-federal" structure. I conducted research in three cities in three provinces: Peshawar in KP, which is described as a Pashtun city, Islamabad in Punjab, which is described as a Punjabi city and Karachi in Sindh, which is described as an (albeit contested) "Urdu-speaking" city. Although I was not able to conduct fieldwork in Balochistan and rural areas, across my field sites and, as journalist and human rights reports show, across the country (Human Rights Watch 2015, 2017), the Afghan experience appeared very similar. The standardization of and a demand for ID cards was combining with a hegemonic anti-Afghan refugee political discourse to make Afghans vulnerable to forms of verbal and/or physical abuse by law enforcement officers. Additionally, the card was central to the process of enabling and/or *coercing* Afghans to repatriate to Afghanistan.

The paper has four main sections and further sub-sections. In the first section that follows this introduction, I introduce the Afghan ID card in Pakistan and conceptualize the border. The next section explains how the Afghan ID card is a tool of population surveillance that embraces Afghans for inclusionary and exclusionary purposes. The following section examines how and why Pakistan's post-colonial trajectory has used identification and documentation at key junctures of border-making and remaking. It also unpacks how the Afghanistan–Pakistan border is fluid and marked by an incomplete project of colonial and post-colonial state consolidation in the Federally Administered Tribal Areas (FATA). And it explores the shifting global, regional and local political reasons as to when, why, and how the fluidity of the border is celebrated (in the Soviet-Afghan War) or condemned (in the GWOT). The section ends by detailing that since the 2000s, the Afghan ID card facilities the performance of the Afghanistan–Pakistan border via AVR programmes. Finally, I detail how the ID card is experienced in everyday life, explaining how the Afghan ID card is a material artefact and a form of media that communicates the non-citizen status of Afghans to the everyday state. In turn the state either violates Afghans for reasons of petty corruption and/or disciplines them into accepting a social – and ultimately physical – exclusion both in and from Pakistan.

ID Cards, Population Mobility, and Border Performativity

During October 2006 and February 2007, the Afghan refugee ID card, a biometric computerized card officially known as the Afghan Citizen Proof of Registration (POR) card (see Figure 1), was introduced by Pakistan and the

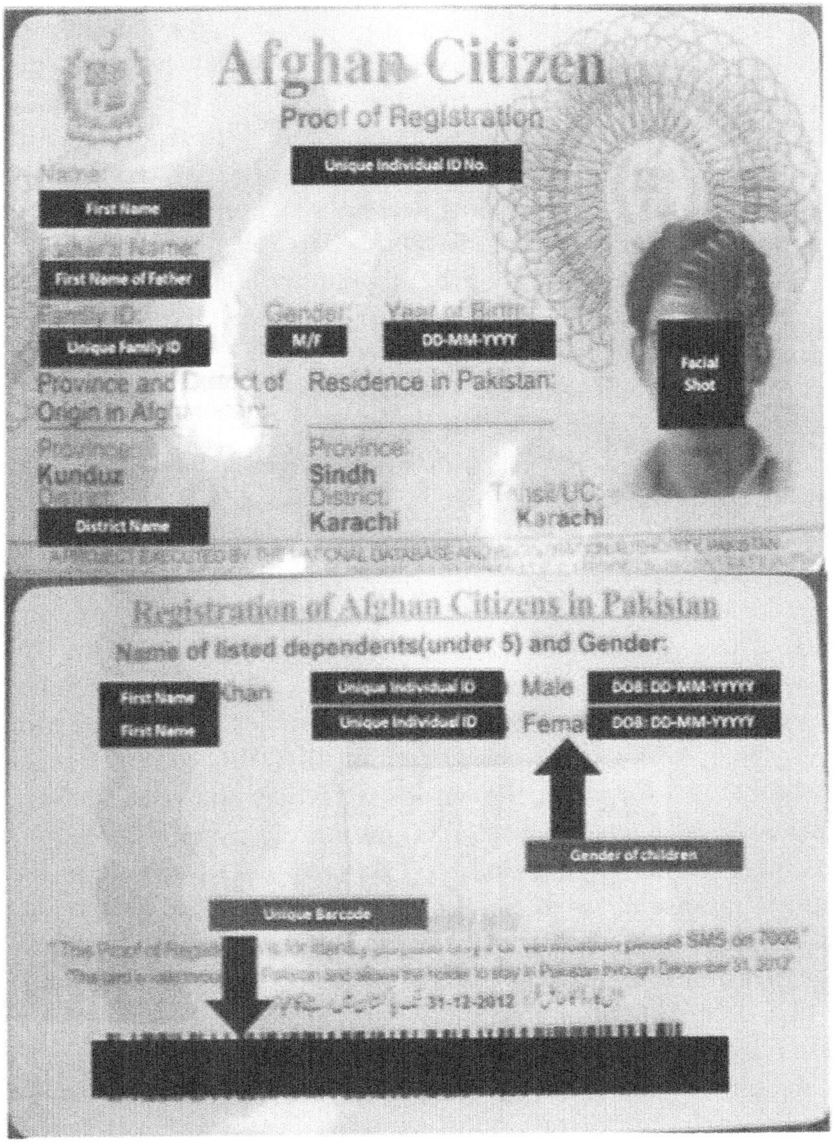

Figure 1. Afghan POR card, front and back, issued in 2010. Collected by author on fieldwork. Unique ID and personal information removed by author.

UNHCR to all Afghans who could prove that they had been living as refugees in Pakistan prior to 2001, that is before the US-led NATO invasion of Afghanistan. Pakistani and UNHCR officials said the POR card would improve the management of this large and protracted refugee group (Khan 2012). The card was introduced after the 2005 Census of Afghans in Pakistan carried out by Pakistan and the UNHCR (Ministry of States and Frontier Region [SAFRON], Chief Commissionerate for Afghan Refugees [CCAR], and United Nations High Commissioner for Refugees [UNHCR] 2005), which itself is based on tripartite agreements among Pakistan, Afghanistan and the UNHCR (Government of Afghanistan [GOA], Government of Pakistan [GOP], and UNHCR 2003). By 2007, some 2.1 million persons over the age of five were registered on a national database and provided with a POR card; all children under the age of five were registered on a parental card (SAFRON, National Database and Registration Authority [NADRA], and UNHCR 2007). In addition, in July 2017, as this paper was being written, an ID card and registration programme for approximately one-to-two million undocumented Afghans was rolled out with the support of the International Organization of Migration (IOM) and other international funders (Khan 2017) (This paper, however, primarily focuses on the POR card). In the 2000s, Pakistan also introduced a computerized biometric ID card for its own citizens, the Computerized National ID card (CNIC). Today 96% of all Pakistanis over the age of 18 are registered with a CNIC (A Reporter 2012). Periodically, ID cards have also been issued for disaster relief to citizens, such as after the 2010 national floods or during the forced displacements from military operations in FATA. There have also been various unsuccessful attempts to register undocumented migrants in Karachi, including Bangladeshi and Burmese nationals (Anwar 2013; BEFARE 2009). These various ID cards are managed by the National Database and Registration Authority (NADRA), which is a self-funded private corporation established in 2000 that sits under the Interior Ministry.[1] Yet the Afghan POR card is different from the CNIC card in its form and impact: the POR card serves the purpose of refuge and relief *and* the legal/documentary, social *and* physical exclusion from Pakistan, the latter of which are acts that perform the Afghanistan–Pakistan border into being – a point I will return to shortly. Afghans also get more attention by the state and international institutions than, say, the Burmese or Bangladeshi populations, because they are constructed as being a more geopolitically significant population that needs careful management (Alimia 2014a).

In simple terms, a national ID card (NIC) is a plastic or paper document that is the physical manifestation of forms of belonging within a nation-state. The card is also a mobile version of the files of information gathered about individuals, such as biometric data and information recorded from state censuses, surveys and other enumeration mechanisms. Today ID cards usually contain an embedded computerized chip that is connected to networked and searchable databases (national registries) (Lyon 2006). This indicates the need to refer to *ID card systems* rather than ID cards alone (Lyon 2006, 6). It also indicates how ID cards systems are a form of modern surveillance, which is linked to the emergence of the colonial and nation-state that are defined by a relationship between sovereignty, territory and population, and industrialization. Here a central problem of the modern and colonial state is how to make societies within its territories "legible" (Scott 1998). This process of legibility is enabled by population surveillance, which is "the focused systemic and routine attention to personal details for the purpose of influence, management, protection or direction" (Lyon 2007, cited in Zureik 2011, 10), and *identification* is "the starting point of surveillance" (Lyon 2006, 6). John Torpey explains how the state surrounds and takes hold of its populations: "In order to extract resources and implement policies, states must be in a position to locate and lay claim to people and goods ... States *must* embrace societies *in order* to penetrate them effectively" (Torpey 2000, 11). Michel Foucault most famously explores how in the modern state, unlike in the medieval state, sovereign power is concerned with the management of life in order to make it governable (Foucault 1977, 1978). Yet Torpey says:

> For all their preoccupation with policing, population, and "pastoral power," ... Foucault's considerations of these matters lack any precise discussion of the *techniques of identification* that have played a crucial role in the development of modern, territorial states resting on distinctions between citizens/ nationals and aliens. (Torpey 2000, 5, emphasis added)

Censuses, surveys, registries and ID cards, internal passes and the passport are all techniques that seek to know who belongs to the territorial nation-state. Indeed, for Torpey, the modern territorial nation-state develops not only to exercise a monopoly over the means of production (as per Marx) or violence (as per Weber) but also to exercise a monopoly over the *mobility of populations*.

With regard to understanding the border, then, the territorial frontier is not the only place worth examining. The border is not simply a line on the map that is simply *there*. As indicated above, it is held together through documentary regimes. To borrow from Torpey, "the notion of national communities must be codified rather than merely 'imagined'" (Torpey 2000, 13). Further, echoing the anthropological works on the everyday state and sovereignty, political scientist Mark Salter explains how the border (and thereby sovereignty) is performed into being by governments, citizens and other agents (Salter 2011). The border is in process and upheld by a series of acts. For Salter "border performativity" has three interlinked registers: formal, practical and popular (Salter 2011, 67). This includes the deployment of military might and resources along territorial entry and exit points (formal), everyday negotiations by citizens and non-citizens (popular), and, relevant for this paper, *the control of entry and exit and the exclusion of certain individuals and groups* (practical) (Salter 2011). Indeed scholars working on deportation emphasize how population transfers, evictions, defections and even forced migrations and ethnic cleansing have historically been central to nation-building and the border-making process (Coller 2012). For the Pakistani state then, the POR card is a document/technology that supports AVR programmes to remove a large non-citizen Afghan population from Pakistan to Afghanistan as a means of performing the Afghanistan–Pakistani border. In addition, changes in transportation, communications and population flows (globalization), and the language of risk in the GWOT means there is an even greater urgency to police the mobile body, which is now facilitated by biometric technologies and identification systems (Zureik and Salter 2005, 4). As ports of entry, such as the airport, are now situated in major cities, the border is deterritorialized (Zureik and Salter 2005, 4), whilst the computerized ID card means that a border is both portable (the plastic card) and virtual (the database) (Lyon 2005). Louise Amoore explains how the "biometric border" also means that the bodies of migrants and travelers are now sites of "multiple encoded boundaries" that are tied to the border (Amoore 2006). The body itself acts as a passcode for belonging (or not).

Philosopher Etienne Balibar also informs us that the border is "everywhere and nowhere." In part, Balibar's statement is a nod to the ubiquitous nature of contemporary borders (Balibar 2002, 78). Yet it is also a metaphor for forms of social, political and cultural exclusion experienced by migrants. This is not the same as legal expulsion or exile; but it does show how migrants, especially poor migrants from poor countries, are constructed as forms of "bare life" (Agamben 1998) or social deviants that are risks to the "purity" (Douglas 1992) of the nation and more vulnerable to forms of direct and indirect violence. Whilst Shahram Khosravi's auto-ethnography of borders explores how racialized migrants in Europe are situated on the "threshold between inside and outside"; they are included without being members and as a result are forced to "be the border" (Khosravi 2010, 98). And as the paper will detail later, the POR card, its different colours, forms and the information contained on it, *communicates* different legal statuses and identities to the everyday state that increasingly demands to see these documents in a context of violence and "risk" in the GWOT. In everyday life the need for ID cards assists the profiling of Afghans who are under pressure to leave Pakistan that leads to a *feeling of "bordering" by Afghans.*

Inclusionary and Exclusionary Surveillance

Most studies on modern and contemporary surveillance are centred on the citizen and/or the Western liberal democratic state. But what can be said about the surveillance of the refugee, the colonized, or the undesired citizen? And what does surveillance look like in the post-colonial and/or Global South state?

Offering a critique of the Western liberal/democratic bias of surveillance studies, Ariel Handel says modern surveillance has undergone three phases, which are not necessarily separate from each other (Handel 2011). These are: colonial/founding, inclusive/biopolitical, which dominate Western surveillance studies and exclusionary surveillance. According to Handel, "Colonial/founding surveillance targets the population as part of the territory's resources" (Handel 2011, 264). Inclusive surveillance is concerned with controlling the mobility of populations and making "normal" citizens (Handel 2011, 262–264). Exclusionary surveillance, however, is meant to divide and to separate specific population groups from the general *demos* (to which inclusive surveillance is still applied) even though all groups live in the same territory (Handel 2011, 264). Exclusionary surveillance chases its subjects and spies on them "in order to prove that they do not belong to it" (Handel 2011, 264). Surveillance is a method used to withdraw state responsibility from certain population groups – those who are considered unnecessary, surplus, or redundant, such as slum populations or refugees (Handel 2011). The ID card thus can be used for delivery of rights, responsibilities and privileges of citizenship (Lyon 2006); yet it can also be used as a form of exclusion from the general *demos*. As scholars of the Holocaust, slavery, colonialism, forced displacements and discrimination detail, state (and sometimes corporate) surveillance and documentation is used to exterminate, experiment on, kill, exploit, exclude and expel populations from the state (Baumann 1991; Cole 2002; Parenti 2003). It is necessary to read the impact of surveillance, documents and technologies within the social and political contexts in which they operate.

In Pakistan, the Afghan POR card is both an inclusionary and exclusionary surveillance tool. At its most obvious, ID cards are a documentary site of national *identity* making; ID does after all stand for "identity" (Lyon 2006). The POR card renders Afghans distinct from Pakistani citizens. It declares that they are "Afghan Citizens" that are tied to the Afghan nation-state and who only have *temporary* protection in Pakistan.[2] Afghans also cannot possess a CNIC and are excluded from the rights and privileges of Pakistani citizenship. Documents bring "refugeedom" and citizenship to life. And, as I will detail in later sections, the POR card facilitates population transfers and efforts of the everyday state to perform the border through violence.

Yet the ID card and its accompanying databases also embraces Afghans to include them within Pakistan, a transnational migration circuit and an international refugee regime. Pakistan is not a signatory to the UN's 1951 Convention Relating to the Status of Refugees and the 1967 Protocol Relating to the Status of Refugees, the main instruments used to define refugees in the international world system, and it does not have an official refugee law.[3] However, since the 1979 Soviet invasion of Afghanistan, the UNHCR has been active in the country and Pakistan has been acting "in the spirit" (SAFRON and CCAR 1981) of the 1951 Convention and 1967 Protocol. Today, UNHCR's main responsibilities are to support POR card registration and AVR programmes, to provide UNHCR-issued birth certificates and to impart "protection by presence" (Khan 2012, 104). In addition, since 1979 there has also been a Pakistani government department dedicated to the management of Afghan refugees, the Chief Commissionerate of Afghan Refugees (CCAR), under the auspices of the Ministry of States and Frontier Regions (SAFRON). Since the 2000s, Pakistan has also signed a series of tripartite agreements with Afghanistan and the UNHCR pertaining to Afghan refugee management that set out principles of refuge and rights for Afghans who are registered as refugees in Pakistan (GOA, GOP, and UNHCR 2003). And in 2017, steps have been taken to manage Afghan undocumented migrants by giving them their own ID cards.[4] The POR card identifies the Afghans whom the state is willing to claim responsibility for as *Pakistan's Afghan refugees.* The Afghan POR card ties its possessors to Pakistan's (albeit legally tenuous) commitment to principles of refuge.[5] In addition, the card facilitates those Afghans who *do* want to return to Afghanistan or apply for asylum in a third country. The card ensures Afghans legally exist in an international system defined by documentation and legality.

Within Pakistan the 2006–2007 Afghan POR card builds on the earlier institutional processes of refuge and relief that emerged from the Soviet-Afghan War. In 1980, Afghan refugees would be registered and then issued with a ration passbook by CCAR, the Afghan *Muhajireen* (Refugees) Passbook, commonly referred to as the *shanakhti* (identity) pass. The *shanakhti* pass allowed Afghans to receive basic services, such as rations, shelter, education and health services. Afghans were also provided with paper documents by other UN-based organizations. For example, UNICEF would provide a document to receive and provide proof of vaccinations. The various Afghan *Mujahideen* resistance parties that were stationed in Pakistan also instituted their own ID cards allowing holders to access relief items issued by the *Mujahideen*, specifically foodstuffs and soap.[6] (See Figures 2–4). In the current moment, the Afghan POR card does not provide direct relief from UN-based organizations (the World Food Program was closed down in 1994–1995), but it does give Afghans legal recognition of their right to remain in Pakistan and a right to mobility, employment and protection (GOA, GOP, and UNHCR 2006).

Furthermore, contemporary Pakistan has witnessed the ubiquity of formal identification. The CNIC and the POR card and their compatible NADRA databases are necessities in nearly all aspects of daily life. They are prerequisites for opening bank accounts, purchasing SIM cards, accessing education and healthcare, purchasing/renting property, paying for utility bills, voting in

Figure 2. ID Card issued by Mujahideen in the 1980s. Collected by author on fieldwork, Peshawar. Unique ID numbers removed by author.

Figure 3. Front and back pages of Afghan Muhajireen Passbook ('shankhti pass') issued by CCAR, circa 1986. Collected by author on fieldwork, Peshawar. Unique ID numbers and names removed by author.

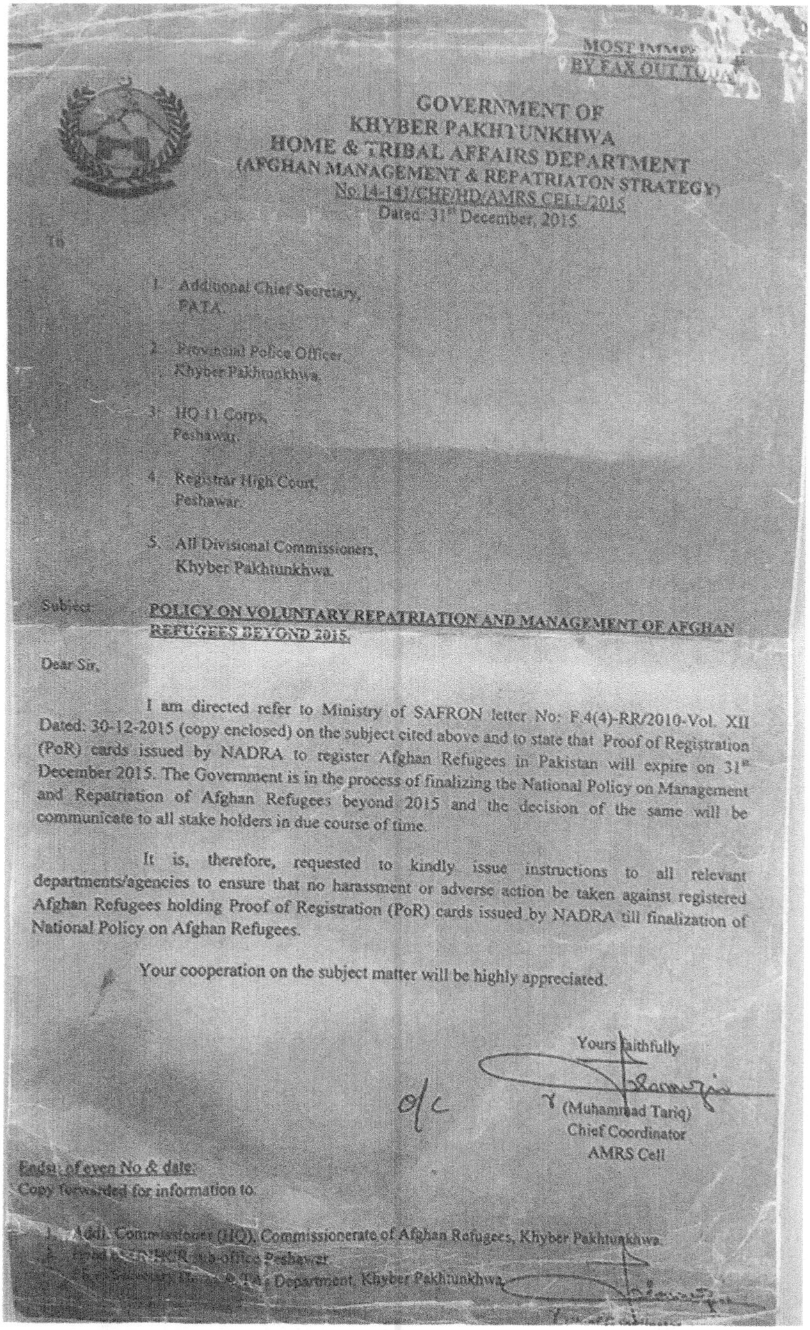

MOST IMM...
BY FAX OUT TO...

GOVERNMENT OF
KHYBER PAKHTUNKHWA
HOME & TRIBAL AFFAIRS DEPARTMENT
(AFGHAN MANAGEMENT & REPATRIATON STRATEGY)
No.14-141/CHF/HD/AMRS CELL/2015
Dated: 31st December, 2015

To

1. Additional Chief Secretary,
   FATA.
2. Provincial Police Officer,
   Khyber Pakhtunkhwa.
3. HQ 11 Corps,
   Peshawar.
4. Registrar High Court,
   Peshawar.
5. All Divisional Commissioners,
   Khyber Pakhtunkhwa.

Subject: POLICY ON VOLUNTARY REPATRIATION AND MANAGEMENT OF AFGHAN REFUGEES BEYOND 2015.

Dear Sir,

I am directed refer to Ministry of SAFRON letter No: F.4(4)-RR/2010-Vol. XII Dated: 30-12-2015 (copy enclosed) on the subject cited above and to state that Proof of Registration (PoR) cards issued by NADRA to register Afghan Refugees in Pakistan will expire on 31st December 2015. The Government is in the process of finalizing the National Policy on Management and Repatriation of Afghan Refugees beyond 2015 and the decision of the same will be communicate to all stake holders in due course of time.

It is, therefore, requested to kindly issue instructions to all relevant departments/agencies to ensure that no harassment or adverse action be taken against registered Afghan Refugees holding Proof of Registration (PoR) cards issued by NADRA till finalization of National Policy on Afghan Refugees.

Your cooperation on the subject matter will be highly appreciated.

Yours faithfully

(Muhammad Tariq)
Chief Coordinator
AMRS Cell

Endst: of even No & date:
Copy forwarded for information to.

1. Addl. Commissioner (HQ), Commissionerate of Afghan Refugees, Khyber Pakhtunkhwa.
2. ... sub-office Peshawar
3. ... Department, Khyber Pakhtunkhwa.

Figure 4. Photocopy of a government issued document that outlines the process of the POR card renewal is underway, December 2015. The photocopy is taken from Afghan students studying in Peshawar who carried this document with them in early 2016.

elections, intra- and inter-city travel and employment. Pakistan appears to be lumbering towards a system of Gilles Deleuze's control societies (Deleuze 1992, 3–7). Transformations in technology mean that the individual is tied to continuous and entangled networks that both limit and create opportunities for individuals. The notion of a seamless and networked society also captures the vision of the former NADRA chairman, Tariq Malik, who in 2012 said with regards to the CNIC:

> The [C]SNIC [Smart National ID card] is a chip-based identity document which will provide unprecedented security and convenience to citizens and will eventually be the only card a Pakistani will ever need... Eventually, every citizen will have the option of using their SNIC as their main identity instrument, as their driving license, school card, hospital card, card for gym membership and numerous other facilities. (Malik 2012)

Although the comments above are a reference to the CNIC, much of what Malik says also applies to the POR card. However, as the remainder of this paper will detail, ID cards for Afghans (and Pakistanis) are not simply about Malik's envisioned networked society of "driving licenses and gym membership." In 2016, for example, Pakistan's networked society turned on its Afghan population to exclude them from their privileges of belonging when the government, in coordination with NADRA, asked mobile phone companies to disable Afghan SIM cards and forced banks to close Afghan accounts (Pakistan Is Driving Out 1.5 m Afghan Refugees 2016).[7] POR cards thus also enable exclusion, which is a route to performing the Afghanistan–Pakistan border into effect because of shifting geopolitical interests. ID cards are also a part of military and intelligence gathering in a conflict zone. ID cards were also introduced in Pakistan as a result of pressure from Western states. And, the physical ID card itself also acts as a form of media in everyday life in that it enables the profiling of Afghans that results in lived vulnerabilities for Afghans. I will return to these points later in this paper. Before that, in the next section and sub-sections, the paper details how identification and documentation is central to the post-colonial state's process of border-making and it will uncover why, since the 2000s, the fallouts of the GWOT and the political status of FATA mean that Pakistan is performing the Afghanistan–Pakistan border into effect.

Border-Performativity in the Post-Colonial Security State

Surveillance, Documents, and Mobility Control in the Making(s) of Pakistan

Post-2001 scholarship on the Western liberal/democratic state explains how we have entered an era of the "securitization of citizenship" (Muller 2004), where states are preoccupied with state security and managing risky bodies through domestic surveillance and the prevention of entry, deportation and restricted mobility of undesirable migrants. Yet for the state that endures European colonial rule, founded on a violent exchange of populations in 1947, has faced various ethno-national secessionist movements, one of which was successful, as well as acrimonious rivalries with its neighbours, the question of who belongs has always been underpinned with existential concerns of state-security and the integrity of borders.

After 1947, Pakistan's colonial inheritance means a security mindset has persisted at the heart of the state (Jalal 1990). Post-1947 Pakistan emerges with an overdeveloped structure of a heavy bureaucracy and military (Alavi 1972); although, since the 1970s, the state has been transformed and fragmented through economic liberalization, urbanization, globalization and a cynical use of Islam by the state (Akhtar 2008). Yet the military and thereby state security interests have deepened and diversified their grip over the state.[8] This is shaped by a number of factors that cannot be discussed in detail here, but include an uneven distribution of power in Pakistan where political power is concentrated in the military-dominated federal province of the Punjab. It is also shaped by the conditions of Pakistan's traumatic birth that placed it in a geopolitically sensitive position next to Afghanistan and India, which with India include three wars (1948–1949, 1965, 1971), and one near-nuclear confrontation with India (1999). The military's grip has been bolstered by US patronage, most notably in the Soviet-Afghan War and then the GWOT. Today, Pakistan's security agenda is being strengthened by the deepening of Pakistan–China relations. It is also adapting and extending its tentacles across state and society via a growing capitalist agenda, which has strong networks with international financial institutions and international capital and Pakistan's civilian administration and its ruling, capitalist and intermediary classes (Siddiqa 2007). Indeed, since the 2000s Pakistan has, to borrow from historian Saadia Toor, emerged as a "neoliberal security state" (Toor 2011) – it is no surprise that NADRA, a corporation, is in charge of the state's population management.

In British India, enumeration and surveillance techniques embraced the colonized populations as resources tied to the "imperial nation-state" (Banerjee 2012) and to prevent rebellion (Bayly 1996; Cole 2002). In 1947, Vazira Zamindar explains that India and Pakistan were not simply defined by a "moment of arrival" in August 1947, with both countries territorial borders emerging as fully formed (Zamindar 2007). Instead, independence and partition unfolded over a period of years (the long partition) that required the *control of population movement, à la* Torpey, through a regime of documentation and surveillance. Permits were introduced in 1948 and passports in 1952. Meanwhile, Muslim refugees from India and their refugee camps were placed under tight state surveillance (Zamindar 2007). Even today, India–Pakistan rivalry means there are firm restrictions on visas issued to Indian citizens and Indian citizens who are granted entry to the country are often placed under surveillance (the converse applies to Pakistanis in India). Charges of Indian visitors to the country being RAW (Indian intelligence) agents and compromising the integrity of Pakistan are common claims made in the media and by state officials.

In addition, after the 1971 Secession of East Pakistan/Independence of Bangladesh, the 1973 National Registration Act led to the introduction of the paper-based NIC for all citizens. In the 1970s, the government was concerned with enacting "foolproof measures to prevent foreign nationals from obtaining Pakistani identity cards" (Ministry of Interior 1976, 54). The NIC was one tool (amongst others) to meet the state's need for securitization and to delineate lines between the new/geographically remade Pakistani state and its former territory (now Bangladesh) and its *populations. Bengalis* who went to Pakistan before 1971 are legal citizens of Pakistan, but *Bangladeshis* who entered after 1971 are undocumented migrants – although the amended 1978 Citizenship Act also required *Bengalis* (in Pakistan before 1971) to legally apply for citizenship through the NIC schemes (Sadiq 2009). The border is performed into being through the control of population movements that is managed by ID cards, documentation and passport controls. The post-1971 ID cards were also important with regards to concerns of internal security, such as Balochistan where the military was embroiled in a 5-year-long war as it attempted to crush an ethno-nationalist movement.[9] Further, whilst beyond the scope of this paper, it is important to note that the impetus for improved population control in the 1970s is also linked to the massive rise of state-contracted labour migrations of Pakistanis to the Gulf Arab region.

Today it is the turn of the Afghanistan-Pakistan border to be performed into being. On first glance, this appears to be somewhat of a chronological anomaly since the Afghanistan–Pakistan border is based on the 1893 Durand Line Agreement signed by the British colonial state and the emerging Afghan state and was later inherited by Pakistan (Haroon 2007; Hopkins and Magnus Marsden 2011, 26–30). Yet the very nature of the Afghanistan–British India/Pakistan border was fluid and marked by a "buffer zone," FATA (then known as the Tribal Areas). Since 1947, Pakistan's project of state-building in FATA has continued to rely on intermediaries and limited intervention. In addition, after 1947 the Afghan state consistently rejected the Durand Line. Since the 2000s, these factors have combined with the political and military impact of the GWOT to push Pakistan to perform the Afghanistan–Pakistan border in to effect, which will be discussed below.

The Afghanistan–Pakistan Border, FATA, and Shifting Geopolitics: From the Cold War to the GWOT

The Afghanistan–Pakistan border has two main official territorial crossing points; the first is at Chaman, Balochistan, the second, Torkham, Khyber Agency, FATA. Yet in FATA there are multiple crossing points that were unmanned until recently. FATA is geographic buffer zone that was administratively created by the British in order to secure the territories of British India from the threat of Russian imperial expansion and the Afghan state. Today, FATA consists of seven different tribal agencies and is governed by the British colonial laws, the 1901 Frontier Crimes Regulation (FCR) (Tahir 2017). FATA sits outside of the Pakistani Constitution via Article 247 in a state of legal and political exception. Pakistani laws do not have full jurisdiction in the areas and neither can the Pakistani police enter the areas. The state maintains its writ in the area by mediating with "tribal society" through sanctioned tribal elders (*Maliks*). Residents of FATA are effectively quasi-citizens who are subject to collective punishment and political and economic underdevelopment, although recently plans have emerged that may incorporate FATA into Pakistan proper (GOP 2016). Pakistan's post-colonial project of state building in FATA is incomplete and FATA's state of exception means that a large tract of the Afghanistan–Pakistan border is porous, which allows ease of movement for populations on either side. The Afghanistan–Pakistan border is something of a formality rather than a lived reality.

During colonial rule and after 1947, the areas that are now KP and FATA faced heavy surveillance in the form of intelligence gathering, but cross-border population movements were not heavily regulated. At first this seems odd, especially given the hostile relationship between Afghanistan and Pakistan. One month after the creation of Pakistan, in September 1947, Afghanistan was the only UN member-state to oppose Pakistani membership of the world organization and did not recognize the Durand Line (Haroon 2007, 189). Historian Shah Mahmoud Hanifi explains how after Afghanistan shed its British protectorate status in 1923 it engaged in a "post-colonial" nation-building project that was dominated by a Pashtun ruling-elite that gave prominence to a Pashtunized national identity over a Persianate one in order to mimic Eurocentric notions of ethno-national purity (Hanifi 2012). After the creation of Pakistan in 1947, the Afghan state consistently rejected the validity of the 1893 colonial border agreement as a means of asserting its Pashtun character. It also interlinked this rejection to the ethno-nationalist movement for the creation of a Pashtun state (Pashtunistan) that emerged in FATA and KP [then the Northwest Frontier Province (NWFP)] and by directly funding and supporting theses movements (Qureshi 1966; Tarzi 2012). Yet despite this, after 1947 the management of population movements across the Afghanistan-Pakistan border was nominal. This is because the scale of the movements was small and the Afghan state's interventions in Pakistan always stopped short of a direct confrontation (Haroon 2007, 192). This was bolstered by the fact that a large chunk of Pashtun nationalists gradually sought to seek gains from *within* the Pakistani political system or were silenced by other Pashtun political actors who were allied to the Pakistani state, in leadership positions in the state, and/or allied to the ideals of Muslim nationalism. There was also no desire to redress FATA's state of exception by the state or the *Maliks* of FATA who benefited from their role as state sanctioned local powerholders. Furthermore, Pakistan's early obsession with the control of population movements and borders concentrated on the country's border with India (Zamindar 2007).

After 1979, however, the story somewhat changes when a massive and unprecedented number of Afghans moved *into* Pakistan. In the late 1970s and in the 1980s, the gradual rise of the People's Democratic Party of Afghanistan (PDPA) and the Soviet invasion of Afghanistan in December 1979 meant some four-to-five million Afghans migrated from Afghanistan to Pakistan.[10] Those who moved into Pakistan were not just regular border-crossers but came as far as Herat, Jowzjan, Kunduz and the closer located Paktia, Qanadahar, Kabul and other areas. Nearly all of these Afghans were given *prima facie* (on first encounter) recognition as refugees and the majority settled in KP, FATA and Balochistan, whilst smaller numbers settled in Sindh (especially Karachi) and the Punjab.[11] The *scale of population movements* creates a need to perform the border into being through surveillance and documentary control. This included registration systems, the creation of the 1980 paper *shanakhti* pass and the surveillance of refugee camps.[12] These were managed by the central government (CCAR/SAFRON) and made Afghans distinct from Pakistanis. The 1980 *shanakhti pass*, for example, includes the disclaimer that "the passbook did not entitle Pakistani citizenship"/"*Is pass book seh Pakistan ka sheriyat ka haq nahiN hota.*" The text also outlines that only one passbook will be given to the family head, which will be taken back when the family leaves Pakistan. (See Figures 2–4).

Yet in the Soviet-Afghan War there was simultaneously a political will to encourage the movements of Afghans into Pakistan. In Pakistan's mainstream (Punjabi-Urdu) discourse, the terms "Afghan," "Pashtun"/"Pakhtun" and "Pathan" are often used interchangeably with each other (Alimia 2015) – although not all modern Afghan citizens (or *Afghanistanis*) are Pashtun but are also Turkmens, Tajiks, Uzbeks, Hazaras and others. This conflation and confusion is shaped by a number of factors, which includes most Afghan migrants into Pakistan being Pashtun. It is also shaped by British colonial legacies (Hanifi 2016), the Afghan state's historic ethno-national rejection of the border, and the nature of political and cultural power in Pakistan being concentrated in the Punjab and/or a Punjabi-Urdu cultural imagining, where Afghans and Pashtuns are lumped into one category. In the Soviet-Afghan War this conflation was constructed as an asset. Indeed, Afghans were managed by CCAR that sits under SAFRON and until 1979 only dealt with FATA. The Afghan refugee issue was understood as an Afghan/Pashtun border issue.

In the Cold War, Pakistan's military dominated state was allied to the US and in the Soviet-Afghan War the military regime of General/President Zia ul-Haq (in power 1977–1988) was the US's frontline ally in the battle against communism. Billions of dollars of military and humanitarian aid poured into Pakistan from the US, Western European states and the Gulf Arab region (Nunan 2016). The Afghan and international Islamist resistance to the Soviets was organized, funded and launched from Pakistan. Meanwhile, refugees were constructed as a moral issue, burning at the conscience of Western liberal democracy (Alimia forthcoming). Pakistan also had its own reasons to welcome Afghans to the country. First, the refugee diaspora offered Pakistan a means to exert potential political influence in Afghanistan by patronizing a sympathetic Afghan opposition in exile who could, in future, potentially be in government – a policy that was initially enacted by Prime Minister Zulfiqar Ali Bhutto (in power 1973–1977). By giving preference to a transnational Islamist identity over an ethnic (Pashtun) identity, albeit still laced with tropes of the good Pashtun Muslim, this would silence the Afghan states claims to border revisionism and the demands for Pashtunistan. Second, the defeat of socialism in Afghanistan would also bolster the military's purge of socialists within Pakistan. Third, after the 1971 loss of East Pakistan, Pakistan was in desperate need of financial support that could be secured through international military and humanitarian aid (Baitenmann 1990). Fourth, a focus on an Islamist outlook would allow post-1971 Pakistan to geographically, ideologically, politically and economically realign itself with the Arab Muslim region and away from the India-dominated South Asia. On balance and broadly speaking, Afghans were an asset in the country. Afghans were made distinct in documentary terms but they were not expelled. Instead ID schemes, such as the *shanakhti* pass were concerned with embracing Afghans to include them in relief efforts and to support military fighting in Afghanistan. These were after all the "glory" years of the Afghan *jihad*. The border is thus not experienced in the same way across time and space. National politics, geopolitical considerations and global power asymmetries mean the Afghanistan–Pakistan border, which is performed through entry and exit of populations, is flexible.

After the Soviet withdrawal from Afghanistan in 1989, in the 1990s a civil war, the rise of the Taliban, and severe cases of drought meant Afghan migration to Pakistan was still taking place. US attention on the region, however, was dramatically reduced (Donini 2011). Yet as the Pakistani military state continued to patronize Afghan militants, specifically the emerging Taliban, many of who lived transnational lives in Pakistan and Afghanistan, an Afghan presence continued in Pakistan (Rashid 2000). However, the 11th September 2001 attacks and the US-led NATO invasion and occupation of Afghanistan, transformed the Afghan position in the country. By the 2000s, an Afghan refugee diaspora in Pakistan is no longer considered geopolitically useful by Pakistan, the US and other states. This has led to the relocation and a refocus of international humanitarian aid for Afghan refugees toward Kabul rather than Islamabad and the support of AVR programmes.

For the US and other Western states the reasons for this shift are multilayered. First, it is related to the war in Afghanistan. Since the GWOT in Afghanistan started, the US and other NATO-based states are concerned with showing the war as a success. Despite the war entering its seventeenth year and some 120,000 Afghans dead, these states project Afghanistan as a "safe country" worthy of capital investment, democratic elections and *return refugee migrations* (Ayaz 2016). This is also supported by the Afghan state's concerns of rebuilding the nation and state through the inclusion of the human, economic and cultural capital of its large transnational diaspora. Second, in the US, Europe and other Western liberal/democratic states right-wing anti-migrant xenophobia is emerging as a part of the political mainstream and has intensified as the GWOT years progress. At the core of homeland security is the need to control the mobility of "risky" bodies (read Muslim, black, brown and poor) from "risky" territories. This is bolstered by the fact that practices of deportation are now an accepted part of state migration policy (Coller 2012). Afghans are one of Europe's largest asylum-seeking populations and European states are intent on curbing and reversing Afghan migration to their states.[13] This neatly dovetails with and, to a degree, informs, Pakistan's post-2001 policy toward Afghans. Indeed, although beyond the scope of this paper, it is important to mention that Pakistan's introduction of identity cards *for citizens and non-citizens* is tied to the migration policies and military objectives of more powerful states in the world system and who are engaged in the GWOT in Afghanistan. Consider that in 2000 Pakistan was placed on a migration watch list of the US and European governments (Sadiq 2009, 131) and told to upgrade its paper passports to machine-readable passports and improve internal population management and by 2000 NADRA was formed. Or that the Pakistani government uses NADRA databases and personnel to collaborate with the UK government to verify the identity of asylum seekers that may be of Pakistani origin (Federal Investigation Agency 2018). Further, in 2009 Wikileaks cables revealed that in a series of meetings at the US embassy between then President Asif Ali Zardari, Prime Minister Yusuf Gilani and Interior Minister Rehman Malik, the US Department of Homeland Security Secretary Janet Napolitano offered to work with Pakistan to improve its border security with Afghanistan (U.S. Embassy 2009). In turn the Pakistani government was considering providing advanced passenger information on passengers travelling to and from Pakistan to the US and Canada. Pakistan also offered to share NADRA's databases with the United States: "A front company was set up in the United Kingdom, International Identity Services, which was hired as the consultants for NADRA to squirrel out the NADRA data for all of Pakistan" (The Julian Assange Show 2012). What exactly the purpose of the sharing of the NADRA databases are is unclear. Yet what is clear is that the control of the Afghanistan–Pakistan border and population mobility is considered to be central to winning GWOT, whilst controlling mobility from Pakistan is central to US homeland security.

For Pakistan, after joining the US-led NATO GWOT, the state aimed to (at least publicly) distance itself from its Taliban protégés. In the 2000's, Pakistan constructed itself as the "Good Muslim" state versus the "Bad Muslim" Afghan state and its people. Yet the war in Afghanistan led to the Afghan Taliban and other militants seeking refuge in FATA (and Balochistan) and the rise of Taliban factions *within* Pakistan. Under pressure from the US, for the first time since the formation of Pakistan in 1947–1948, Pakistan stationed troops and conducted military operations in FATA. The war has also seeped in to the rest of Pakistan. Post-2001 Pakistan is shaped by insurgencies, military operations, US-led drone strikes in FATA and KP, and militant violence. The GWOT has killed over 67,000 persons (Crawford 2005) and displaced over five million persons, mainly civilians from the northwestern areas, including FATA and Swat (KP) (Internal Displacement Monitoring Centre 2013). Bombings (suicide and other) are a routine part of the everyday urban landscape. In addition, by the mid-2000s, the US constructed one foreign policy for Afghanistan and Pakistan, commonly referred to as "Af-Pak." Meanwhile the rebuilt Afghan state has again vocally rejected the Durand Line agreement.[14]

Issues of internal security, external pressures from the US in the GWOT counterinsurgency, and a rivalry with the Afghan state have motivated Pakistan to make clearer its autonomy in terms of territory and population from that of Afghanistan. The state's once celebrated blurred Afghan/Pashtun borderland is now being made distinct. This "border performativity" is executed in a number of ways, including the control over Afghan mobility and extending the writ of the state in FATA and parts of KP via military operations. With regards to Afghans, as early as 2001 *prima facie* recognition of Afghans was stopped and migration into Pakistan was illegalized (Khan 2012, 4–5). Since then the state has also enacted stricter border controls at Afghanistan–Pakistan crossing points, engaged in military skirmishes at the border (Al Jazeera and Agencies 2016), closed all Afghan refugee camps in FATA[15] outlined plans for new visa regimes for Afghans, and as I will detail next, introduced ID cards and AVR schemes. In addition, in FATA and KP local political actors and state institutions are vocal in articulating a distinction from Afghans/Afghanistanis, whilst in FATA there are demands to be incorporated into Pakistan proper. These articulations are done in the hopes of avoiding the fallouts of Pakistani military operations and to secure state protection from the violence of the Taliban and now, Islamic State. Indeed, it is the KP and FATA that have borne the brunt of the military and militant violence of GWOT. Consider, for example, that over 33% of Pakistan's terrorist attacks take place in KP and 19.6% in FATA (Khan 2014).

Post-2001 Exclusionary Surveillance and Border Performativity: AVR Programmes and the NADRA Database

Since the 2000s the central policy for managing Afghans in Pakistan is geared towards "voluntary return and sustainable reintegration."[16] The government's 2010–2012 Afghan Management and Repatriation Strategy explain that border management requires the control of "illegal" Afghan nationals crossing the border and is essential to improve state security (CCAR and SAFRON 2010). From 2001 to 2016 some four million Afghans repatriated from Pakistan to Afghanistan as a part of the process of border performativity ("3.9 Million Afghan Refugees Repatriated" 2015). Today, some 2.5-to-three million Afghans still live in the country, 74% of whom were born in Pakistan (SAFRON, CCAR, and UNHCR n.d., 12). Yet these remaining Afghans are also under pressure to leave Pakistan and "return" to Afghanistan, much of which is being facilitated through the POR card.

The POR card and its databases are the lynchpin of AVR schemes that seek to move Afghans from Pakistan and back into Pakistan. Habibullah's opening comment, "They want to know how many of us there are," indicates an awareness of being watched, identified and registered for removal. In order to know whom to physically exclude from the country via AVR programmes, Pakistan and the UNHCR first needed to identify and count the Afghan population. This was completed with the 2005 Census and then the 2006–2007 POR card scheme. Since then these have been supplemented by national surveys, more registration schemes and the regular renewal of POR cards, which includes updating the card and database technologies.

The POR card is written in English and not Urdu, like the CNIC, so it is compatible with UNHCR's international rules. In addition, the data encrypted onto the card is used by databases in UNHCR voluntary repatriation centers (VRC) in Pakistan and Afghanistan. In Pakistan Afghans (usually families) register their plans for return to Afghanistan with a local VRC using their POR card. Here they are *de-registered* from Pakistan and the international refugee regime through biometric verification, which includes iris scans. The body is a passcode on the route to non-belonging and border enforcement. In addition, individuals and families are eligible for a financial lump sum payment (a financial incentive) to support return and reintegration. This is received at UNHCR encashment centers in Afghanistan but only after individuals authenticate their identity through the POR card and biometric verification (again). The encashment center is one of the steps of Afghan reintegration into the Afghan nation-state.

There are, of course, always ways to circumvent the system. Political scientist Kamal Sadiq uncovers the vast informal economy of counterfeit documents that allows refugees/undocumented migrants to become what he calls "paper citizens" (Sadiq 2009). Here individuals steadily accumulate documentation to prove that they have a right to belong to the state. Yet since Sadiq's publications in 2005 and 2009 even these "paper citizens" are being clamped down on through the combination of political will and new technologies. The 2010–2012 Afghan Management and Repatriation Strategy issued by SAFRON and CCAR specifically says:

> NADRA should launch a special drive to detect and cancel NICs [,] passports etc., fraudulently obtained by refugees and discourage the tendency of obtaining illegal NICs, passports, and domicile certificate (CCAR and SAFRON 2010, XI, xxix).

Using the examples of the advanced Western liberal/democratic state, Lyon explains that whilst ID cards are a sensitive point of political discussion it is actually the "database that is likely to have the largest long-term impact" as information can be cross-checked with other information in an instant (Lyon 2005, 74). Certainly much of this statement applies to Pakistan. NADRA's databases are used to identify any Afghans who may have informally appropriated Pakistani citizenship. Once found their status as citizens is revoked in the database. In NADRA's Afghan POR card registration centers in urban Pakistan you will find hundreds of Afghans waiting from early morning until evening to be photographed, have their fingerprints scanned and have personal information taken, rechecked and stored in national databases.[17] Meanwhile, NADRA data processers sit at their desks and crosscheck their POR databases with the CNIC ones to check if any Afghans have informally appropriated, *a la* Sadiq, Pakistani citizenship. At one registration center, Shah Jahan, a data processer, eagerly explained to me, "Now if anyone possesses an Afghan card and a Pakistani *shanakhti* card it [the Pakistani identity card] immediately gets flagged up on the system when they come in for registration. This is how we catch them out." Indeed, in theatrical style, with raised voices and a show of potential force, when individuals who have both Pakistani and Afghan identity card are caught, a commotion ensues as individuals are held aside for interrogation by a government representative and/or an intelligence officer. Confusion and fear are publicly created by the everyday state as other Afghans observe the border transgressors being castigated for their acts. After this, the Afghans who have been caught have their Pakistani identity revoked on the NADRA database. The border is performed in an urban center through the policing of Afghans via virtual servers and databases. The body is a passcode on the route to unbelonging by the removal of individuals from the database registry.

Importantly many Pakistanis also find themselves being placed under surveillance for the purpose of exclusion – what Sadiq calls a purposeful state policy of creating "undocumented natives" (Sadiq 2009, 76) or what Handel calls the removal of "surplus populations" (Handel 2011, 264). Cases of Pakistani Pashtun CNICs being blocked in the Punjab, KP and Balochistan have been frequent in the GWOT years (Tahir 2015; Residents of Border towns in Balochistan Denied ID cards 2015; Khan 2015). In other cases state and/or private investors development plans on potentially lucrative urban land have led to attempts to create undocumented natives by saying individuals do not have CNICs and are not in the NADRA database (Qazi 2015). However, in these cases local community organization and political lobbying by Pakistani actors and local "intelligence" allows these "natives" to keep their position as Pakistanis nationals within the state. This is a luxury that is not afforded to Afghans who are also considered as non-nationals within local communities that leads to its own forms of social policing and xenophobia.

Profiling Afghans with the ID Card: Media and Materiality

The impact of the POR card does not stop at removal from the database or repatriation. The POR card is a material artefact and form of media that *carries* meaning in everyday life. As Habibullah's comment in the opening section of this paper indicates, the POR card transforms lived experiences and mobility for Afghans who remain in Pakistan. More specifically, for Afghans the POR card facilitates their profiling by the everyday state that targets Afghans for state security interests, everyday border performativity and/or petty corruption. Whilst in Lyon's Western liberal/democratic state the database and ID card system are game changers, in Pakistan it is also the ID the card itself that carries significant (and sometimes lethal) power (Tawil-Souri 2011, 231). It is necessary to unpack how documents engage with people, places and things (Khan 2014). The final section of this paper details how ID cards are material artefacts and form media that makes Afghans particularly vulnerable to violations by the everyday state for reasons of petty corruption and/or everyday performances of the border and sovereignty within the city.

Writing on Israel and the Occupied Palestinian Territories, Helga Tawil-Souri proposes that in a very basic sense the ID card is a form of media and a material artefact (Tawil-Souri 2011, 231). It is a media in so far as it is "a tool used to store and deliver information or data; a mode of communication that incorporates multiple forms of information content and processing" (Tawil-Souri 2011, 231). The ID card is also a form of media since it is *standardized, reproduced* and *personalized* (Tawil-Souri 2011, 231). It also serves the national goals of a dominant group – in this paper, the military-dominated Pakistani state. The card is a material artefact as, in its plastic composition and via its different colours, it is a form of one-way communication to the everyday officer (Tawil-Souri 2011, 231). It is necessary then to ask: how do documents evoke meaning in daily life? How are they experienced by their subjects? And how are they used to mediate social and political relationships.

The clearest indication of the POR card as communicator to the everyday state is seen when the POR card is about to expire/has expired; this is the time that individuals face the intense levels of state violence, including the mass arrests that Habibullah refers to at the start of this paper. When the POR card expires cardholders have no legal protection from Pakistan and the UNHCR. Instead they are a form of "bare life" that can be easily violated. The POR card is issued on a temporary basis. The date of expiry is printed on the back of the card. However, the date of the card expiry is negotiated in the tripartite agreements between Pakistan, Afghanistan and the UNHCR (see GOA, GOP, and UNHCR 2017), and it is always only after the card expires that the process for either extending or renewing the card takes place. This extension/renewal process is conducted on an *ad hoc* basis and with muddled communication between government departments and the multiple federal and provincial law enforcement agencies that will interact with the card.[18] The delay in the extension process is because of bureaucratic shortcomings in communication methods. It is also a purposeful tactic used by the state as a way to exert diplomatic pressure on Afghanistan by threatening to send back millions of Afghans to a state that cannot cope with a mass population re-entry. In practice what this means is that Afghans in Pakistan possess an out-of-date POR card. This impacts individuals in a networked society when they want to, say, open a bank account and the POR card is read as invalid. Yet, its most powerful impact is reserved for everyday engagements with law-enforcement agencies, which is a near daily occurrence as post-2001 Pakistan is marked by checkpoints, stop-and-searches, and a growing surveillance regime. The expired card communicates an "illegal" and threatening status of the cardholder making them vulnerable to arrest, deportation and harassment and verbal and physical abuse by everyday state, which are acts carried out both as forms of border performativity and/or petty corruption.

I conducted fieldwork in the months after the POR card expired in December 2009 and across my three field sites in Islamabad, Karachi and Peshawar groups of 2–250 (as per Habibullah's opening statement indicates) Afghans were being arrested at a time and were facing increased harassment at checkpoints, stop-and-searches and legal rulings calling for their deportation (despite having a right to stay).[19] This was repeated when the card expired again in 2013, 2015 and 2016.[20] Police arrests were justified through the POR card having expired and the 1946 Foreigners Law that says:

> Section 3(2)(c) of the Foreigners Act, 1946 which allows the Federal Government to make orders providing that a particular foreigner or prescribed class of foreigners "shall not remain in Pakistan or in any prescribed area therein." (Khan 2012)

It is difficult to document if any official declaration for the harassment of Afghans has been ordered, and if so, by which government or military departments. Further, more research on why the everyday state targets Afghans and other marginalized groups for everyday violations is needed – although government officials have sporadically admitted that Afghans are harassed as a point of state policy (Khattak 2017). Yet what is clear is that the POR card – and its dates of expiry – are used to justify the individual and mass arrests of Afghans. When individuals and groups were put on trial for having an out-of-date card, judges appeared unsure of the legal position of Afghans in Pakistan. This uncertainty is the result of poor communication between government departments *and the information contained on POR card*. Here, the POR card and the expiry date acts as a "discursive construct." (Tawil-Souri 2011, 232). It is a "contested text that is subject to interpretation by police officers, border officials and soldiers, on behalf of the state," and in this study, also the courts (Tawil-Souri 2011, 232). In one judicial magistrate's court case in Peshawar in February 2010, for example, an Afghan refugee was arrested under Section 14 of the Foreigners Act, 1946, which was upheld on the basis of the POR card. The verdict states:

> This court feels that Afghan Citizens who are/were refugees, but their statues of refugees have ended on 31-12-2009 and their status have not been renewed by the concerned officials, hence they have become foreigners in circumstances and hence they should not be entitled for bail on concession on the basis of old Afghan Citizenship card.[21]

In order to mediate the expiry of the POR card, some Afghan nationals have taken to carrying photocopies of circulars issued by SAFRON and CCAR stating that they have the right to remain in the country.[22] (See Figures 2–4). These photocopies are an attempt to prove a right to belong. Yet these documents are not an accepted form of media or a material artefact. It is only the ID card, a standardized nationally issued document that is considered as legitimate, and it is always preferred if the card in question is a CNIC rather than a POR card. Meanwhile, for undocumented Afghans, life is even more precarious with localized and limited mobility.[23]

Checkpoints and the ID Card

As mentioned earlier, on one level ID cards in Pakistan are used to deliver rights and privileges of belonging, be it of the citizen or non-citizens. They are also a reflection of a shift toward the seamless society. Yet unlike Deleuze's liberal state or the NADRA chairman's idealization of ID cards, in everyday life in the security state of Pakistan, ID cards are most important on issues of internal security and/or to assist in counterinsurgency campaigns. Fingerprint technology on ID cards is used to identify victims and perpetrators of terror attacks, which is then used for military and intelligence gathering. ID cards are also now a requirement for "legitimate movement *within* [the] state's territory" that is in conflict (Tawil-Souri 2011, 224). In North Waziristan Agency (NWA), FATA, residents were registered with an additional biometric ID card to the CNIC, the Watan card, in order to distribute humanitarian relief and to manage population mobility of residents in the light of ongoing military operations that required the area to be emptied of all populations in order to sift out the militants from non-combatants. Meanwhile, across the country, security checkpoints dominate road networks, urban spaces and entrances to local neighbourhoods.

In Islamabad, Karachi and Peshawar the checkpoint is a surveillance tool that is used to enhance public security. It is a site of "public site of theatre" (Handel 2011) to survey, police and deter subversive political actors and it checks if individuals passing through have the right of movement. Yet the checkpoint also serves other purposes. First, the checkpoint can be a publicity stunt by political parties and/or state actors who want to create an impression that they are managing security issues: for example, checkpoints often appear *after* a major terrorist attack. Second, the checkpoint is a site of economic opportunity for underpaid and overstretched law enforcements agencies, namely the police, who wish to earn extra income because of structural shortcomings in pay or norms of petty corruption (Abbas 2011, 9). The state, as embodied in the individual local actor, is not a consolidated entity solely acting to maintain public order. It is also located in the person who is shaped by individual interests and rationales. Yet everyday violations by law enforcement officers are much more likely to take place on individuals/groups that are stigmatized and criminalized in hegemonic discourse and/or those who are in the most vulnerable structural positions – the poor, marginalized groups, migrants. Here the ID card – or its absence – communicates one's status within a social hierarchy. Third, the checkpoint is a site of border performativity by the everyday state. The everyday state in the guise of a policeman performs sovereignty (and the border) through acts of direct and indirect violence. A body of scholarship informs us how sovereignty must be performed and reiterated on a daily basis in order to be effective – one way of which is through violence as it is only the state that has a legitimate monopoly over violence (Blom Hansen and Stepputat 2005, 7). Repeated acts of violence create emotional responses, such as fear, humiliation and discomfort, and discipline the citizen or non-citizen to change their behaviour and accept a social and political order. Yet for Afghans and other marginalized groups, these are not disciplinary actions in order to include individuals in the state but to exclude them from it.

For Afghans the POR card, whether expired or not, flags up Afghans as non-citizens and risky bodies and makes them vulnerable to routine physical and verbal abuse, detention and extortion, especially at the time of no legal status. These experiences lead to a feeling of "bordering" by Afghans; here the border is a metaphor for social exclusion but also can lead to a change in behaviour, namely the physical exit from Pakistan. More and more Afghans are leaving Pakistan for Afghanistan or, more often than not, Europe, Turkey, or other states (Alimia 2014b, 159–181). This is not forcible expulsion *per se*, but in the very least it reflects a process of coercive rather than voluntary repatriation or outward migration.

When I first interviewed Junaid in 2011 he was 26-years-old, living in Peshawar, and working as a high school teacher. He moved to the city in 1996 with his father and younger brothers – his father was a former civil servant with the PDPA and facing persecution from the Afghan *Mujahideen* who had returned to Afghanistan in the early 1990s. Junaid is an Afghan Pashtun, as are some 82% of Peshawar's Afghans (SAFRON, CCAR, and UNHCR n.d., 5). However, Junaid was fully aware that his Afghan/Afghanistani presence in Peshawar was no longer acceptable – Pashtun or not. He (as did others) found that police harassment was a routine affair. Trying to engage in basic mobility in the city, for example, to go to work, the shops, visiting friends or take public transport was not easy. On one occasion he was asked for his POR card at a police checkpoint and violently assaulted. He recalled, "The police officer slapped me across my face when I was coming home from teaching at college one day. He asked me what I was still doing here [in Pakistan], that we create trouble here." He continued, "Without fail, they [the police] always target Afghans. We are used to it now." Police harassment is a rite of passage that proves one's national identity. On another occasion, he was informed that he was being arrested because his POR card was out of date. Whilst at another time he and his friends (also Afghan) were stopped by a police officer at the checkpoint near his home, asked for his ID card, and then asked to pay a bribe in the currency of *chai* and *samosas*. Here the everyday state official confirms Junaid's Afghan national identity via the POR card and seeks to discipline Junaid into accepting his social and physical exclusion *in* and *from* Pakistan. The everyday state in the guise of a policeman is performing sovereignty (and the border) through violence. It is also violating a marginalized resident in order to earn some extra income in the form of a tea and snack. Eventually in 2016 Junaid left Peshawar for Kabul, as did thousands of others (HRW 2015). He explained to me over a *Whatsapp* telephone call that he was tired of being harassed and arrested for being Afghan.

Profiling Citizens and Non-Citizens: Marginalizing FATA Pashtuns and Pushing Out Afghans

Of course, it is not only Afghans who are subject to ethnic/national profiling and/or class profiling that make it hard to pass through a checkpoint or engage with law enforcement officers. In Pakistan the police are understood as being notoriously corrupt (Abbas 2011). In addition, class, ethnicity, nationality, location in Pakistan, gender and political positions mediate one's vulnerability to violations by the everyday state and cases of surveillance. These various intersections affect how likely it is that an individual will be asked to show their ID card at, say, a checkpoint and what one's experience will be like. Women are rarely stopped at the checkpoint, which reflects how threats to state security are gendered. However, in a society based on interconnected nuclear, intergenerational, and/or joint family units, women are affected when their social, emotional and economic male dependents are arrested, harassed, abuse and/or deported. In terms of class, the ease of which one can pass through a checkpoint is determined by the vehicle being used (no vehicle, bicycle, rickshaw, taxi, private car – expensive or cheap), the style of clothing worn and phenotypes, even before documentation is requested. Here class and ethnicity are *à la* Pierre Bourdieu a habitus that is performed in clothing and transport type (Bourdieu 1981). Driving a well-maintained and high-end car means you are unlikely to be stopped (Afghan or not), whereas travelling in a low-end car, motorbike, or bicycle almost guarantees you will be stopped (Afghan or Pakistani). Profiling is also experienced by the Baloch, residents of FATA and others, which is now compounded by the ID card and its ability to communicate information in more "accurate" ways. The POR card confirms if one is an Afghan national and the CNIC indirectly confirms ethnic identities by the inclusion of "permanent residence" (province or tribal area) on the card, that is which "ethnic" area you belong to, and a unique 13-digit identification number that also identifies one's province of origin.

In Peshawar, these intersections of ethnicity and class manifested when I was told, "They always stop the *mazdoor* (worker), Afghans, or 'tribal' Pashtuns [i.e. from FATA]." In Karachi I was informed by male residents, day labourers and factory workers – Sindhi, Kashmiri, Punjabi, Pashtun and others – about the manner in which they were often stopped by authorities while returning from work in various locations across the city. Cousins, sisters, mothers, aunts and wives of these men expressed concern at the punctuated movements of their male relatives because of police harassment. Whilst in Islamabad students from Balochistan related to me how they were regularly stopped and searched on their ways to and from classes. Afghans, however, are non-citizens who are facing pressure to return to Afghanistan. Afghans are subject to the everyday state engaging in forms of border performativity and as geopolitically significant non-citizens are rendered as "risky" bodies (Khosravi 2010, 27).

My three field sites of Karachi, Islamabad and Peshawar are notably different in their demographics and political, economic and infrastructural capabilities, and histories. Yet, across these sites the POR card was making it easier to identify who was an Afghan, resulting in increased verbal and physical abuse, extortion and arbitrary detention. This was accompanied by calls for the Afghans in question to leave Pakistan. Consider that Karachi has a population of over 23 million persons and is a microcosm of Pakistan and the wider Indian Ocean and Central-South Asian region. The city is also the site of ethno-political tussles over power, which were spearheaded by the Muttahida Qaumi Party (MQM), which claims to represent "Urdu-speaking" *muhajirs*, and other secular, ethno-national and religious political parties, such as the Awami National Party (ANP), or the Pakistan People's Party (PPP) (Gayer 2014). The MQM periodically positions itself against the military dominated state, Sindhis, who are native to the Sindh province and dominate rural areas and often politically represented by the PPP, and Pashtuns, who have migrated to the city from KP, FATA and Balochistan, and are often politically represented by the ANP. Notably, the MQM's repeated efforts to control the city are shaped through the construction in the public imagination of a looming "Pashtun"/ "Afghan" threat. Islamabad is, meanwhile, a predominantly Punjabi city and the capital city with a population of approximately one million people. However, in recent years thousands of residents from KP and FATA have also relocated to the city and are transforming its demographics. The capital city is nonetheless closely intertwined with the political and military establishment.

In cities, such as Islamabad and Karachi, which are nuclei of Pakistan's hegemonic Punjabi and sometimes Punjabi-Urdu political and cultural discourse, Afghans (*Afghanistanis*) and (Pakistani) Pashtuns are often understood as one and the same, or with very tightly bound shared interests, which, again, is despite the fact that not all Afghans are Pashtun and cities such as Karachi are very diverse in their Afghan population. This is also shaped by the GWOT years, where conflicts in Afghanistan *and* Pakistan's northwestern Pashtun regions mean that these territories and their peoples are also associated with a particular form of "Afghan"/"Pashtun"/"Pathan" "terror" (Alimia 2015), with all three terms and peoples seen to be bleeding into each other (this also builds on the earlier mentioned colonial legacies and the uneven ethno-federal structure of the Pakistani state). A major consequence is high state surveillance and profiling of Afghan citizens *and* Pakistani Pashtuns, and in the latter category, especially residents of FATA. Consider that in Islamabad 5,400 residents of FATA were placed under strict surveillance in 2016 (Asghar 2017 cited in Ahmad and Mehmood 2017). Whilst in Karachi residents of NWA face routine harassment; some have also been killed in "encounters" with the police because of their "tribal" origins (Hashim 2018; Rehman 2015).

Peshawar, on the other hand, is a Pashtun-majority city and situated on the northwest of Pakistan bordering Afghanistan. It has a population of four to five million persons and also hosts the most Afghans in the country, the majority of whom (some 82%) are also Pashtun. Yet some of the most vocal calls for the expulsion of Afghans come from political voices within KP and FATA. Simply having a shared ethno-linguistic background does not always mean shared social, political and economic, and other interests. The nation-state, power relations, social relations, political and economic interests, and "intra-group" dynamics undermine the assumption that it is possible to talk about a singular "Afghan"/ "Pashtun" identity.[24] In Peshawar, a "Pashtun city," differences of nationality between Afghans and Pashtuns carry importance – indeed *within* Pakistani Pashtuns village of origin, tribe of origin, class, and whether one is a resident of FATA or not (and then which agency in FATA) are important social categories. The result is that it is mainly Afghan nationals and residents of FATA who are subject to everyday violations at checkpoints. And, of course, within this for Afghans who are non-Pashto speakers, such as Uzbeks and Tajiks, there is a higher likelihood of being profiled.

Yet, across these three sites and even within the ethnically diverse Afghan national group, national identity is being standardized via ID cards. Thus, whilst Pakistani Pashtuns in general are subject to discrimination in Islamabad and Karachi at checkpoints, they can – to a degree – mediate their right to the city (and nation) as citizens through the standardized CNIC – albeit a *de facto* unequal right of belonging. In addition, Afghan Uzbeks in Peshawar may be, for example, more susceptible to profiling than Afghan Pashtuns, but now both are placed on the same standardized national *Afghan* ID card. For Pashtuns of who originate from FATA, however, their quasi-citizen status signifies that belonging continues to be a vulnerable and lethal reality across Peshawar, Islamabad and Karachi (Rehman 2015) and, of course, within FATA where these "peripheral" peoples have been made landless and displaced in their millions and killed in their tens of thousands in the GWOT (Crawford 2005). In Peshawar, Islamabad and Karachi the mobility of FATA residents is punctuated, which is the result of profiling and the data carried and communicated on the CNIC. At the same time, the standardized CNIC card nevertheless communicates a right to belong to the territorial nation-state of Pakistan or, at the very least, the buffer-zone that falls within the state – one which may potentially be included within mainland Pakistan via the FATA reforms. Afghans, however, are non-citizens facing mounting pressure to repatriate to the territorial Afghan nation-state. Afghans do not have a precedence that they will be naturalized into the state. For Afghans, in everyday life at checkpoints, stop-and-search, or other forms of policing, the POR card signifies and authenticates them as non-citizens who are constructed as a fifth-column and/or potential site of terror and/or as non-nationals who do not belong and should return to Afghanistan. Residents of FATA, then, are subject to the performativity of the buffer-zone into effect – a buffer-zone that may soon be in the state proper – whilst Afghans are subject to (international) border performativity via daily harassment, AVR schemes, and in the cases of undocumented Afghans outright deportation.

Conclusion

Surveillance, documentation and control over population mobility make the border. Pakistan has historically been shaped by a need to control the mobility of citizen and non-citizen populations in order to "perform" its borders into effect and to manage internal security concerns. After the independence and partition of British India in 1947 it was the border with India that was performed into being through a regime of documentation and a control over population mobility. Then, after the secession of East Pakistan in 1971, it was the new territorial constitution of Pakistan that was performed into being through the introduction of the national identity card and a control over population mobility of "new" and "old" Pakistanis. In 1979 after millions of Afghans migrated to Pakistan after the Soviet invasion of Afghanistan it was the turn of Pakistan's western border to be performed into effect through the issuance Afghan refugee ID cards and a regime of surveillance on Afghan nationals. Yet at the same time, the geopolitical considerations of the Soviet-Afghan War and later the Pakistani state's patronage of the Afghan Taliban meant that the Afghan population was able to remain in Pakistan as a useful asset (albeit still as non-citizens). Then, the border was enacted in documentary terms but not through the removal of populations. In the post-colonial security state of Pakistan, the border is not experienced in the same way across time, but mediated by geopolitical considerations. In the 2000s and 2010s as the GWOT spills into Pakistan and as the Afghanistan-Pakistan relationship reverts to one of mutual antagonism, the need to perform the Afghanistan-Pakistan border into effect is being pushed by the state and the US A large Afghan population in Pakistan is being carefully controlled, monitored and pushed back into Afghanistan or, more-often-than not, outward to third countries.

Notes

1. The registration of undocumented migrants in Karachi, including Afghans, was first managed by the National Aliens Registration authority (NARA) that sat under NADRA. This, however, soon shifted to NADRA and in 2015 all NARA activities were transferred to NADRA.
2. Afghans were given *prima facie* (on first encounter) *refugee* status in 1979. However, this was never formally granted to Afghans by way of a Ministerial declaration. Indeed, in archived UNHCR Pakistan "Information Sheets" and "Fact Sheets" from 1982–1985 Afghans are referred to as refugees but by 1987 they are referred to as having "temporary asylum." See UNHCR Pakistan, Fact Sheets and Information Sheets collection 1981–1987, Oxford Refugee Studies Centre [RSC] archive; see also Khan (2012, 4–5) and GOA, GOP, UNHCR (2003).
3. Efforts to develop a national Refugee Law started in the 2010s but have yet to be passed in to effect.
4. Interviews with CCAR officials, Islamabad March 2016 and UNHCR officials, Islamabad September 2017.
5. In Pakistan Afghans are managed under the various tripartite agreements among the GOP, GOA and UNHCR and the 1946 Foreigners Laws.
6. Interviews in Peshawar.
7. A number of cases of POR cards being rejected are recorded by the Society for Human and Prisoner's Rights (SHARP), an implementing partner of UNHCR that offers legal aid to Afghan refugees in Karachi, Lahore, and Islamabad. See: SHARP ALAC Cases 2008–2010 (Private archive, collected by author).
8. In Pakistan's history the armed forces have directly taken power through three coups (1958–1971, 1977–1988, 1999–2008).
9. The issue of ID cards in Balochistan is discussed in 1972 Cabinet Office documents, with decisions about implementation proposed to be negotiated by the Ministry of Interior and Government of Balochistan. See: Ministry of Interior (MOI 1972, 132).
10. CCAR, Khyber Pakhtunkhwa, 'Afghan Refugee: Statistics', Peshawar 2012. Private archive, collected by author.
11. Afghans were not restricted to live in refugee camps or specific provinces, although the government had a preference that Afghans would stay in KP and Balochistan. See SAFRON and CCAR, 1981, p. 1.
12. Interview with CCAR officials, Peshawar, Islamabad 2011.

13. In 2016, the European Union (EU) used the leverage of aid to enforce a secret agreement with Afghanistan that allows EU member states to deport unlimited numbers of Afghan asylum seekers. The agreement also proposes building a terminal dedicated to deportation flights at Kabul international airport – despite the fact that many Afghans in Europe were born and raised in Pakistan or Iran. European Commission [LEAKED: Restricted File, MIGR 43; COASI 19] European Commission and European External Service (EEAS) to COREPER Ambassadors. "Joint Commission-EEAS non-paper on enhancing cooperation on migration, mobility and readmission in Afghanistan," Brussels, 2nd March 2016.
14. In March 2017, Hamid Karzai, the former Afghan prime minister (2004–2014), tweeted 'We remind the Government of Pakistan that Afghanistan hasn't and will not recognize the Durand line' (See Siddiqui 2017).
15. In 2005, all Afghan refugee camps in FATA were closed down.
16. Interview, CCAR office, Islamabad, October 2015, March 2016; GOA, GOP, UNHCR, "International Conference on the Solutions Strategy for Afghan Refugees to Support Voluntary Repatriation, Sustainable Reintegration and Assistance to Host Countries (SSAR)" (Geneva 2012).
17. During 2010 and 2011, Afghans who had missed the first round of registration for the POR cards were eligible for registration through the Unregistered Members of Registered Families (UMRF) scheme.
18. As noted in the following documents: CCAR KP, "Home & T.A's Department Letter to: The Provincial Police Office re: NWFP Arrest of Afghan Refugees," Document No: DCAR/ACRHQs/214–17, dated 5th November 2009, Peshawar; "Letter to: Additional Chief Secretary, Home & TA's Department, Government of NWFP, Peshawar Re: Arrest and Deportation of Afghans Holding Valid POR Cards (CC: Mr. Felipe Camargo: Head of UNHCR, Sub Office, Pesh, wrt letter No. Pesh/Exec/235 dated 17th November 2009)" Document No: CAR: 262–63. "This is with reference to the Head of UNHCR, Letter No. Pesh/Exec/235 dated 17th November 2009 on the subject cited above (Copies A&B enclosed)." Peshawar. CAMP archive, Islambad.
19. As documented in the sources cited in note 18.
20. Interviews in Islamabad, Karachi, and Peshawar and private collection of court cases, for example: AJ son of GK, Afghanistan, presently Peshawar vs. the State, FIR No. [redacted], U/S: 3/4 / 14 Foreigner's Act 1946, Police Station: Daudzai, Peshawar, status: bail rejected, February 2010; The State vs. NK and Others, FIR No. [redacted], U/S: 3/4 / 14 Foreigner's Act 1946 Police Station: Maripur, Deportation Ordered (Karachi West), December 2009.
21. Pakistani Judicial Magistrates Courts Legal Rulings: February 2010, AJ son of GK vs. the State. Bail rejected (Private Collection).
22. Interviews with Afghan students, Peshawar, March 2016; CCAR Khyber Pakhtunkhwa, Home & T.A's Department Letter to: The Provincial Police Office re: NWFP Arrest of Afghan Refugees. Document No: DCAR/ACRHQs/214–17, Dated 5th November 2009, Peshawar.
23. The impact of the 2017 ID card for undocumented Afghans has not yet been assessed.
24. Karachi's Afghan population is 59% Pashtun, 20% Tajik, 10% Uzbek, 5% Hazara, and 2% Baloch. See SAFRON, CCAR, and UNHCR (n.d., 54).

Acknowledgments

In addition to the reviewers at Geopolitics, the author would like to thank Sami Raza, Usman Shah Zahirzai and Matthew J. Nelson for their comments and insight as this paper was written.

Funding

This work was supported by the Dahlem Research School, Freie Universität Berlin [COFUND Postdoctoral Fellowship] and Zentrum Moderner Orient.

References

3.9 Million Afghans Repatriated, Senate Told. November 3, 2015. *Pakistan Today*.

A Reporter. 2012. 96pc Adults Registered in Pakistan: NADRA. August 18, 2012. *Dawn News*. Accessed August 18, 2012. https://www.dawn.com/news/743082.

Abbas, H. 2011. *Reforming Pakistan's police and law*. Washington, DC: United States Institute for Peace.

Al Jazeera and Agencies. 2016. Afghanistan-Pakistan Border Clashes Kill Two Soldiers. *Al Jazeera* News, June 14, 2016. Accessed 14 June 2016. http://www.aljazeera.com/news/2016/06/afghan-soldier-killed-border-clash-pakistan-160613075159320.html.

Agamben, G. 1998. *Homo sacer: Sovereign power and bare life*. Palo Alto: Stanford University Press.

Ahmad, M., and R. Mehmood. 2017. Surveillance, Authoritarianism and 'Imperial Effects' in Pakistan. *Surveillance & Society* 15 3–4: 509.

Akhtar, A. S. 2008. The Overdeveloping State: The Politics of Common Sense in Pakistan, 1971–2007. PhD Thesis, London: SOAS.

Alavi, H. 1972. The state in post-colonial societies: Pakistan and Bangladesh. *New Left Review* I (74):59–81.

Alimia, S. 2014a. Who counts as a refugee: The geopolitics of Afghan and Bangladeshi migrants in Pakistan. *Himal South Asia* 27 (2):260–69.

Alimia, S. 2014b. Afghan (Re)Migration from Pakistan to Turkey: Transnational norms and the 'Pull' of Pax-Ottomanica?. *Insight Turkey* 16 (4):159–81.

Alimia, S. 2015. *On discrimination against Pashtuns: Reflections from Peshawar*. *Tanqeed*, 9, Summer.

Alimia, S. forthcoming. *Afghan refugees in Pakistan*. Philadelphia: University of Pennsylvania Press.

Amoore, L. 2006. Biometric borders: Governing mobilities in the war on terror. *Political Geography* 25:336–51. doi:10.1016/j.polgeo.2006.02.001.

Anwar, N. H. 2013. Negotiating new conjunctures of citizenship: Experiences of 'Illegality', in 'Burmese-Rohingya and Bangladeshi migrant enclaves in Karachi. *Citizenship Studies* 17 (3–4):414–28.

Asghar, M. 2017. *People of Fata-origin put under surveillance in Pindi division. Dawn News*.

Ayaz, G. 2016. *Officials count around 30,000 war dead in Afghanistan this year. Voice of America*.

Baitenmann, H. 1990. NGOs and the Afghan War: The politicisation of humanitarian aid. *Third World Quarterly* 12 (1):62–68. doi:10.1080/01436599008420215.

Balibar, E. 2002. *Politics and the other scene*. London: Verso.

Banerjee, S. 2012. *Becoming imperial citizens: Indians in late victorian empire*. Durham: Duke University Press.

Baumann, Z. 1991. *Modernity and the Holocaust.* Cambridge: Polity.

Bayly, C. A. 1996. *Empire and information: Intelligence gathering and social communication in India, 1780–1870.* Cambridge: Cambridge University Press.

BEFARE. 2009. *Baseline study on illegal migration, human smuggling and trafficking in Pakistan.* Karachi: BEFARE.

Blom Hansen, T., and F. Stepputat, eds. 2005. *Sovereign bodies: Citizens, migrants, and states in the postcolonial world.* Princeton: Princeton University Press.

Bourdieu, P. 1981. The forms of capital. In *Handbook of theory and research for the sociology of education,* ed. J. Richardson, 241–58. New York: Greenwood.

CCAR and SAFRON. 2010. Afghan management and repatriation strategy (AMRS). Islamabad: CCAR and SAFRON.

Cole, S. 2002. *Suspect Identities: A History of Fingerprinting and Criminal Identification.* Cambridge: Harvard University Press.

Coller, M. 2012. Deportation and the micropolitics of exclusion: The rise of removals from the UK to Sri Lanka. *Geopolitics* 17 (2):277.

Crawford, N. C. 2005. *War-related death, injury, and displacement in Afghanistan and Pakistan 2001-mid-2016 in Costs of War Project.* Providence: Brown University.

Deleuze, G. 1992. Postscript on the societies of control. 59:3–7. http://links.jstor.org/sici?sici=0162-2870%28199224%2959%3C3%3APOTSOC%3E2.0.CO%3B2-T

Donini, A. 2011. Between a rock and a hard place: Integration or independence of humanitarian action? *International Review of the Red Cross* 93:141–57. doi:10.1017/S1816383110000639.

Douglas, M. [1966] 1992. *Risk and blame. Essays in cultural theory.* London: Routledge.

Federal Investigation Agency. Human trafficking and migrant Smuggling Newsletter' (date unknown). Available via UN Office on Drugs and Crime. Accessed January 25, 2018. https://www.unodc.org/documents/pakistan/3_FIA_Newsletter.pdf.

Foucault, M. 1977. *Discipline and punish.* New York: Pantheon.

Foucault, M. 1978. *The history of sexuality,* vol. 1. New York: Pantheon.

Gayer, L. 2014. *Karachi: Ordered disorder and the struggle for the city.* London: Hurst.

Government of Afghanistan (GOA), Government of Pakistan (GOP), and UNHCR. 2003. 'Agreement Between the Government of Islamic Republic of Pakistan, the Transitional Islamic State of Afghanistan and the United Nations High Commissioner for Refugees Governing the Repatriation of Afghan Citizens Living in Pakistan,' March 16, 2003, Geneva.

GOA, GOP, and UNHCR. 2006. Memorandum of Understanding Between the Government of Islamic Republic of Pakistan and the Office of the United Nations High Commissioner for Refugees on the Registration of Afghan Citizens Living in Pakistan. April 19, 2006, Islamabad.

GOA, GOP, and UNHCR. 2017. Extension Agreement between the Governments of the Islamic Republic of Pakistan, the Islamic Republic of Afghanistan, and UNHCR Governing the Voluntary Repatriation of Afghan Citizens Living in Pakistan. February 15, Islamabad.

GOP. 2016. *Report on the Committee of FATA Reforms.* August 2016. Islamabad: GOP.

Handel, A. 2011. Exclusionary surveillance and spatial uncertainty in the occupied palestinian territories. In *Surveillance and control in Israel/Palestine: Population, territory, and power,* eds. E. Zureik, D. Lyon, and Y. Abu-Laban, 259–76. London: Routledge.

Hanifi, S. M. 2016. The Pashtun counter-narrative. *Middle East Critique* 25 (4):385–400.

Hanifi, S. M. 2012. Quandaries of the Afghan nation. In *Under the drones: Modern lives in the Afghanistan-Pakistan borderlands,* eds. S. Bashir and R. D. Crews, 83–101. Cambridge, MA: Harvard University Press.

Haroon, S. 2007. *Frontier of faith: Islam in the Indo-Afghan borderland.* New York: Columbia University Press.

Hashim, A. 2018. Police Killing of Naqeebullah Mehsud Angers Pakistanis. Al Jazeera News. Accessed January 19, 2018. http://www.aljazeera.com/news/2018/01/police-killing-naqeebullah-mehsud-angers-pakistanis-180119081758397.htmlm.

Hopkins, B. D., and M. Magnus Marsden. 2011. *Fragments of the Afghan frontier*. London: Hurst.

Human Rights Watch [HRW]. 2015. *"What are you doing here?" Police abuses against Afghans in Pakistan*. Islamabad: HRW.

Human Rights Watch [HRW]. 2017. *Pakistan coercion, UN complicity: The mass forced return of Afghan refugees*. Islamabad: HRW.

Internal Displacement Monitoring Centre. 2013. Massive New Displacement and Falling Returns Require Rights-Based Response. Accessed 15 August 2014. http://www.internal-displacement.org/south-and-south-east-asia/pakistan/2013/massive-new-displacement-and-falling-returns-require-rights-based-response.

Jalal, A. 1990. *State of martial rule: The origins of Pakistan's political economy of defense*. Cambridge: Cambridge University Press.

Khan, I. 2014. Pakistan Most Terror Hit Nation. *Dawn News*. Accessed February 23, 2014. www.dawn.com/news/1088864.

Khan, M. B. 2012. *The legal environment in Pakistan for registered Afghans*. Islamabad: CAMP.

Khan, S. 2017. Afghans Dream of Stepping out of the Shadows with Pakistan ID Scheme. UNHCR. Accessed July 28, 2017. http://www.refworld.org/docid/5975bc8b4.html.

Khan, T. 2015. Denial of Existence. *The Express Tribune*. Accessed May 10, 2015. https://tribune.com.pk/story/884091/denial-of-existence/.

Khattak, I. 2017. SAFRON Ministry, NADRA Sign MOU on "Carrot-and-Stick" Policy for Undocumented Afghan Nationals. *Dawn News*. Accessed May 11, 2017. https://www.dawn.com/news/133244.

Khosravi, S. 2010. *'Illegal' traveller: An auto-ethnography of borders*. Basingstoke: Palgrave.

Lyon, D. 2005. The border is everywhere: ID cards, surveillance and the other. In *Global surveillance and policing: Borders, security, and identity*, eds. E. Zureik and M. B. Salter, 66. Portland: Willian Publishing.

Lyon, D. 2006. *Identifying citizens: ID cards as surveillance*. London: Polity.

Lyon, D. 2007. *Surveillance studies: An overview*. Cambridge: Polity Press.

Malik, T. 2012. *From an idea to reality: Pakistan's smart card. The News*.

Ministry of Interior [MOI]. 1972. Document No: 596, 123/CF/72. Cabinet Records Office, National Documentation Centre, Islamabad.

Ministry of Interior [MOI]. 1976. Report on the problem of issuance of identity cards to the foreigners. Document No: 705, 129/Prog/76. Cabinet Office Records, National Documentation Centre, Islamabad.

Ministry of States and Frontier Region (SAFRON), Chief Commissionerate for Afghan Refugees (CCAR), and [UNHCR] United Nations High Commission for Refugees (UNHCR). 2005. *Census of Afghans in Pakistan*. Islamabad: SAFRON, CCAR, and UNHCR, 2005.

Muller, B. J. 2004. Disqualified bodies: Securitization, citizenship, and "identity" management. *Citizenship Studies* 8 (4):279–94. doi:10.1080/1362102042000257005.

Nunan, T. 2016. *Humanitarian invasion: Global development in Cold War Afghanistan*. Cambridge: Cambridge University Press.

Pakistan Is Driving Out 1.5 m Afghan Refugees. 2016. *The Economist*. Accessed September 16, 2016. https://www.economist.com/blogs/graphicdetail/2016/09/daily-chart-11.

Parenti, C. 2003. *The soft cage: Surveillance in America from slavery to the war on terror*. New York: Basic Books.

Qazi, N. A. 2015. Is the CDA Bulldozing our Constitutional Rights? *Dawn News*. Accessed August 5, 2015. https://www.dawn.com/news/1198354

Qureshi, S. M. M. 1966. Pakhtunistan: The frontier dispute between Afghanistan and Pakistan. *Pacific Affairs* 39 (1/2):99–114. doi:10.2307/2755184.

Rashid, A. 2000. *Taliban: The story of the Afghan warlords*. London: Pan Books.

Rehman, Z. 2015. *Footprints: The crimes of being Mehsud. Dawn News*.

Residents of Border towns in Balochistan Denied ID cards. February 6, 2015. *Newsline Pakistan*. Accessed February 5, 2015. http://www.newslens.pk/residents-of-border-towns-in-balochistan-denied-id-cards/.

Sadiq, K. 2009. *Paper citizens: How illegal immigrants acquire citizenship in developing countries*. Oxford: Oxford University Press.

SAFRON and CCAR. 1981. *Official handbook on refugee management in Pakistan*. Islamabad: RSC archive.

SAFRON, CCAR, and UNHCR. n.d. Population profiling, verification, and response survey of Afghans in Pakistan. Islamabad: SAFRON, CCAR, and UNHCR.

SAFRON, National Database and Registration Authority (NADRA), and UNHCR. 2007. *Registration of Afghans in Pakistan*. Islamabad: SAFRON, NADRA, and UNHCR.

Salter, M. 2011. Places everyone! Studying the performativity of the border, in Interventions on rethinking "The Border" in border studies. *Political Geography* 30 (2):66–67.

Scott, J. C. 1998. *Seeing like a state: How certain schemes to improve the human condition have failed*. New Haven: Yale University Press.

Siddiqa, A. 2007. *Military, Inc.: Inside Pakistan's military economy*. London: Pluto Press.

Siddiqui, N. 2017. Afghanistan will never recognize the Durand line: Hamid Karzai. *Dawn News*. Accessed March 4, 2017. https://www.dawn.com/news/1318594.

Tahir, Z. 2015. 100,000 Pakistanis Lose Nationality for Being 'Suspect Aliens'. *Dawn News*, May 29, 2015. Accessed May 29, 2015. https://www.dawn.com/news/1184905.

Tahir, M. 2017. The ground was always in play. *Public Culture* 29 (81):5–16.

Tarzi, A. 2012. Political struggles over the Afghanistan–Pakistan borderlands. In *Under the drones: Modern lives in the Afghanistan Pakistan borderlands*, eds. S. Bashir and R. D. Crews, 17–29. Cambridge: Harvard University Press.

Tawil-Souri, H. 2011. Orange, green, and blue: Color-coded paperwork for palestinian population control. In *Surveillance and control in Israel/Palestine: Population, territory, and power*, eds. E. Zureik, D. Lyon, and Y. Abu-Laban, 219–38. London: Routledge.

The Julian Assange Show. Episode 10, 2012. Interview with Imran Khan. Accessed January 25, 2018. http://worldtomorrow.wikileaks.org/episode-10.html.

Toor, S. 2011. *The state of Islam: Culture and cold war politics in Pakistan*. New York: Pluto Press.

Torpey, J. 2000. *The invention of the passport: Surveillance, citizenship, and the state*. Cambridge: Cambridge University Press.

U.S. Embassy. 2009. Secretary Napolitano Discusses Border Security and Passenger Name Record Data Sharing with GOP Officials. *Wikileaks Cable: 09ISLAMABAD 1642_a*. Accessed January 10, 2013. https://wikileaks.org/plusd/cables/09ISLAMABAD1642_a.html.

Zamindar, V. 2007. *The Long Partition and the making of modern South Asia: Refugees, boundaries, histories*. New York: Columbia University Press.

Zureik, E., and M. B. Salter, eds. 2005. *Global surveillance and policing: Borders, security, and identity*. Portland: Willian Publishing.

Zureik E. 2011. Surveillance and population control. In *Surveillance and Control in Israel/ Palestine: Population, Territory, and Power*, eds. E. Zureik, D. Lyon and Y. Abu-Laban, 10. London: Routledge.

Tribal Women, Property and Border: An Auto-Ethnographic Critique of the *Riwaj* (Tradition) on the Pakistan–Afghanistan Borderland

Noreen Naseer

ABSTRACT

This paper explores the cultural status of tribal women living in the Pakistan–Afghanistan borderland. Pakhtun tribes, a patriarchal and paternalistic society, practising tribal customs *(Riwaj/Dastoor)*, inhabit this borderland. Owing to these tribal customs, the tribal Pakhtun society treats women much like property of their men. This essay focuses on how a tribal woman is socially discriminated by denying her certain fundamental rights. I discuss six tribal customs, by giving examples based on my field work, through which tribal women are treated as personal property by her male kin—father, brother, uncle or husband. These customs include *shamilaat* (denial of the right to inheritance in shared family's and tribe's property), *miratah* (declaring a woman as issueless in the absence of a male kin and thereby denying her property), *rasnama/valver/khawara* (bride-money), *ghairat/nang* (honour and pride), *badala/swara* (barter, as in getting father or brother a bride or as in exchange for settlement of dispute) and *ghag* (pronouncing the desire to marry a specific woman or in some cases to spite a family).

Introduction

چرته ښځه چرته لور یم
آبادی زه ستا د کور یم
هُم دی متی هُم دی زور یم
هُم زه ستا لره پیغور یم

Daughter or Wife
Your house is home because of me,
I am the prop you lean on,
I am the power that runs you,
Yet, you think I am a slur against your honour.

In the above Pakhto poetic verse, a Pakhtun woman is complaining about her status in the tribal society, which is centred on her position as man's honour and property. Her status is also reflected in the three aspects of *Pakhtunwali*, the ideal code of life of the Pakhtun tribal people and their honour: *zer, zen* and *zameen* (gold, women and land). In various ways, these aspects are codified and embedded in the *Riwaj*, the traditions of the borderland Pakhtuns. It is intriguing and ironic to see that women are placed with gold and land, that is, with non-living material that constitutes private property. In the *Riwaj*, a tribal woman without a father, brother, husband or a son has literally no socially recognised identity and hence lacks rights, which is a reflection of a predominantly patriarchal society. Her identity in much eulogised patriarchal *Riwaj* is, in fact, a suffering of women in a Pakhtun borderland society. Thus, the social status of the tribal Pakhtun woman under the *Riwaj* is symbolic of domestic violence and oppression. In this essay, I mainly illustrate the oppressed social status of women on the North-West frontier through a number of auto-ethnographic narratives, which I obtained during my fieldwork research.

I employ the auto-ethnographic method to give voice to the oppressed tribal women through their self-narration. Moreover, I also want to relate them to my own (author's) experience of the *Riwaj*. This method enables me to explore my own as well as that of the other tribal women's constructed identities in the social and cultural structures of the borderland tribal society. Hence, this work contains pieces of autobiography expressing the life experiences of tribal women living under tribal *Riwaj*. A number of scholars describe the method of auto-ethnography "as both process and product, where a researcher can use the tenets of autobiography and ethnography to do and write auto-ethnography" (Denshire 2014, 831–850).

I have collected the life experiences of the tribal women that I mention in this article through my family and tribal connections. Moreover, I also identify myself as one of them. It is pertinent to mention that my identity as a tribal woman enabled me to collect data/information, which otherwise does not surface in society due to strict codes of honour. In addition, I took into confidence the tribal women (victims or relatives of victims) by giving them my word/assurances (*Jabba*), telling them that their stories will be a trust (*Amanat/Bawar*), and used carefully for academic purpose only. I hope to narrate their stories to highlight the plight of victims of the Riwaj. Thus in narrating these life experiences/events, I want to create and expect respect and encouragement for the tribal women.

I want to highlight at the outset that unlike tribal women living in the erstwhile FATA, the educated tribal women in the settled areas of Pakistan enjoys certain rights, but they still suffer indirectly and at times directly from the tribal cultural traditions. Like the tribal women of the tribal territorial agencies, they are also expected to be the custodian of their family honour. This indirectly makes them hostage to the *Riwaj* even in settled areas where the state institutions and constitutional rights are available. They are also denied the right to private property and are not allowed to make certain personal decisions like choosing a profession of their choice or to marry persons of their choice, especially if their decisions risk affecting family relations or honour.

I explore how *Riwaj* has passively affected me. I observe that in carrying out the auto-ethnographic method, it was not easy to step out of constructed cultural values. Thus, it is even more difficult to write a critique of *Riwaj* and self-interrogate too. Hence, the purpose of this essay is not to degrade or belittle the borderland *Riwaj* or its utility/accomplishments in the everyday course of peaceful life, but to make a conscious effort for the emancipation and protection of the borderland women. By highlighting the plight of borderland women, I seek the removal of certain forms of inequality, domination and oppression through the creation of a just, social and economic order inclusive of women.

My analysis is based on the argument that "the old *Riwaj*" was framed on survivalist strategies of a low production society. However, in the present time, we notice that Pakhtun tribesmen are no more "acephalous" and/or "segmentary". Their social arrangement of kinship and society has undergone considerable change owing to the state policies on both sides of the border, especially in the wake of the war and changing economic concerns. Nevertheless, the social status of women has not seen much change. Therefore, to understand the *Riwaj*'s treatment and dealing of the tribal women, several cases are discussed from the borderland of Pakistan.

An Auto-Ethnographic Critique of the *Riwaj* (Tradition)

Fazeelat Bibi

In Landi Kotal Khyber Agency, Fazeelat Bibi was brutally murdered by her brothers-in-law on 10th August 2016. However, the news could not make it to the national televisions but the locals of the Landi Kotal communicated it to the tribal women rights activists. Two men named Naseem and Fakhr-e-Alam, the victim's brothers-in-law, colluded to kill Fazeelat Bibi and their maternal uncle Kher Ullah on the pretext of saving their family's honour. The main cause behind the Fazeelat Bibi's murder is a money dispute between Naseem and his uncle Kher Ullah. Thus, to avoid family's enmity, they implicated Kher Ullah and Fazeelat Bibi, using the practice of *Tor* (dishonour) to settle the score with their uncle. Bibi's husband Shakoor, who is an economic migrant in the Middle East, was not present in Pakistan at the time of his wife's killing by his brothers. On his return, he filed a case with the agency's Assistant Political Agent (APA), who is a magistrate and arranges *Jirgas* (quasi-judicial council of elders) under the Frontier Crimes Regulations. APA put together a *Jirga* of five elders on the application of the victim's husband. The *Jirga* decided with a majority of four members in favour of the defendants, thus approving Bibi's murder on the account of saving the honour of the family with/without the willingness of the victim's husband. The APA in his official verdict wrote that the decision of Jirga is in accordance with the local *Riwaj* and that the majority members endorsed it. Therefore, Shakoor's application was dismissed (Jirga Award Khyber 2016, 1–4). *Riwaj* has frozen time for the tribal women living in the borderland.

Janna

Another murder case of a woman on borderland that I want to highlight is that of an Afghan migrant in the Orakzai Agency, Janna. Her family migrated to the Orakzai Agency via Kurram Agency from Afghanistan during the Afghan War of the 1980s. She fell in love with a local tribal man. Janna and Iqbal Khan wanted to marry but their families refused. Khan's family self-consciously thought of itself superior to Janna's family because they owned land and property. In the tribal society, land and property are a symbol of status and power. Thus, Khan's family thought it is below their dignity to allow Iqbal Khan to marry Janna whose family was landless and migrant. Against all odds, they eloped and got married at friend's house. Later Janna's father Khanum Gul reconciled, but claimed bride money under the *Riwaj* for elopement[1] and left the agency as his daughter's elopement dishonoured him.

After a few years, Janna's husband died in a landmine accident on the border. Janna was left in the care of her brother-in-law, Ali Khan. It is interesting to note that in the tribal *Riwaj* a widow cannot go back to her father's house or anywhere else without the permission/willingness of her husband's family. In the majority of cases, she is either remarried to her brother-in-law if he is willing to take her as his wife or left to do household chores and can live as a widow. Ill-fated Janna had a tragic destiny; her brother-in-law took her as his wife, but only with the purpose to sell her off to another man without divorcing. The so-called suitor Arbab Khan from Tirah Orakzai had a murderous plan. He bought Janna as a bride without confirming divorce and wanted to use her as a scapegoat by killing her and his enemy in a family honour case. Somehow, elders of the village came to know about the plot and rushed to rescue Janna. After a *Jirga* intervention, Janna was rescued and brought back to her house. She was still left in the care of a person who had sold her in a murderous scheme. Soon afterwards, an unknown person comes to her house and kills her. There are different explanations of her murder. Some say her husband's son in law killed her, while others say that the person who had bought her killed her (Janna's Family 2014)

Janna's murder is quite tragic. When she was a child, she became a victim of war, and when she grew up as a young woman, she became a victim of the *Riwaj* of border areas. On her several dimensions of *Riwaj* were played: father took the bride money in lieu of elopement (*Valver*)[2]; her brother in law took her as his wife per *Riwaj* that is ownership after her husband's death (*Kaween, Izzat.*)[3]; another person bought her and wanted to use her to avenge his honour against an enemy (*Tor, Ghairat*); and eventually she is brutally murdered as she had no male to protect her at home (*Miratah*).

Eid Bibi

For a long time, before even the War on Terror began, women living on the north-western border of Pakistan had no safety and peace in their lives especially owing to the *Riwaj*. Eid Bibi, daughter of Sardar Hussain, a resident of Sameer, Kurram, tribal agency of the erstwhile FATA, was one of the unfortunate tribal women who was killed by her step-nephew for inheriting her father's property. She was an unmarried woman in her late 50s, living with her sister and maternal nephews after her father's death. Her father Sardar Hussain (who had codified the *Riwaj-e-Kurram)*[4] and was a signatory to it (Hussain and Kakakhel 1947, 2–30), had two wives. From his first wife, he had two daughters, Eid Bibi and her sister. His second wife bore him a son and from him five grandsons. In his life, he gave some property to his unmarried daughter Eid Bibi. He also took fatwa[5] from two Maulanas (religious clergies of Kurram) that he could give a share to his daughter. He distributed rest of his property amongst his grandsons. Sardar Hussain giving a share of his property to daughter and justifying it with religion shows that tribal men are ready to transform their behaviour towards their women if *Riwaj* allows them.

After her father's death, her paternal step-nephews started bothering her to give them her share of the property. In Kurram, land distributions are recorded. Hence, any transfers and cancellations are formally required on paper for properties and lands. On refusing, Hur Hussain, one of her step-nephew shot Eid Bibi several times while she was coming from Sameer Abbas (a Sufi Saint Tomb). She died on the spot. The people soon apprehended the killer. *A jirga* of four elders was formed to hear the case of Eid Bibi. In his defence, Hur Hussain stated that his motive behind the killing was to save his family honour, as she was accused of maligning family's name by living in her sister's house and having illicit relations with her brother-in-law. Out of four, three decided in favour of Hur Hussain that he saved family's honour and one dissented stating that Eid Bibi known as Haji Gula for her piety cannot bring any dishonour to her family. The dissenting member thought she was innocent. Later the case was referred to the Political Agent of Kurram Agency for a detailed investigation. Her maternal nephew (sister's son) wrote an appeal to the Political Agent and other higher authorities, stating that his aunt was killed for property and land. The Political Agent on pressure from higher authorities and village people investigated the issue and then awarded three years imprisonment to Hur Hussain. Ironically, the property of Eid Bibi is left to her murderers, her step-nephews, as per *Riwaj*—only paternal nephews, cousins and distant cousins can inherit a woman's share if she is issueless and unmarried. Her close friends and family say that when she was bothered and threatened by her step-nephews, she would say that she wished she had a son or brother to protect her from them (Najeeb 2015)

It depicts how a tribal woman's identity is defined and rights are protected by the presence of male members of the family. Moreover, it reinforces the notion that Pakhtun men's obsession with property and women can take them to any level, where he can use an excuse of defending honour, a part of *Pakhtunwali*. In this case, it is observed that it is not only a property but also hurt his Pakhtun ego—masculinity, as he considered himself the only legal heir of his grandfather. To Hur Hussain, Eid Bibi was herself a property like other tribal women, hence when her father tried to empower her that irked him. He is a product of centuries-old *Riwaj*, where man is an owner and shareholder of everything around him.

Sakina Bibi

Unfortunately, tribal Pakhtun women suffer equally due to *Riwaj* even in the presence of laws and protection mechanism in the settled areas of Pakistan. The case of Sakina Bibi daughter of Ulas Khan from Mohmand family settled in Peshawar is a glaring example of how tribal men assert their *Riwaj/Dastoor/Pakhto*. She was married to Ijaz Khan from Peshawar city and he paid the *Valver* to bride's father according to the Mohmands' *Riwaj/Dastoor*.[6] In the tribal families, a newly married daughter pays a visit to her father's house on the seventh day of her marriage and stays overnight. Hence, like many tribal brides, Sakina Bibi came for the overnight stay. However, her father refused to send her back to husband's house. Thus, Ijaz Khan filed a suit in the Peshawar's family court for restitution of conjugal rights and the return of his wife. He also pleaded that he had paid the bride money (Peshawar Family Court 2013, 1–10). In return, Ulas Khan, father of Sakina Bibi, claimed that his daughter's husband had not paid her dower (*Mahr*). The family court ordered Ulas Khan to produce his daughter based on the evidence that the bride's money was paid. Therefore, he was not entitled to any dower. Even on court's order, Ulas Khan refused to bring his daughter in the court under the pretext of tribal honour relating to *Pardah*.[7] The case showed that the tribal woman while living in the urban/settled areas have no freedom, and treated as men's property. In such cases from border areas, the state is equally responsible for not protecting the tribal women even in the settled areas that has a judicial system and other law enforcement bodies.

Anjum Ara

Anjum Ara, daughter of Fazal-e-Nabi, from Mohmand Agency also became a victim of the *Riwaj*. She lived in the city of Karachi. Ara fell in love with a non-Pakhtun man from Karachi. On finding out, the grandfather of Ara, Haji Fazal Mohmand a chieftain of Mohmand tribe, and self-conscious custodian of the *Riwaj* shot Ara and her man. The shooting resulted in the killing of the man, while Ara suffered severe injuries. She was taken to a hospital by neighbours and after treatment recovered. Meanwhile, Fazal Mohmand was arrested. He confessed the killing of the man in the name of saving his honour that he thought was demanded of him in the *Riwaj*. Afterwards, he was released due to a settlement with man's family. When he was released, he took his granddaughter Anjum Ara to his native village, killed her and buried her in an unmarked grave (Arqam 2016, 4). The killings show how tribal men living in another part of the country uphold the *Riwaj*. Tribal women are not safe even in the urban area where the rule of law exists. Educated and economically independent tribal women living in the settled areas of Pakistan are passive victims of the *Riwaj* too. They uphold all the values that are prescribed in the tribal system for an honourable tribal woman. The limits of the cultural system transcend the borders of borderland and haunt them if they violate any of the practice.

The *Riwaj*, Borderland Pakhtun Woman and Homo-Sacer

The world has experienced first, a second and third wave of feminism in the last two centuries, thus recognising social, political and economic rights of women not only in the developed world but also in the developing world including settled urban parts of Pakistan (Lorber 2010, 1–4). However, feminism and issues related to gender-based violence are always considered one of the most notorious themes in general social sciences discourse in Pakistan. Although with all the controversy regarding feminism, Pakistani urban women have three decades of activism and some scholarly work against the gender-based violence in Pakistan, but a tribal woman living on borderland is absent from their work and activism. This neglect, either intentional or unintentional, has adversely affected tribal women living in the periphery. She is trapped in a centuries-old system of *Riwaj* and suffering both in the borderland as well in the cities of Pakistan.

The Pakhtun woman living in the borderland under the *Riwaj* is like a figure of woman homo-sacer, as she is denied rights and can be killed without fear of justice. Giorgio Agamben defines homo-sacer "the sacred man is the one whom the people have judged on account of a crime. It is not permitted to sacrifice this man, yet he who kills him will not be condemned for homicide"; in the first tribunitian law, in fact, it is noted, "if someone kills the one who is sacred according to the plebiscite, it will not be considered homicide. This is why it is customary for a bad or impure man to be called sacred" (Giorgio 1998, 47). Hence, like Roman law, *Riwaj* judge her on the account of certain behaviour that is culturally constructed as an offence. She is killed (sacrificed) for honour, yet he who kills her will not be condemned for homicide and considered acceptable in the society. Thus, if a tribal woman living on the borderland violates the traditional laws of *Riwaj* she is like a cursed person and killed with impunity.

Why have I found the character of archaic Roman law closer to the tribal women status in the border areas? Homo sacer is a cursed and outcaste person by a law—may be killed by anybody but may not be sacrificed in a religious ritual. In early Roman religion, sacer denotes anything "set apart" from common society and encompasses both the sense of hallowed and that of cursed (Giorgio 1998, 54–56). The tribal woman is a character like homo sacer in the centuries-old *Riwaj*, she is a person expunged from the society and deprived of certain social and economic rights, if challenge cultural practices, then stripped off certain civil religious rights too. Thus, her murder in the name of defending honour is *Pakhto/Ghairat* and is legal in *Riwaj*; she is someone who can be killed with impunity whilst the killer is regarded as a defender of honour. A woman living under *Riwaj* is that sacred human and may be understood as someone outside the law, or beyond it. Her murder under *Riwaj* is not a crime against state and society as it happened in the cases of Fazeelat Bibi and Anjum Ara.

A tribal woman living on the borderland transforms into a homo-sacer if she breaks an oath of *Riwaj*. An oath breaking is challenging cultural practices, thus invoking divinity's wrath and asking for punishment (Hussain and Kakakhel 1947, 2). Thus, a tribal woman will be punished if deceive or challenge gods (men and their constructed *Riwaj*). She is killed as an oath-breaker or challenger of *Riwaj*. Her killing with impunity is understood as the revenge of the men into whose power she had given to herself as it happened in the case of Eid Bibi. She challenged the *Riwaj* and men of the family by inheriting her father's property gifted to her.

Agamben's discusses homo-sacer as reduced to 'bare life' in the state of exception, hence deprived of any rights. In border areas, the state of exception is created with the special status and *Riwaj Act*, thus marginalising tribal women through *Riwaj*. The tribal woman is an individual, accorded limited citizenship by the state. Her life regulated by the *Riwaj* is placing her outside the state's law, thus reducing her to "bare life" in the eyes of the judicial powers *(Jirga)*. In such state of exception, the boundaries of power are precarious and seldom threaten to destabilise not only the law but also one's humanity, as well as their choice of life or death. A tribal woman (living in erstwhile FATA or other parts of Pakistan) is in a state of exception, she is excluded as well included in the traditional juridical system. She is discussed as a subject in the context of both property and life, excluding her by denying individual rights and including her when her productivity is discussed or questioned (Giorgio 1998, 18–29).

Historically, women living under the *Riwaj* neither had asked for nor were granted rights. There are several reasons for such a passive attitude. One of the reasons is that patrilineal (not entirely patriarchal) tribal society was once nomadic and matrilineal (not matriarchal); women played a significant role in relocation, assisted men in wars, helped in building tribes and social structures. However, when tribes started settling down, wars ended and properties acquired, then the role of the women started to decline, and she started to become complacent, thereby leaving public space to tribal men (Kakakhel 1965, 42–170). Only recently have women rights activists raised voice for their rights and oppression. In addition, state's policies towards Pakhtun borderland alienated tribal women from raising voice against the somewhat misogynist *Riwaj*.

This transformation from nomadic to sedentary life changed the dynamics of tribes and tribal structures. As the matrilineal society transformed into patriarchal and patrilineal, tribal men started believing that men are born to dominate, women to be subordinated and his property in the form of his honour. The *Riwaj* reinforced the notion among men that they were biologically superior and women as inferior, which they thought is universal and natural, and hence irreversible. After settling down on the borderland, they did not acquire land only but also started to own everything that failed to resist or rebel. Land and property earned with wars and force (*pa matto gatalay*), hence now owned jointly by influential tribesmen in the borderland (Hussain and Kakakhel 1947, 7–9). The concept of combined/jointly owned property (*Shamilaat)* is a necessity to survive in hostile situations together. Under the pretext of land earned by the men only (*pa matto gatalay zmaka*), and women's compliance, is a masculine notion.[8] It is interesting to know that according to western scholarship, patriarchy developed with private property. Frederick Engels in his book, "Origin of the Family, Private Property and the State", believed that women's subordination began with the development of private property, "the world historical defeat of the female sex took place" (Engels 1820-1895, 34). In the borderland, the property is jointly owned by the tribes but divided amongst the male members only.

The concept of combined property ownership by the tribesmen (*Shamilaat*) has defined the tribal women identity and rights too. A woman without a man (father, brother, husband and son) has no identity or protection and is known as *Miratah*, one without male as in the case of Eid Bibi. For a tribal woman, having a father, brother, husband and son is not only her identity and protection but a symbol of status too. Property or land that her father, brothers, husband or sons inherit defines her position, and in return, she protects her family honour and does not trespass certain set codes of the *Riwaj*. A married woman without a son is also described as *Miratah* in the *Riwaj* and after her husband's death; she cannot inherit his land or property. Her son's inheritance is hers and can enjoy individual rights. Hence, a married woman needs a man to give her financial and other protection.

Depriving the borderland woman of property and economic rights traps her in an honour syndrome, which is explicitly discussed in the *Riwaj* with a context of either land or women. The tribal woman, like private property, is considered as the honour of family (*Ghairat, Nang*). It classifies her in the category of "his honour" (read property like gold and land), takes away her rights and justifies her killing with impunity. She is his personal belonging, and if she does something against his honour, then the man can punish and kills her anywhere like Anjum Ara. She survived the fatal incident and was given a second chance; however, honour prescribed in the *Riwaj* did not let her live.

Ironically, in defence of his honour, he can use her to take revenge (*Badal*) from his enemies too as it happened in the case of Fazeelat Bibi. Honour in *Riwaj* is man defending and protecting his land, property and women. In case of woman, honour is her obeying certain set standards of culture and if she tries to challenge it then it is tantamount to man's dishnour. For example, the tribal man's honour is affected if she interacts with any other person without the consent of her father, brother and even cousins. If she does so, it is tantamount to breaching the tribal man honour. If she is given property or married to a man of her choice and in some cases, if a male member of a family disapproves her education then she cannot pursue her studies. In any case, if she defies then again in saving a family's honour, male members can take any action to stop her. Marriage is strictly based on men's permission. She has no choice or consent, but to follow the tribal tradition that is to respect the decision taken by the elders/male of the family. Hence, like Homo Sacer, a tribal woman is sacred in the form of his honour and to safeguard his honour she can be killed without breaking any law.

After marriage, woman's honour/ownership goes to her husband, the change of ownership comes with *Rasnama/Valver/Khawara*, the amount of bride price that husband pays to bride's father or brother and in some instances to a former husband. The *Riwaj* is very explicit about the bride money and amount paid to the owner (father, brother, uncle, former husband) of the virgin, widowed, divorcee, high class, working class and the eloped woman. The fate of the tribal woman belonging to the upper class and working class is not different, but the difference is of the bride prices (Hussain and Kakakhel 1947, 10). In places like Peshawar city, she is sold, refused access to the court, take an independent decision about her life or marry as it was in the case of Sakina Bibi.

In some instances, a tribal woman is exchanged or bartered for father or brother's bride known as *Badala* (Ghulam 1969, 13). In the case of an exchange for a bride, there is no amount paid. In such cases, if one bride gets divorced, the other is also divorced in revenge. Hence, in such exchange—marriages, a sense of insecurity amongst the brides prevail—if one of them is unable to develop good relations in the family. In one case of exchange of brides, Piyao Mohammad of Orakzai Agency now settled in Hangu (a settled district of Khyber Pakhtunkhwa) appealed to the government to intervene. His marriage was *Badala*—exchange marriage—15 years ago. Unfortunately, his sister was divorced and thus he was asked by his family to divorce his wife. However, he refused to be a part of such cruelty and did not divorce or separate from his wife, which resulted in enmity between him and his family. After 15 years, now his brothers and their sons are taking revenge for that divorce through *Ghag*—declaring that if anyone tried to propose his daughters, then he will buy enmity with them (Tribal News Network 2016, 12). It was an exchange of brides of the first generation that turned ugly and transformed into enmity that is victimising the second generation.

Ghag, literally a masculine roar, is the anger of the man if his marriage proposal for a woman is turned down. He expresses his dismay and anger by aerial shooting outside his proposed woman's house, such declaration is a symbol that if anyone tries to propose her he will have to first deal with him. It is not a romantic gesture, but a reflection of the tribal mindset of a woman being a commodity and property, devoid of choices, rights and feelings. It is to humiliate and disgrace the woman and her family that how dare they refused a proposal. In the case of Mohammad's daughters, it is used as a tool of revenge for one woman's divorce to punish the other seven young girls, taking away their choices, declaring enmity with their suitors. In this case, the nephews of Mohammad's have no desire to marry his daughters but to punish him and his daughters.

A tribal woman like a scared commodity is also bartered or used as a tool for settlement of family vendettas. If her father or brother kills someone, then a *Jirga* might settle the dispute by ordering to give a woman to the aggrieved family in *Swara/Veenay*. However, the *Riwaj* gives protection to the woman given in *Swara/Veenay*. Recently in Mohmand Agency's Sapary village, the local Jirga gave over five-year-old girl to resolve the blood feud between the two warring families. Due to public pressure, created by the civil societies and NGOs, the Assistant Political Agent of Mohmand tribal agency intervened on the ground that a girl is a minor and cannot be given in a *Swara/Veenay* (Jirga Award Mohmand 2013, 1–4). It was possible as in the *Riwaj*; a girl should be an adult and of marriageable age, otherwise, it is near to impossible to convince or intervene in the *Jirga*'s decisions.

The *Riwaj* and the State

The Pakhtun border areas have traditionally been treated as Yaghistan (the land of the rebels) by the Afghan governments and used it mostly for recruiting young men for wars. Home to different tribes, who live according to their tribal codes of conduct, these areas did not have any administrative setup and had not seen any developmental work (Dupree 2014, 12). Similarly, British treatment of the tribal areas was no different; being a periphery, the only utility of the place was to use it against the Russian Czars as a shield. This policy led to only building forts and forces rather than investing in the development of infrastructure or protection of basic human rights, especially those of women. The special semi-autonomous status of the erstwhile FATA grew from derogation of the colonial rule of law. Thus, the colonial period is the time when the roots of a formal marginalisation of tribal women took place. The British system of the colonial rule shows its clear marks of discrimination and suppression of women. They had two primary goals to achieve through the Frontier Crimes Regulations[9]: one was to include the tribal territory in the political and economic ambit of the British Raj and the other was to create an impression of tribals being independent in their internal affairs by allowing them to practice the *Riwaj* (Nicholos 2013, 60). The enforcement of the FCR excluded women from the political and economic system. They were left to centuries-old outdated Riwaj that has nothing to offer to women regarding their rights.

Robert Nichols in his edited book "The Frontier Crimes Regulations: A History in Documents", has collected certain letters of official correspondence exchanged between different British officers posted at this frontier in September of 1892. In these letters, it is highlighted that the Riwaj treats women "like a cow or other chattel and they belong to their nearest male relative". In the correspondence, it is however not recommended to change such conditions because it would offend "good conscience or public policy". When it came to wider colonial political interests, women were the ones to be sacrificed. All of this was being done in the garb of the greater cause of reforming the "wild tribals" (Nicholos 2013, 50–54). In striking a balance, British through article 30 of the FCR legalised tribal violence against women. Under this section, "a woman charged with adultery can be fined, punished/imprisoned for five years or more, and fined on the complaint of her husband". From the policy point of view, it is not clear whether the intention of the Raj was to save women from the violence of stoning or they just wanted to include them in colonial oppressive regulations (Pakistan Human Rights Department 2005, 5). On the other hand, Raj did not take any steps to stop the discriminatory practices such as *Swara, Badala, Ghag* and *Miratah* through FCR. Family laws and other issues related to women are left to the *Riwaj/Dastoor*. Thus, shutting state machinery on tribal women.

After 1947, Pakistan inherited the British system of colonial governance, including FCR. The new Pakistani state continued with the policy of semi-autonomous tribal system based on the *Riwaj*. In the last 70 years, different governments have introduced certain amendments to the FCR, but not much has changed with regard to women's rights. It is ironic that instead, the state takes pride in preserving the *Riwaj*. Presently, the debate on reforms has heated up, but the state is adopting a stance that retains the patriarchal structures and the *Riwaj* intact and reluctant to change the status of tribal woman. An educated tribal woman from the erstwhile FATA is aware of her deprivation in the system but she has no support. The government claims that the reforms in border areas are according to the aspiration of the tribal people's customs and traditions, safeguarding their fundamental rights. However, the problem is, most of the people consulted by the state during the reform process are men who already have a voice, agency and power. Women's aspiration and fundamental rights are excluded systematically under the name of culture, thus giving them limited citizenship (Naseer 2017, 4).

The state is also treating the tribal women as homo-sacer for its national interest; it has converted erstwhile FATA into a zone of exception with the "special status". Thus, the fateful tribal women are experiencing the worst form of cruelty due to the state perpetuated violence and its subsequent militarisation. The special status is like the state of exception according to the borderland in the 1973 Constitution that somehow resulted in granting limited citizenship to the tribal women. She is left at the mercy of the cultural system, hence transforming her body into a battleground for preserving man's honour. With no fundamental rights, she turned into an invisible being with no voice or freedom and at the mercy of temperamental, overprotective Pakhtun man and *Riwaj*.

Her limited citizenship in the militarised border can be seen through the lens of both misogynist state and *Riwaj*, which says that men will inherit land as the men have earned it. She is his honour like land and gold, thus defend it by killing her with impunity. She is a commodity; purchase her as a bride or even in some instances exchange it for a bride, a cheap labour and production machine of sons. If she fails to produce the male heir, then her identity and security are at stake too. In addition, tribal man can use her for settlement of disputes; she can be sacrificed for her father, brother, uncle or cousin's misdeeds. Ironically, both state and *Riwaj* is not clear on the issues of her forced marriage by such inhuman practices. Although, it is mentioned and accepted in every *Riwaj* that Islamic Sharia would be the guiding principle for decisions and dispute settlement (Hussain and Kakakhel 1947, 2; Khan 1964, 2) although it is never implemented in the letter and spirit. In fact, the state allows the tribesmen to use religion and *Riwaj* interchangeably for their convenience.

Conclusion

Unfortunately, a tribal woman living on the periphery of peripheral Third World has never been a part of any movement or struggle for women's rights; hence, it is very difficult to develop an argument in the framework of Western feminist discourse or other coloured women's struggles. Jacqui Alexander and Chandra Talpade Mohanty in their edited work "Feminist Genealogies, Colonial Legacies, Democratic Futures" discusses coloured women of Third World, social identities and global feminism. It provided a comparative, relational, and historical based conception of feminism, one that differs completely from liberal-pluralistic understandings. It also examines that some theories and movements are feasible and carry explanatory weight in relation to certain experiences but they have no value or relation to the rest of the world (Alexander and Mohanty 2012, 9–15). Therefore, I have tried to develop an argument and case for tribal feminism[10] in the context of given circumstances. It is also pertinent to mention that unlike other women in traditional societies, tribal woman has no qualms about the practices that deprive her of social and economic rights including her right to life. Born and raised in such oppressive patriarchal structure and system, she has reduced herself to a bare life too. Ingrained and brainwashed with the 'honour discourse', she accepts her deprivations including honour killings. In many instances, mother, aunt and elder sister are also colluders in the killing of a woman if she trespasses the set values of *Pakhto* or *Ghairat*. To instigate a man, the mother or other elderly women use *Paighore* (taunts), challenging his masculinity and bravery. For her, man's masculinity is attached to woman's honour. Thus, tribal man romanticising his centuries-old outdated *Riwaj* and taunted by the women folk fails to distinguish between a chattel and woman while killing her under different reasons that is also legit in the cultural structure.

Five million tribal women with a 7% of literacy rate and raised in the oppressive system are completely isolated socially, politically and economically from the world (Naseer 2015, 4–10). For a social change in the border areas, they need indigenous tribal feminism and struggle to create a humane society for themselves. Tribal feminism for me is a struggle for equity of the oppressed women living on the Pak-Afghan borderland. It should be understood as the creation of feminism that would educate tribal woman about misogynist *Riwaj* and apathy of the state towards them. During my work and interviews with the tribal women, I have concluded that it is not possible to convince a woman with the values foreign to them. For a tribal woman, international rights, women rights and United Nation resolutions passed for the protection of women are completely alien and against their cultural values and religion. Unfortunately, cultural practices are created as ultimate dogma that led to their alienation towards the acceptance of universal declaration of human and women rights. Therefore, the religious debate can be used for the deeply conservative society to denounce inhuman practices such as *Ghag, Sawara, Badala* and *Miratah*. The debate of Muslim's holy book Quran can be used to convince them about their rights.

It is prescribed in Quran that woman can inherit her father and husband's property; she has the right to marriage of her choice and has the right to divorce. Bride money is not permissible; instead, she is protected by the dower in the marriage contract (*Nikah*) (Al-Quran 2, 229–236, 4, 1–34). I believe that if tribal men and women are convinced that Western concepts of human rights and equality are compatible with their religious discourse then they might be able to accept such values.

In addition, it is important to de-construct the notion in the minds of both tribal men and women that *Riwaj* is not above their religious and fundamental rights. In the *Riwaj*, the present economic paradigm promotes the masculinised notion of powerful man being an owner of gold, woman and land, which is gained through force and power (*pa matto gatalay*). A male child as the inheritor of the land is valued and like land, a symbol of status in the tribal society. The woman is not only the other, the marginal but also inferior. It appears that the tribal woman in the *Riwaj* is a primitive version of a man due to her biological makeup and intelligence. She is an ideal woman if submissive, nurturing, sacrificing and compassionate. Moreover, if rebels, challenges and questions then she will face dire consequences. At times, *Riwaj* is placed above religion; it has developed a tribal society's understanding of family, marriage, divorce, ownership, sexuality; by prescribing normative behaviour and roles of men and women, determining their status, inheritance, guardianship and defined women's identity.

Ironically, a mosaic of outdated and inhuman traditional practices has created a woman homo-sacer, the scapegoat of man's violent masculinity in the form his honour (*Nang/Ghairat*). The tribal man violent masculinity transforms into criminality. The demonstration of physical strength and particular behaviour of aggressiveness such as *Nang, Ghag and Badala* are criminal in nature. The notion of honour in the *Riwaj* has secluded women, controlled her mobility, choices, and decisions, and even threatened her life. The primary objective of such practices is the subordination of the woman and strict control over her body, identity and thinking. The mechanism of control operates through several devices and levels. The first is reinforcement of the notion of tribal man's honour and linking it with woman, translating her submissiveness and fidelity as the highest expressions of his *Ghairat* and *Nang*. The second is customs and practices in the social code to keep a deviant woman (if she rebels, refuses proposal or differs) under patriarchal control. The third is state that has patronised the tribal culture of masculinity and absolved itself from the responsibility of creating a just society and system for tribal women living in a borderland.

To change and rectify centuries-old system, it is pertinent to construct "tribal feminism" even if it involves religion and tribal men in the transformation of the present system. It will be only possible if the tribesmen recognise the existence of sexism, male domination, patriarchy and masculinity in the *Riwaj* and accept her rights given in the religion. Moreover, it is also important that tribal women are willingly striving for conscious action and efforts to change it. It is equally important that the state also recognise the plight of tribal women living in the conflict-ridden erstwhile FATA and her suffering at the hands of *Riwaj*. The tribal woman should not be discriminated because of her geographical location and prevailing situation. The state has introduced reforms and merged FATA with the settled Khyber Pakhtunkhwa but retained *Riwaj* to absolve itself from the responsibility of protecting women living on the borderland.

A woman's decision to educate herself to pursue a career, not to be humiliated, her refusal to be crippled by *Pardah*, choose a man of her choice as a life partner and have other rights is not a rebellion or against the honour of the tribal man. These are basic and her religious rights, which are recognised universally, and it has not challenged any order or society. It is equally important for tribal women to sensitise the men towards their needs and rights. It can happen only if they raise gender sensitive sons to create a humane society, a son that can respect women, less violent and masculine. Therefore, the responsibility falls on both tribal men and women to construct tribal feminism to curb all such practices that are anti-women, masculine, patriarchal and criminal. Moreover, a tribal feminism will be materialising if women's role in the society is recognised by the state, her contribution to economy and family is acknowledged by giving her a share in the land and property as prescribed in the religion. Above all humane system can be possible if tribal women living in the borderland recognise the misogynist *Riwaj's* practices against her. The Stockholm syndrome of romanticising the misogynist and the patriarchal *Riwaj* will not let her breath or develop into an independent individual with freethinking that can challenge the system in a prudent way.

Recently, to enlighten the tribal women, several educated women from erstwhile FATA settled in the cities have started a network by the name of *Qabailee Khor.*[11] Their focus is advocacy and awareness about the rights of tribal women using religious discourse interchangeably with fundamental rights prescribed in the 1973 Constitution of Pakistan for her rights and shuns practices such as *Ghag* and *Sawara*. They include religious debate due to several reasons; one tribal society is conservative and religious, thus tribal women can be convinced on her rights if the religious appeal is used. Secondly, the people in erstwhile FATA are asked to choose either *Riwaj* or Sharia law (religious laws) to settle issues and family-related problems, hence the women rights debate can be built on the religion in the tribal *Jirgas*. Thirdly and most importantly even a state of Pakistan cannot challenge or suppress tribal women if religion is involved in the context of her rights.

A tribal woman can be a family honour and pride if allowed the individual rights. Her honour should not be attached to her body and men's control with cruel practices such as *Swara, Ghag* and *Badala*. Her identity should not be defended with her father, brothers, husband or sons. She is an individual with feelings, needs, emotions and expectations. *Riwaj's* certification of *Miratah* makes her vulnerable to every sort of violence against her. She is not a commodity; selling her like a chattel (*Valver*) is equivalent to the present day slavery. The most atrocious act and legalised by the *Riwaj* is her killing for honour while using different excuses. All such inhuman practices need to end and state must take the responsibility of her protection and grant her basic fundamental rights prescribed in the constitution.

Notes

1. Riwaj/Dastoor is practiced and applied on both sides of Pak-Afghan borderland. Hence marriages on elopement, abduction amongst Pakhtun and taking bride money as per Riwaj is considered acceptable and legal.
2. The boy or boy's family pays according to Riwaj that is the amount against marriage for elopement.
3. In Riwaj, there is no serious punishment if you sell your wife without divorcing, however, according to old records, a man who bought/eloped/abducted married woman has to pay 85 Kabali and 1 goat to husband or his family as repentance (Nanawatey).
4. It was compiled by Abdul Rashid Khan, Assistant Political Officer on request of the Lieutenant Colonel W. C. Leper, O. P. E. I. P. S., Political Agent, Kurram Valley and is the only written/codified Riwaj available in FATA.
5. Fatwa an opinion and ruling on Islamic law by an expert in religious law. Hence Sardar Hussain took Islamic cover for his daughter too that according to Sharia Mohammadi a girl could inherit his father's property. Every Riwaj-Nama and Dastoor pledge that decisions making would be according to Shariat; however, it is only a formality that the majority living in the area are Muslims tribes. In Riwaj, no single clause reflects the influence of religion in the context of discussing women's rights.
6. Bride money is fixed according to tribe's prevailing Riwaj and economic situation.
7. Pardah literally means veil; however here it was used an excuse that being a tribal Pakhtun man he cannot bring his daughter to court and in public that would breach her chastity.
8. Also for details on the combined property, honour and women's issues in Pakhtun's customary laws see Riyasat-e-Dir Western Pakistan, 'Dastoor-e-Aml Riyasat-e-Dir Termeem Shuda', 1963. Zafar Ali Khan, 'Riwaj Nama Malakand Agency', 1964. Ghulam Habib, 'Riwaj Nama Swat' (Saidu Shareef Swat, 1969).
9. It was civil and criminal procedural document enacted 1848 in Punjab and North West. Later reformed in 1901 with an aim to punish any individual or tribe guilty of acting in a hostile manner or unfriendly manner towards the state.
10. Tribal is used as an identity of women living on the borderland and is not taken as a tribal structure or system.
11. *Qabailee Khor* (tribal sister) is a network formed by educated tribal women in 2015 to educate tribal women about their rights. From every agency, there are several volunteer women known as Qabailee Khor Representatives and in different congregation, functions, deaths and marriage parties hold informal talks and try to educate them about their basic rights.

References

Alexander, J. M., and C. T. Mohanty. 2012. *Feminist genealogies, colonial legacies, democratic futures*. New York: Routledge Taylor & Francis Group.

Arqam, A. 2016. 'Die they must'. *Newsline*. August 15.

Assistant Political Agent Khyber. 2016. *'Jirga Award'*. Landikotal Khyber Agency.

Assistant Political Agent Mohmand. 2013. *'Jirga Award'*. Prang Ghar Mohmand Agency.

Denshire, S. 2014. Autoethnography. *Current Sociology* 62 (6):831–50. Australia: Sage Publications.

Dupree, L. 2014. *Afghanistan*. 1980th. ed. New Jersey: Princeton University Press.

Engels, F. 1820-1895. *The origin of the family, private property and the state*. 4th ed. 2010. London, UK: Penguin Classic.

Family Court Judge. 2013. *Case Ijaz Khan Vs Ulas Khan*. vol. 10. Peshawar: PLD (Pakistan Legal Decision).

Ghulam, H. 1969. *'Riwaj Nama Swat'*. Saidu Shareef: Swat Publisher.

Giorgio, A. 1998. *Sovereign power and bare life*. Translated by Danial Heller -Roazen. Stanford: Stanford University Press. Available on URL www.opaa.org/dissensus/wp-content/oploads/2008/03/agamben_giorgio

Hussain, N. 2015. (Haji Gula maternal nephew) in discussion with author. 9 September.

Hussain, S., and S. G. Kakakhel. 1947. *'Qanoon-e-Riwaj Kurram (Turizuna) Urdu*. Kohat: Kohat Publishers.

Janna's Family 2014. (Distant cousins) in discussion with author. 2 February.

Kakakhel, B. Z. 1965. *Pukhtana da tareekh pa ranna kay (Pashto)*. Peshawar: University Book Agency.

Khan, Z. A. 1964. *Riwaj nama malakand agency*. Dragai: Malakand Agency.

Lorber, L. 2010. *Gender inequality*. 4th ed. New York: Oxford University Press.

Naseer, M. 2017. Limited citizenship of tribal women in FATA. *The Nation*, May 7.

Naseer, N. 2015. FATA women voiceless/invisible entity: Victim of cultural structure and state system. *Pakistan Journal of Women Studies: Alam-e-Niswan* 22 (2):1–13.

Nicholos, R. 2013. *The frontier crimes regulations: A history in documents*. Karachi: Oxford University Press.

Parliamentarian Commission for Human Rights. 2005. *FATA, FCR & Human rights: Challenges & responses*. Islamabad: Human Rights Department.

Riyasat-e-Dir Western Pakistan. 1963. *'Dastoor-e-aml riyasat-e-dir termeem shuda*. Dir: Government of Pakistan.

Robert, N. 2013. *The Frontier Crimes Regulations : A history in documents*. Karachi: Oxford University Press.

Tribal News Network. 2016. 'Tribal custom "Ghag" bars seven young sisters from marriage'. Available on URL www.radiotnn.com/father-seek-justice-for-daughters-serving-inhuman-tribal-custom.

Pashto Border Literature as Geopolitical Knowledge

James Caron

ABSTRACT

In this article I read a selection of Pashto literatures against the grain of world history, as critical thought about geopolitics. Drawing on Michael Shapiro's concept of aesthetic subjects, as well as on border theory, I argue that the authors, the content, and the literary networks of these works all critically comment on global relations of power, ranging from the local bordering effects of geopolitics, to systems of knowledge embedded in the spatiality and temporality of empire. I argue that past and current imperial processes have led to fragmenting effects in Afghan society, and literature both reflects and analyses this. More than that, though, I argue – using the lives of authors as well as their work – that literary activity in Pashto has actively negotiated such processes throughout its recent history, and offers strategies for different notions of global connectivity. The decentralized and multiperspective images of life in these works sit in counterpoint not only to the systems-oriented views that drive military and other policy in Afghanistan during the ongoing US moment, but also to universalist perspectives upon which disciplines like world history and geopolitics have traditionally relied. This contributes to the aesthetic turn in IR by arguing that it is not only the aesthetic vision in works that can challenge dominant forms of knowledge: the shape of the Pashto literary formation itself, organic with its contents, is an alternate form of knowledge-in-practice about the contemporary world.

Introduction

In the first decades of the twenty-first century, all the world is living through a watershed moment in the understanding of societies. In this, Afghanistan is a stage for innovation. Since the War on Terror era began, the most globally influential body of knowledge about Afghanistan has involved ever less conversation with Afghans, and ever more a conception of people as 'human terrain' that can be modelled by systems-engineering specialists, to represent reality more faithfully than people themselves can narrate it. In one multimillion dollar project that emerged on the back of the Human Terrain Systems programme of military-embedded ethnographers, the data that social scientists collected was combined with physical and environmental data to create social simulations of clusters of villages (Stockman 2016), able to predict social trends better than any individual in that society itself would, for the purpose of forming military policy.

This echoes, builds on, and even outstrips the processes of the formations of colonial knowledge that Jon Anderson (1992), among others, describes: processes that were part both of imperial management of the Afghan border region, and of subsequent writing about that region. Dan McQuillan (2018), for instance, notes how the epistemology of 'machinic Neoplatonism' that undergirds such modelling is generally still susceptible to the same coloniality of power embedded in older imperial knowledge processes. Taking both cases together maps a trajectory in which Afghans have been placed as ever more peripheral to knowledge of their own modern world. Ever more provincialized visions of Afghanistan and Afghans are locked into the bounded situatedness – a dynamic objectification, but an objectification – of systemic models that help determine policy. Enormous amounts of aggregated fact-fragments produced from such projects, embedded in metadata that are used to produce bounded data ontologies, were released to academics and the public at large from the US military's SIPRNet databases as part of the 2010 Wikileaks affair. Some future history-writers may see this archive as an unparalleled windfall. For others, either history or geopolitical thinking that relies on this sort of archive might represent a nightmare of quantitative dehumanization, the worst excesses of an approach to humans that reduces some to (provincialized) terrain that (universalized) others write themselves onto. In contrast, the content of the literature I read in this article, and the experiences of their authors, both register a tentative imagination of reconstituting better futures from the shifting relationships between ever-evolving individuals in the midst of such dystopia.

In arguing this I take a cue from the same thing I describe: the critical border vision of Pashto literary knowledge, which is enacted in the content of its art, and in the social history of its literary formation and the networks that it moves through. I argue that intellectual production from Afghanistan, figured as what I describe presently as a 'global borderland', challenges dominant visions of what knowledge of the world-at-large can be. In place of a state-centric will to fixity, to monopolizing the meaning of any historical encounter by placing it in a matrix of hegemonic narrative, I show, Pashto literature often focuses on the openness and indeterminacies of such encounters – in this case, those of violent bordering and territorialization amid decades of war. This vision is akin to Walter Benjamin's (1968) secular-messianic ethics of recovering the 'exiled' potentialities of history (Ware 2004), ones effaced by the state's repertories of violence that it uses to constitute itself, and its technologies of destruction (or in this case, the state's, plus those of other violent local and global organizations). By recovering past potentialities, Pashto literary production focuses on future redemption. It does so, I will show, through producing what Foucault (1986) calls 'heterotopias': "something like countersites, a kind of effectively enacted utopia in which the real sites ... are simultaneously represented, contested, and inverted," and by stringing them together into new patchwork cartographies.

There are sociological factors that contribute to this ethos. The historically subordinate position of Pashto literature contrasts with the bureaucratically and hegemonically dominant languages of Persian, Urdu, and English; which even Pashtuns have historically used to project objectifying discourses of power and civilization when they have occupied spaces of authority. This has meant that operating in Pashto literature – since at least the sixteenth century – involves self-conscious participation in a linguistic zone of 'rhizomic' space (Deleuze and Guattari 1987) at the aesthetic fringes of empire.[1] This has often been the case in the social space created by poetic networks, but in the late twentieth century prose has been interlinked to this realm as well. And, as we will see in the works discussed here, this has consistently involved reflexive attention, in literary works, of 'Pashto literature' as a process: one that interlinks multiple aesthetic worlds outside of, and arguing against, the fixity that imperial processes of bordering and ordering seek to impose. Thus the Pashto case, like other borderland literatures, contributes to the 'aesthetic turn' in IR by presenting a case in which the sociological conditions of aesthetic production are themselves a form of enacted knowledge, inseparable from that which they convey in their content.[2]

In order to argue all this, in this article I read Pashto literature composed since 2000 – short stories, poems, and a novella. These literary works, their authors, and their networks critically negotiate the many ways in which Afghanistan has been created as what I provisionally call a 'global borderland'; and with this term, I point to a specific kind of long-term history. The regions centred on the Hindu Kush were textured in antiquity and in the early modern period by Persian and Indian influence; and then colonized in the modern period by British empire. In all these periods, imperial political-economic and sociocultural hierarchies built centralizing authority structures that pulled regional social networks – state institutions, trading solidarities, tribes, religious networks – in various disparate directions, making them at least as responsive to their ties beyond any local horizon as they were to each other locally, and creating new 'borders' between them in that way. The mid and late twentieth century brought Eastern European, Soviet, and US influence, first through development aid and later through military intervention. This created borders between multiple outward-looking factions in the government and in society. Moreover, in the US case, military intervention was indirect, exerted through local powers including Pakistan's intelligence services and its religious parties. This, along with official and private Saudi partnership in the covert war, resulted in reformulations of Islamic authority via *mujahid* and *talib* factions that reordered and segregated Afghan life into yet more hierarchic factions, as much as direct imperial control has done. On top of all this sits, now, a direct overlay of neoliberal restructuring of social relations. This was brought first by the influx since the 1990s of western

NGOs in Afghanistan and their increasingly central role in managing social, especially including under the Taliban. It was accelerated further by the occupation of Afghanistan amid the US-led intervention that removed the Taliban from power.

But finally: shaped by, yet cutting across, all the above are the global and local, physical and aesthetic, worlds of Afghan mobility. The energy of migrant Afghans negotiating plural worlds, and the social connectivities that this creates in Afghanistan and beyond its borders, have been both integral to and marginal to colonial modernity (Crews 2015; also Green 2008; Digby 1965; Nichols 2008). This has always been a counterpoint to imperial fragmentations, even if this counterpoint enjoys less global visibility. And it is this bottom-up globality in which the stories of our authors' lives and their characters' lives are situated. As I argue in the next section and throughout, using Michael J. Shapiro's (2012) concept of 'aesthetic subjects', these two kinds of stories are not separable.

Aesthetic Subjects and History in a Global Borderland

The work of Pashto short story author 'Abd al-Wakil Sulamal Shinwari and his biography, together, are an entryway into these themes. Sulamal was born in the upland Haska Mayna district in Nangarhar Province, which borders on Pakistan. Faced with a choice between military conscription or Soviet education in service to the Afghan state, he obtained a Masters' degree in military pedagogy in Minsk before returning to work in the Afghan Ministry of Defense. Somewhat after the fall of the People's Democratic Party of Afghanistan [PDPA], he emigrated to Peshawar where he worked as a journalist with the Writers' Union of Free Afghanistan [WUFA]. This body was originally created as a non-partisan patronage alternative both to the PDPA's circles of state-sponsored intellectuals and to the militant *mujahidin* factions' patronage structures of recorded and written literature, structures that grew into durable transnational political-economic and cultural hierarchies during the period that they were funded and even cultivated by the intelligence services of the United States, Saudi Arabia, and Pakistan. It eventually brought together authors who emerged from the communist writers' unions, from the *mujahidin*, and expatriate intellectuals who were formerly tied to older state institutions and who now worked with western news and intelligence services. As literary scholar Zarin Anzor (1993) describes, their solidarity recombined elements from all these networks even as that solidarity, and the new physical and social space it created, was a response to these authors' discontent with those networks.

In short the WUFA's, and Sulamal's, creation of networks in such spaces is an illustration of the border processes I introduced above, and his life after that traces more than one of the global spaces to which local ones were tied.

After working with the WUFA for a number of years but searching for stable employment to no avail, Sulamal left Peshawar for further afield, spending many years in Bratislava until he then moved to London. Amid all this, as we will see soon, Sulamal's work too stands in contrast to the literatures colonized either by the communist PDPA or by the *mujahidin* factions that asserted forms of local territorialization and bordering, both social and geographic.

I begin with Sulamal's biography, because it is in keeping with my argument that the literary formation and the contents of Pashto production are two parts of the same rhizomic knowledge form: that is, the characters in these stories and the lives of their authors are inseparable. Following the work of Michael J. Shapiro, I see these literary authors, as well as the characters they enact, as 'aesthetic subjects' who operate in realms that may include, but subsume and exceed, rational argument, and who mobilize alternatives to dominant frames of knowledge through aesthetic production (Shapiro 2012; Opondo and Shapiro 2012). Just as Sulamal's life moves across geopolitical territory in macrocosm and across various forming-and-disintegrating literary institutions in microcosm, Sulamal's characters both inhabit and describe extreme plurality in a set of societies configured by empire as a global borderland. They also critically theorize, through narrative, the processes of fragmentation that they describe; and provide alternate imaginations. Before fleshing this out, though, I should pull back and read a few narratives that focus on the production of borders – geopolitical, geographical, and psychosocial – in Afghanistan. I will return to the issue of alternate imaginations, and the refiguring of bordering as potentiality rather than fixed event, in subsequent sections.

Sulamal's story 'The Old Fort' is a good example of a narrative of bordering, as well as an exploration of the limits of its subversion.[3] Before the eyes of our narrator, a recently returned expatriate, the inhabitants of his ancestral village uproot all of its architecture in an attempt to purify its inauspicious past by erasing all memory of their 'ignominious cousins': those who had embraced the communist party. As his own family joins in, the narrator appears to be the only one who notices that they are destroying the very structures they live in. While the narrator has not been affected by a decade of ideological change, due to his absence, this has fragmented his perspective away from that of his family. He leaves, disillusioned. The story then moves forward in time. The narrator returns years later and finds the entire village living in tents. New coloured banners demarcate new, fragmented rural geographies that restrict movement.

The narrator's experience serves as a reminder that human mobility and ties of kinship constantly place histories of memory in tense discussion with histories of forgetting. The point is not just the fragmentation of locality, but also fragmentation of past and present. Engagement with even older pasts, marginal but still existing, draws the Pashto reader into the same role as the narrator's – the individual who remembers – and places the reader in a position of empathy with yet other aesthetic subjects. That is, as the dismantling of social life proceeds apace, the village's past lives, existing in traces as domestic utensils and mysterious Hindu and Buddhist effigies buried in the soil, no longer abide in anyone's memory except that of the very poor, those with no stake in the local partisan factions created by transnational militancy. Other villagers excavate this once-shared past as objectified artefacts, which represent idolatry to them but which are marketable to foreign collectors and which will hence further fund local militarization. As he walks on past this scene, the narrator leaves the village, resolving never to return.

The geopolitical dimension here is unsaid, but is understood to its readers: the spatiality of the present is colonized in part through fragmentation of the past, and this is not only a local process. The *mujahidin* era, to which this story refers, came after successive waves of influence from ever-farther sources: foreign investment from the Eastern Bloc followed by local communist revolution and then direct Soviet intervention. This was succeeded by Islamist counterrevolution that brought global funding through the militant organizations based in Pakistan, each of which developed its own cultural programmes alongside its own transnational political and economic redistribution structures. When the international funding dried up, leaders throughout the hierarchies of each faction began cannibalizing its own client base for resources, fostering civil war on highly local levels. The various elements of the story give a spatialized trajectory of ever-greater fragmentation when seen from the perspective of rural life: a transregional past reflected in the pre-Islamic artefacts; a national-state constructed amid early Cold War superpower rivalry and represented by the structures built by the 'ignominious cousins'; a postnational, presentist wartime imagination of space in which even neighbourhoods have borders between and within them. The deterritorial subject of the narrator, existing in global space, is as powerless as the reader is to address this local fragmentation, in the face of the much more dominant global forces that drive local territory-creation.

Sulamal's even darker farce 'Fifty Million' (Sulamal (Shiwari) 2010) comments on a new era of globalized fragmentations that run even deeper: rewriting the meaning given to bodies and their most intimate relationships, those of kinship. It fixates on the trope of an influx of naked cash as a metonym to explore one aspect of neoliberalized society during military occupation. Here we see an image of how identities and affect are produced between geopolitical demands and colonized populations directly. The main character 'Jandad' rethinks his circumstances upon hearing a radio announcement: a bounty of fifty million dollars for Osama bin Laden, dead or alive. His once-jovial nature fades as he joins the Taliban in an increasingly obsessive and desperate search for the terrorist. His self-respect as a patriotic *mujahidin* commander, and the propertied husband of two women, is rewritten in starkly monetized terms as penury as Jandad is confronted by new standards of wealth. His comfortable life now feels paltry...perhaps, although the story is not explicit on this point, when compared to the lives of those few in Kabul with access to internationalized corridors of power in neoliberal-era Afghanistan, those who can comfortably conceive of what 50 million dollars would actually mean in practice?

The geography of Afghanistan is remapped as Jandad wanders across it, objectified and transformed into a list of the places he has searched for, and failed to locate, bin Laden. Eventually, after years of failing to find 50 million dollars hiding 'under any rock or in any tunnel', Jandad returns home. He and his young wife hatch a plot, as they stare at the walls in silence: is not the picture hanging there, the picture of Jandad's beloved, younger, full-blooded, and only brother 'Zardad', the spitting image of bin Laden? American policy in this scenario drives people in the Afghan landscape to think of themselves and others in terms of categories – 'terrorist', 'collaborator', 'commodity' or 'irrelevant' – by attaching monetary value to these categories, even though in their agentive manoeuvring they may sometimes inhabit more than one category at once. Like the landscape of Afghanistan itself, Zardad's body is objectified and rewritten in Jandad's mind as the potentiality of 50 million dollars. But Zardad's body fails to live up to his name just as surely as Jandad's actions fail to live up to his: Jandad ('Gift of Life') slays his brother and brings his head to an American outpost, while the grisly remains of Zardad ('Gift of Gold') inevitably fail the test of identification and fetch a mere pittance, a token pay-out in recognition of Jandad's good intentions towards US policy objectives.

These are only two among many of Sulamal's short stories, published in at least six collections since the 1990s. At this point, rather than focusing on individual stories, I would like to highlight the overall sort of picture that emerges from stringing together a series of such individual images, as Sulamal's collections and his combined oeuvre do. Sulamal's individual vignettes may not approach a unified Afghan history of the recent world in their scope; but this is part of the point. Pashto literary production illustrate a need to think of 'the whole' in different terms altogether. As Vinay Lal (2011) notes, histories of globalized cross-cultural encounters look quite different on the micro-level when it is the provincialized and situated subject who is the world historian. This is true when imagining fragmentations, but it is also true when imagining recompositions from the local perspective of nodes in a network, rather than from the top-down survey vision of colonial forms of knowledge. And as the influential poet, theorist, and activist Gloria Anzaldúa highlights, the act of negotiating between and forging bridges among such nodes, and their situated rather than universal forms of knowledge, is both an epistemological act and a normative one (Anzaldúa 1987, esp. Ch. 7). In the next section, then, I move on to introduce works that not only pessimistically interrogate processes of fragmentation, but also ask about possible recompositions of life across and outside of those fragments. As we will see, some of these works directly theorize this point in abstraction. Others, to which I turn first in the next section, intuitively dramatize reconstitutions of space by shifting their narration to subjects building the realm, as Michel de Certeau would put it, of the 'tactical' everyday, rather than negotiating the 'strategic' level of dominant regional and global actors (Certeau 1984).

Negotiating Fragments to Imagine a Multiperspective World

A longer work by Muhammadajan Yar, a novella titled 'An Eyewitness Account of the Dasht-i Layli', attempts at linking the remapping of one experienced locality's present to a long-term history of increasingly global interactions (Yar 2004). The novella traces the fictitious eyewitness account of an unnamed farmer who was caught in a Northern Alliance sweep through Pashtun villages near the town of Sheberghan, close to the Turkmenistan border, after the 2001 fall of the Taliban in Kunduz; detained with other non-combatant Pashtuns alongside Taliban POWs; loaded in the hot sun into a blistering metal shipping container with them, and transported to the Dasht-i Layli desert for execution. It is framed as the account of this man after he miraculously escaped the scene of the atrocities, set off through the hinterland, eventually reached his family's ancestral homeland in Pashtun-majority Nangrahar province, and met the author in a small store in Jalalabad. But this trauma is only the backdrop for an exploration of the mutability of local historical experience, in the face of geopolitical change.

The story begins with a recitation of the narrator's historical memory: his father had once claimed that Pashtuns originally came to 'Turkistan' in the 1930s under a state policy designed to make the north productive, and to link it to the rest of the country as Afghanistan consolidated its internal geography as an independent state. The steppes had been a wasteland, the narrator was told; and once these Pashtun pioneers had created settlements, building agrarian productivity through painstaking labour, then 'Tajiks, Uzbeks, and a few Turkmens' also started settling in the region. Roads and infrastructure were built, consolidating a national domestic geography. Back-and-forth flows of people increased, further consolidating it. Things were fine, our protagonist recalls, up until Daud Khan's 1973 coup. From that point, 'each day was worse than the last'. The Taliban were the worst, he says. They rewrote history and cultural heritage, effacing the past. And, they inadvertently heralded a new era of invasive globalization: they 'brought the world's attention to Afghanistan' such that the United States and the United Kingdom were 'driven to intervene and take the country from them'. As American B-52s bombed Taliban positions, we hear, local Northern Alliance commanders took the opportunity to mislead their credulous new US allies into destroying innocent Pashtun villages, and conducted a new series of anti-Pashtun pogroms themselves also under cover of war. At one point the protagonist realizes (as his Turkic and Tajik neighbours had presumably long known) that one can be suddenly deprived of one's subject position in the face of externally created identities, encouraged by geopolitical forces. As he, a Pashtun farmer, is captured by Northern Alliance forces, he pleads with an adolescent gunman that he has done nothing. He is beaten and told, in Persian, "Be silent; you're all savage, culture-less Taliban!" (Yar 2004, 24).

Now, there is more than one way to read this narrative. The story is in Pashto, which marks it as sectional from the outset in any reading oriented towards the breakdown of a nation-state consciousness, in a country where Persian is the lingua franca and generally seen as a language of high culture. And this particular massacre at Dasht-i Layli, one of a series of them, is an event that has been used by Pashtun political groups in a way that echoes Veena Das's words from a different context. That is, a focus on this particular trauma has often functioned in Afghan public discourse as a way to "open up suspect spaces in which stories of suffering are deployed in the dividing practices of separating 'innocent' victims from 'guilty' ones" (Das 2003, 297). So, the historical narration in this novella might provide an opportunity to reiterate older histories of innocence that legitimate resentments in the present, thereby participating in a spiral of communitarian violence and revenge. In my reading, though, this well-worn narration is supplied at the outset in order be interrogated later. It becomes unsustainable through the course of the novella, and rather than this being a story that opens up wider fractures, it becomes a story about the possibilities and limits of overcoming them. The violence visited on the narrator and his community occupies less than half the book, while the remainder traces encounters with members of other ethnic communities as the narrator flees.

Staggering from settlement to settlement, the narrator encounters numerous other individuals including a powerful Turkmen *arbab* and a Tajik Jami'at militia commander. They help him as individuals, even as the larger identity politics taking shape in the region constrain them to tell him why, historically, the ethnic cleansing of the north must happen; why he must continue fleeing. For the first time he encounters alternate pasts, *their* pasts, which sound less like the history he had been told, and more like settler colonialism by Pashtuns onto a pre-existing Turkic population. History in this region has *long* been fragmented under the weight of transregional power, even if the relatively privileged place of Pashtuns in official-nationalist constructions of the north has blinded him to that fact. And new locally dominant pasts are forming as older hegemonies are dismantled, even though those pasts are based on the same set of events. But this is not the extent of the story. When its characters are forced to negotiate with each other in concrete transactions, rather than abstract collective ones, new possibilities emerge from the empathy that can result from displacement of absolute narratives. In such contingent, face-to-face situations, individuals may potentially address others as individuals; and unique relationships of selflessness, rather than identity boundaries, can be negotiated in real time. This story is history as potentiality, built out of new recompositions of past ways of being, knowing, and feeling. This is so, even as these contingent and localized relationships are fleeting.

Yet, not all such transactions are necessarily so fleeting. Their effects accumulate over time, in borderland space. Let us return to Sulamal. While much more allegorical, his story 'The Village and the Bus', like Muhammadajan Yar's novella, is a stage for both fragmentation and new recomposition. At its base, it narrates a crime of passion. A bus arrives in an isolated and starving village on a bus. It has temporarily broken down but it is part of a route that has finally relinked this unfortunate settlement to its more prosperous neighbours 'in the next valley over the mountains'. The story describes the local meeting of two returnees arriving on the bus, one who had relocated to Europe and one who was raised over the mountains in Pakistan, both vying for ideological influence over the future of 'the village': a localized backdrop for the story, and a metonym for Afghanistan. At the same time the bus is an allegorical stand-in for the Afghan state. The first newcomer, a westernized and scarcely recognizable native son who was born in the village, argues for a hasty blanket repudiation of the bus's drivers, whom he sees as hopelessly inept, the very reason that the bus has broken down in the first place. He gets into an argument with, and is soon slain by, the second newcomer: a hot-headed young rifleman, one who was born and raised just on the other side of the mountain and who is nativist in his ideology despite never having seen the village itself, and who is rather more compassionate toward the drivers than the first newcomer is.

Importantly, though, the murder is not the end of the story. As a shocked village discusses what happened, each person produces a phrase-length commentary on the events. Their discrete and even conflicting narrations merge into the consensus of an abstraction, and their sentences fuse into a folkloric song of self-criticism that the entire village participates in. The story is a powerful literary image of new metanarratives in formation, and of their simultaneous internalization by individuals in the community through participative exchange. As in 'The Old Fort' and in Yar's novella about Dasht-i Layli, these perspectives consolidate themselves and exclude older, prior metanarratives in the process. But in this case, the global cross-cultural interaction is not an omniscient narrator surveying the rise of new narratives amid local fragmentation, as in 'The Old Fort'. Instead the meeting of two differently globalized intellectuals is what produces violent conflict. This both obliges, and creates opportunity for, local collaboration at one node of a network-in-formation to build countering solidarities of a qualitatively different sort. Here the newly dominant perspective, the song of self-criticism among villagers situated on the bus route, bears the suggestion that it may be less stabilized and fixed due to its participative nature. And yet this exists in durable literary space: it is not only an issue of fleeting individual transactions, as in Muhammadajan Yar's narrative. Here, constantly emergent, collaborative self-reflection on the divided present may optimistically invite the possibility of a more humane future at the same time as older geographies, forgotten but persisting as metaphorical bus routes, are regenerated through new activity. The song may seem to be an odd anti-climax if we read it as a story about murder, but if we read attuned to decolonial space-time, the song is itself the climax to a different story, bearing an oblique suggestion to which I turn now: the reflexivity of a transregional literary formation, along with the basic fact of its existence, is part of what stitches together fragmented networks into new, and less-violent, kinds of cartographies.

Border Literature as Theory-in-Practice

In looking at ways that older fragmented space-time can be recalled by aesthetic subjects in Pashto literary production, and new, less-violent cartographies can be constructed out of the ruins of the old, poetry is at least as interesting as narrative prose. Take for example a cycle of long poems, published in the 2000 collection *Da Xaperay Warghoway* by poet Pir Muhammad Karwan, about war, dislocation, and shifts in aesthetic knowledge. The entire poem cycle is a disjointed series of images, impressions, and vignettes written from a variety of loosely autobiographical subject positions, all linked at various points by the voice of 'The Wilderness' writing letters to Karwan. Taken as a whole it builds a kaleidoscopic impression of fragmenting time, space, and ontology within a single subject; but external fragments are productively reassembled into 'new life' through the life of its protagonist: a boy who used to hold conversations with a speaking mountains cape that knew no borders; a youth who worked in cross-border camel caravans smuggling weapons in the 1980s; a man who became a transnational poet based in Peshawar and Kabul and who founded one of Afghanistan's premier literary salons. This organization, the Afghan Adabi Bahir, now includes not only live meetings in Kabul but also radio call-in programmes that attract participation from men and women, urban and rural, across Afghanistan. Thus Karwan linked oral, literate, and electronic networks of Pashto literature through his personal subject-formation across domains, through his social activities that place his art in concrete social space and build space for others' as well, and through art that comments on these boundary crossings in its content.

Leading into the excerpt below from this cycle, Karwan has already described a recent encounter with his publisher in Pakistan who asked him to produce market-oriented love songs in place of his earlier preoccupation with trauma. He then has moved on to recall a much earlier encounter in his childhood with the oral poetic world: an impromptu performance by a party of ecstatic *mujahidin* youth in the Khost mountains that drew on much deeper sedimentations of affects of love and concern, in a traditional micro-genre, the *tappa*, that is in part defined by such affects. After a description of the *mujahidin* party's subsequent clifftop encounter with a Soviet jet, Karwan then pulls back from these disjointed vignettes; and in the personified voice of the Khost border wilderness, he addresses both reader and poetic subject directly, in order to reorient the reader's attention to a wider conceptual view of social and intellectual life in the globalized conflict that gripped his region. Creating a metaphor for social and cultural fragmentations and recombinations amid war, the sentient landscape itself describes fragments of abstract space falling to earth and giving rise to new interactions. The Forest-as-Storyteller writes, in a letter to Karwan:

> In the middle of this story/There are many deserts, mountains, crags/Arrows ripped from chests/Arms chopped off by swords/It's very reckless/Fighting with dragons/In the middle part, houses turn into cemeteries/Emptying out filled beds/We'll leave aside this middle part of the story/By God, it gets really bitter/So anyway, it's hardly even twilight/Not yet fully night/Droplets of the dragon's venom/Will form themselves out of white stars/And you'll see its teeth/Made from some other stars/All the wounds of the young-men/Will form themselves out of golden stars/You'll see all these stars/Fighting with each other/Some will flee their orbits/Some will fall to earth/They'll smash on the cliffs/They'll fall into the springs/And there, from inside the two halves of their husks/As their kernels swell up, new life will emerge. (Karwan 2000, 37–39)

Returning from the sensory world of nature and war violence to the affective and cognitive worlds of literature in a later poem in the cycle, 'Give them a tongue with *tappas*', Karwan completes the circle and unifies experiential knowledge of a devastated wartime environment to human literary interaction, in recompositions of new meaning. The Poet and The Forest collaborate to use the skins of predatory mammals, and the discarded munitions casings that litter and poison the forest, to build drums. The Poet and the Forest hope in turn that the act of repurposing these materials will neutralize the violence built into them. They hope that the drums will once again propel the songs, *tappas*, that mountain women improvise. These will then provide a new language by which entities who have not found a voice in the violent setting they find themselves in – human and non-human entities alike – can conceptualize new modes of justice: incorporating to themselves the environmental and human devastation that they live in, and remaking it into new life. And in the poem completing the cycle, Karwan finally ties these regional impressions into an image of transnational literary networks through allusions to multiple current poets who do the same, and who thereby sustain transregional connectivities between environment, village, city, and wider worlds.

Karwan's folk-surreal style is distinctive in Pashto literature, but his juxtaposition of pluralist knowledges and aesthetic expression to describe processes of fission and recombination is not new. Into these border spaces irrupt traces of prior interregional geographies, alive in the aesthetic subjects that gave them life. The aesthetic subject Karwan links print-sphere lyric in global circulation among Afghans into concrete performance by transborder itinerants. Those subjects in turn channel much older structures of feeling that pre-date any of the states or empires around them. The *tappa*, the two-line micro-genre that Karwan's *mujahidin* party sing and that re-emerges to the sound of wolf-mortar drums later, is also a major, and highly formal, genre preserved in James

Darmesteter's 1870s Pashto/French anthology *Chants populaires des Afghans* which, compiled as the British empire consolidated rule on the Afghan frontier, is our earliest comprehensive archive of Pashto folklore. Often composed impromptu as part of everyday interaction, Darmesteter's *tappas* circulated in piecemeal networks from Qandahar to Peshawar to South India with mobile traders and labourers and poets, cutting across the imperial and state bordering that was progressing even as Darmesteter was collecting them.[4] And other poems in that anthology, sung by the same mobile people, dramatize similar mobility in yet older settings. One is the *qissa*, a genre of ballad or verse romance, of Fateh Khan and Rabia: two lovers from the trading hub of Qandahar whose relationship, set in the sixteenth century, transgressed local patriarchal power. They rode off along with a retinue of friends into the Mughal heartlands to the east, enjoying success after success in a series of narrated episodes until their party was eventually defeated at the gates of the Delhi fort (Darmesteter 1888, 117). In this *qissa*, like so many other Pashto folk narratives that survive, the anti-structural desire of romantic love is mirrored in the act of overcoming fixed identities determined by imperial geography and lineage patriarchy.

There is a continuity between Karwan's folk surrealism and the fragments from earlier oral worlds that he incorporates into his work. Karwan's poem cycle, emerging as a fragmented *qissa*-autobiography of sorts, rewrites folk knowledge of body, place, and mobility into a story about the everyday perception of rupture and fragmentation. At the same time, *tappas* link deep sedimentations of affect to contingent circumstances. The song that the village composes impromptu in Sulamal's short story 'The Village and the Bus' does something similar. These nested genre fragments are all quite separate, but they all emphasize transactions in everyday life that link across space and time to form a counterpoint to the violence of geopolitics. The genres are not the same either, but in each case, as they build webs from episodic fragments of experience, as subjects interact at the interstices of empire and across them, they create worlds that exceed imperial reach in space and time both. Moreover, like Karwan's poem cycle suggests, the long-term cumulative effect of this sort of activity has built it up as a *reflexive* approach to aesthetics and life alike.

Conclusion: Afghan Knowledges of Globality; Alternatives to History

In my reading of literary practice as critical thinking about geopolitics, I draw on themes from the work of the poet and literary theorist Heriberto Yépez, particularly '*La frontera como falla*' ('Borderland as Faultline'), as well as the work of the historian and anthropologist team Ben Hopkins and Magnus Marsden in their monograph *Fragments of the Afghan Frontier* (Hopkins and Marsden 2012). Yépez describes a 'border' as a non-concept; it is not a thing or a place, but rather a process in which loose 'systems' of politics, economy, and culture reach their limits, meet, and undermine and fracture each other's system-creating authority. But also, as Yépez argues in abstract and Marsden argues empirically, actors at the epicentres of these processes also reassemble the political-economic, cultural, and even psychosocial 'fragments' that result from them, in dialogue with their own plural long-term histories. Such actors reassemble them into new worlds with their own senses of space and time and meaning, which can then potentially ripple back to start reshaping the more centralized systems around them. That is, even as they describe processes of 'bordering' and 'frontierization' and 'fragmentation', Yépez, and Hopkins and Marsden, also centre the productive potential of both actors and modes of thought in such spaces. In so doing, they undermine the idea of borderlands as a periphery (or even, really, a 'borderland' or 'frontier' in most commonplace senses), and re-centre such spaces' own salient space-time and their global importance.

However, the works I discuss here already know all this, and they point to more still: they show that this kind of vision is not only an analysis, but leads to an ethics as well. In engaging these literary works we are faced with alternate visions of geopolitics and world history that are embodied in the lives of their authors as aesthetic subjects, as much as they are represented in the characters of the stories as aesthetic subjects. And in some, like Karwan's work, the literary formation itself even becomes a sort of aesthetic subject. Their experiences force us to rethink spatiality and systems of knowledge, but also present us with an alternate politics of temporality and the nature of events. The stories and poems introduced in this essay together revive older spatialities and alert us that similar processes of border living are on-going now in global space, to those that have been going on for centuries. At the same time, narratives of disassembling and reconstituting relationships from contingent events are both the inheritance of a long-term history of the same, and a practice aimed at the future. I discuss these points, and the relationships between these narratives and the world, in this concluding section, before moving on to the point that I began with: literary activity in a 'global borderland' poses a countering approach to knowledge of geopolitics through aesthetics; this is related both to the dramatic content of the work and the sociological conditions it emerges in; and this is not an imagination of alternate worlds, but an enaction of them as well.

I read the works above as examples of a particular fiction genre, one sometimes labelled 'historiographic metafiction' (Walsh 2007): work that, while creating narratives, itself meditates on the process through which narratives are created. And, this has a distinct politics to it in this context. Sulamal and Yar are expatriate writers and migration has informed their work. Karwan never left Afghanistan, yet he draws abstract theory from the fact that migrant subjects and plural local ones – both in the literary formation and in everyday life – are not separable, in a transregional society that has been configured as a 'global borderland' but that has pushed back against this configuration constantly. In their destabilization of historical memory, as well as in the fluctuating spatial awarenesses to which they devote such attention, all these authors place an emphasis on how everyday yet global space-time beyond empire can be, and is, created. Theirs is a combined social and aesthetic practice that negotiates bordering, and that reconstitutes new formations out of the fragments that result from it. After a mobile society was encapsulated by British imperialism, the brief interlude of a territorial Afghan nation-state in the mid twentieth century meant that the sheer scale of new dislocations in the late twentieth century was shocking yet familiar for many Afghan Pashtuns in particular. This cumulative history – of mobility, then hierarchic centralization, and then mobility again – appears to have fostered a polycentered, subaltern globality in contemporary Pashto literature that reflects a broader experienced truth. Sulamal's vignettes, taken together, reflect a greater degree of decentralization of perspective, allowing him to draw a broader picture in aggregate without any single prognosis. Meanwhile, Yar draws one particular Afghan history of the world in greater depth, to maintain hope in the face of trauma, with his idea of reconstituting more humane relationships from the rubble of competing histories. So does Karwan. All three focus on an aesthetic of constantly fragmenting and reconstituting knowledge; all focus on the formation of aesthetic subjects on the shifting and contingent level of the everyday even if they comment on this as a long-term historical process too. None of these authors are uncritical of the possibilities for new violence that emerge from these moments. But the key point is the maintaining of open space in all its ambiguous potential for subjects to constitute each other outside of globally dominant power relations, or the local manifestations of geopolitics, and to build constantly new forms of life on that intersubjective level.

In these works, it is the authors' experienced absence of the fixity of either imperial or nationalist perspectives, in everyday subjective life amid war and migration, that is itself ultimately the key point about 'what happened'. This absence is an opportunity: equally a concern of these authors is the repeated constraint over time that the crystallizing facts of dominant histories place on potentialities for subjects as well as for better collective futures. Stories like Muhammadajan Yar's reflect on the way that memory of the past, disassembled and reconstituted in erratic and unpredictable ways, can be a quasi-political, or alterpolitical, strategy that is useful for the future instead. At the same time, as both Karwan the poet and Sulamal the prose author describe, aesthetic activity and its networks in actual life have themselves frequently been a reflexive manifestation of that strategy. Literary interlinking of this sort escapes the forgetfulness of much geopolitical policy-thinking regarding longue-durée subaltern pasts – the geopolitical thinking that reduces Afghan society to its present, so as to manage it.

In sum, the literary activity I have described here is an actually existing practice, a spatial and temporal reality, and a loose system of knowledge that comments on and refines both these things. It does so by recasting moments of bordering and violence, ever-pervasive in the historical geopolitical experience of Afghan life, as opportunities for a better set of futures. These futures exist as potentiality in the continuous contingency of reconnections between everyday subjects – subjects whose aesthetics of life blur binaries of past and present, individual and collective, 'fictional' and 'real-world'. In the context that opened this article, the rise of systems-engineering computational models that are based on a concept of humans as terrain, activity like this is the cumulative preservation of unpredictable life against the objectifying and foreclosing imagination of data.

It is no coincidence that in the current Pashto view from the border is a globality without a unified set of hierarchies; is phrased as quasi-allegorical fictive experience rather than fixed data; and focuses on radical contingency among aesthetic subjects as a tactic to undo the foreclosing effects that fixed answers about the past and the present can exert upon the future. The global borderland view from Pashto literary formations adds to the many-layered and polycentric approach to coloniality that scholars such as Madina Tlostanova, among others, have taken in the field of decolonial border thinking, and it certainly intervenes in Eurocentric visions of geopolitical space in international relations and world history, if readers choose to listen (Mignolo and Tlostanova 2006; Tlostanova 2013). But more generally, its nodal view is also the exact opposite of, as Heriberto Yépez puts it, the holistic 'cybernetic' imagination – the systems-engineering perspective – in all respects (Yépez 2007, 53).

This is important beyond Afghanistan, and argues for the salience of this mode of border knowledge to all readers here. What can Afghan literary knowledge share with the entire world, beyond an increased understanding of Afghan lives? That much would be sufficient, of course. However, we are all, worldwide, increasingly managed through data – in our scope for actions as people, and in our very constitution as beings fragmented into bundles of measureable characteristics. While this is a common claim at least as far back as Deleuze's (1992) 'Postscript on the Societies of Control', it has become clear that there is an older colonial persistence here too: a difference between those whose personhood is managed by potentialities like consumer choices, financial choices, medical information, and interaction with social media; and those subaltern populations in regions like Afghanistan whose digital personhood is constituted in large part by state suspicion and is fixed into bundles of very different characteristics by a military gaze. However, this latter too has become a global technology of control, just as the disciplinary technology of the colonial prison was reimported to the nineteenth-century metropole. The same sort of systems modelling that was developed for deployment in Afghanistan has been applied to the study of neighbourhoods and crime in the United States, with predictive models that shape resource allocation and distribution of heavily militarized police forces and that seem to increase forms of insecurity and violence as a result (Lum and Isaac 2016). In a situation where Afghans are once again on the front lines of imperial experimentation in techniques of epistemic and physical violence, and in a world in which imperial experimentation at the borders has frequently returned to reshape societies worldwide, Afghan pasts provide a reflexive tradition of resistive ways of knowing and being. Thinking modern global history through Afghan literary eyes in particular – a vision centred on the creative and inherently unpredictable productivity of individual relationships in history and as history – may offer something to all the world in understanding and contesting violent forms of knowledge in the future.

Acknowledgements

I am grateful to the anonymous reviewer for *Geopolitics* and to Amna Chaudhry for their careful reading of this article, and their extensive guidance on improving it.

Notes

1. One illustration to this effect is contained in Caron 2016; see particularly the discussion of the oral poetic formation. This conceptualization of Pashto literature as a whole is the narrative of my monograph in progress.
2. It is perhaps emblematic of this that Pashto literary culture itself is highly developed, while critical commentary on it, including in Pashto, has been almost non-existent: much Pashto literary work, as this article highlights, already contains a comment on its own social existence as cultural-political and aesthetic intervention.
3. I should note that I have worked, in the case of Sulamal, from electronic files of these stories that the author himself provided me. In cases where I have not given citation information for individual stories, we have been unable to locate full bibliographic details; most of the older collections are not available outside South Asia.
4. Darmesteter (1888) discusses the provenance of his sources in passing, throughout various sections of this work.

References

Anderson, J. 1992. Poetics and politics in ethnographic texts: A view from the colonial ethnography of Afghanistan. In *Writing the social text: Poetics and politics in social science discourse*, ed. R. H. Brown, 91–115. New York: Aldine de Gruyter.

Anzaldúa, G. 1987. *Borderlands/la frontera: The new mestiza*. San Francisco: Aunt Lute Books.

Anzor, Z. 1993. *Da Sawr pa Trazhedey ke Farhang, Adabiyat, aw Azadey*. Peshawar: Da Azad Afghanistan da Likwalo Tolana.

Benjamin, W. 1968. Theses on the philosophy of history, trans. H. Zohn. In *Illuminations: Essays and reflections*, 253–64. New York, NY: Schocken Books.

Caron, J. 2016. Sufism and liberation across the Indo-Afghan border: 1880–1928. *South Asian History and Culture* 7 (2):135–54. doi:10.1080/19472498.2016.1143667.

Crews, R. 2015. *Afghan modern: The history of a global nation*. Cambridge, MA: Harvard University Press.

Darmesteter, J. 1888. *Chants populaires des Afghans*. Paris: Imprimerie nationale, E. Leroux.

Das, V. 2003. Trauma and testimony: Implications for political community. *Anthropological Theory* 3 (3):293-307. doi:10.1177/14634996030033003.

de Certeau, M. 1984. *The practice of everyday life*. Trans. S. Rendall. Berkeley: University of California Press.

Deleuze, G. 1992. Postscript on the societies of control. *October* 59 (Winter):3–7.

Deleuze, G., and F. Guattari. 1987. *A thousand plateaus: Capitalism and schizophrenia*. Minneapolis: University of Minnesota Press.

Digby, S. 1965. Dreams and reminiscences of dattu sarvani: A sixteenth century Indo-Afghan soldier. *Indian Economic and Social History Review* 2:52–98. doi:10.1177/001946466400200104.

Foucault, M. 1986. Of other spaces. *Diacritics* 16:22–27. doi:10.2307/464648.

Green, N. 2008. Tribe, diaspora, and sainthood in Afghan history. *Journal of Asian Studies* 67 (1):171–211. doi:10.1017/S0021911808000065.

Hopkins, B. D., and M. Marsden. 2012. *Fragments of the Afghan frontier*. New York, NY: Columbia University Press.

Karwan, P. M. 2000. *Da Xaperey Werghowey*. Peshawar: Danish Tolana.

Lal, V. 2011. World history and its politics. *Economic and Political Weekly* XLVI (46):40–47.

Lum, K., and W. Isaac. 2016. To predict and serve? *Significance* 13 (5):14–19. doi:10.1111/j.1740-9713.2016.00960.x.

McQuillan, D. 2018. Data science as machinic neoplatonism. *Philosophy & Technology* 31 (2):253–72. doi:10.1007/s13347-017-0273-3.

Mignolo, W., and M. Tlostanova. 2006. Theorizing from borders: Shifting to geo- and body-politics of knowledge. *European Journal of Social Theory* 9 (2):205–21. doi:10.1177/1368431006063333.

Nichols, R. 2008. *A history of Pashtun migration, 1775–2006*. New York, NY: Oxford University.

Opondo, S. O., and M. J. Shapiro, eds. 2012. *The new violent cartography: Geo-analysis after the aesthetic turn*. Abingdon: Routledge.

Shapiro, M. 2012. *Studies in trans-disciplinary method: After the aesthetic turn*. Abingdon: Routledge.

Sulamal (Shiwari), A. W. 2010. *Panzos Milyuna*. Peshawar: Danish Tolana.

Stockman, F. 2016. Knowing the enemy, one avatar at a time. *Boston Globe*, Online May 30, 2010. Accessed December. 12, 2016. http://archive.boston.com/news/nation/washington/articles/2010/05/30/knowing_the_enemy_one_avatar_at_a_time/

Tlostanova, M. 2013. Transcultural tricksters beyond time and space: Decolonial chronotopes and border selves. *Language. Philology. Culture* 2 (3):9–31.

Walsh, R. 2007. *The rhetoric of fictionality*. Columbus: Ohio State University Press.

Ware, O. 2004. Dialectic of the past/disjuncture of the future: Derrida and Benjamin on the concept of messianism. *Journal for Cultural and Religious Theory* 5 (2):99–114.

Yar, M. 2004. *Da Layli Dashta da Stargo Lidalai Hal*. Peshawar: Da Pashtunkhwa da Pohane Dera.

Yépez, H. 2007. La frontera como falla. *Metapolítica* 11 (52):49–53.

OPEN ACCESS

Writing Stars in the Sky or Decentring the Glocal Discourse of the 'War(S) on Terror' through Narratives of Those Displaced

Andrea Fleschenberg and Tariq Saeed Yousufzai

ABSTRACT

Inscribing names into the firmament of symbolic orders is crucial argues Rancière who traces the symbolic distribution of bodies into those that 'one sees' and those that 'one does not see'. The issue of accounted visibility-cum-audibility does not only lie within the specific conflict configuration but also within the geopolitical dynamics of the 'border' as well as 'body-borders' within individuals and communities concerned. One such case can be found at the borderlands of Pakistan with Afghanistan, of the trans-local post-9/11 'Wars on Terror' as well as at the borderlands of Pakistan itself, subjected to invisibility and rumbling noises of conflict and displacement through hegemonic centring of discourses and exclusionary, violent practices of the 'Wars on Terror'. This article is a collaborative work on experiences of conflict-induced displacement, political violence and narratives of everyday life negotiations thereof, based on field research and interviews (individual as well as group ones) conducted in Khyber Pakhtunkhwa and around the capital of Islamabad with those internally displaced from North Waziristan, South Waziristan and Kurram Agencies. The aim is to juxtapose vociferous and deliberate hegemonic practices of invisibility and de-solidarisation in public discourses and counter-insurgency interventions vis-a-vis certain marginalised communities and citizens with the latter's own narratives about their experiences and understandings of state-society relations, relevant stakeholders, public discourses and labelling practices used (such as 'polio threat' and 'terrorist'). We attempt to trace and map how people experience and negotiate political violence, (protracted) conflict-induced displacement and the paucity of governance service provisions in a wider context of contested nation-building and transnational high-intensity conflict. Given repeated, cyclic and/or protracted experiences of displacement, flight and migration, combined with emerging narratives of marginalisation, exploitation and socio-political exclusion, one needs to ask what are the consequences of such transnational conflict and displacement configurations for individual as well as collective social resilience, withstanding ideological manipulation and cooptation into the conflict theatre, as well as for the capacity to develop and implement (alternative and sustainable) livelihoods in the different spaces one has to move in as an individual as well as a family-cum-community member in times of protracted conflict and displacement.

'When I looked behind, it seemed to me as [if] all the stars are falling from the sky.'[1]

Inscribing names into the firmament of symbolic orders is crucial, argues Rancière, in particular when those names are part of a collective destiny, such as a simple citizen vis-à-vis those engaging in promises (such as fighting terrorism) or in contracts (such as peace deals, multilateral military cooperation or border regimes) – because 'whoever is nameless cannot speak' (Rancière 2006, 24ff). Rancière traces the symbolic distribution of bodies into those that 'one sees' and those that 'one does not see'; into those who have 'visible', recognised accounts vis-à-vis those who may actually speak, but whose articulations are not accounted for, but are regarded as 'noise' rather than as 'voice' (Rancière 2006, 24ff). The issue of visibility-cum-audibility lies not only within the specific conflict configuration but also within the geopolitical dynamics of the 'border' as well as 'body-borders' within individuals and communities concerned (i.e. borders inscribed through discourses and practices between citizens). One such case can be found at the borderlands of Pakistan with Afghanistan, of the trans-local post-9/11 'Wars on Terror', subjected via its people to invisibility, rumbling noises of conflict and displacement through the hegemonic centring of discourses and exclusionary, violent practices of respective military actions.

Reflections on Research Objectives and Concerns of the Case Study

This article is a collaborative exploration of experiences of conflict-induced displacement and political violence and the narratives of the everyday life negotiations thereof. It is based on field research and over 50 interviews (individual as well as group ones) conducted by the authors during late 2015 to mid-2016 in Peshawar and Lakki Marwat (a district of the province Khyber Pakhtunkhwa [KPk]) and around the capital of Islamabad with internally displaced persons (IDPs) from North Waziristan, South Waziristan[2] and Kurram Agencies.[3] Interview partners hail from various walks of life in terms of literacy/education, profession/employment, site of displacement, religion, gender and age. The data were collected using an interview guide in English and Pashto language with a list of issues for questions on the experiences of displacement, but allowing for flexibility in the semi-structured interview process given the often traumatic nature of the narrative, the lack of experience of being interviewed, as well as the high level of suspicion among the internally displaced towards interviewers. Interviewees were approached in common places of assembly of IDPs or via friends and relatives at their home, using cues from local contact persons familiar to the research team members as well as snowball sampling to identify further interview partners. We decided to approach those living outside of camps, who represent the overall majority of the internally displaced, thereby avoiding problems with security agencies known for restricting access to camp communities. One problematic side effect was the difficulty of reaching female IDPs, who are mostly restricted to their homes and are far less present in the public gatherings and public spaces used to identify potential interview partners. We rely therefore for that part to a large extent on data provided by our research team member mentioned later, who is a local from Kurram Agency and who collected this data as part of her thesis work. A number of interviews took place in a group setting as people were suspicious, unfamiliar or wary of individual interviews 'behind closed doors', more familiar and comfortable with the notion of a 'hujra' – a room in a house used for social entertainment, assembly and discussion in Pashtun society (or rather its male members one must emphasise). For reasons of protecting our interview partners' identity and safety and addressing their concerns and suspicions about being interviewed, only limited demographic background information was collected (e.g. age, family status, professions and income level, timing and trajectory of displacement), while names and exact dates are entirely omitted in our work. Interviews were thus conducted off the record, often only taking notes or making memory protocols; in quite a number of cases audio we were allowed to record the interviews, whenever interview partners were comfortable with it. These omissions are not without problems, reminding us of Rancière's concern that 'whoever is nameless cannot speak' and of the importance of writing names into the sky of the symbolic order of the post-9/11 'Wars on Terror' (see Rancière 2006). For whatever it is worth and in whatever limited way, we attempt to upload at least voices to the sky and hope that one day names can follow.

In this article, we attempt to trace and map how people experience and negotiate (protracted) conflict-induced displacement and the paucity of public and private relief and service provisions, within a wider context of contested nation-building and transnational high-intensity conflict. For the scope of this article, we focus on two major themes emerging from the interviews conducted as well as additional testimonies and material consulted: first, the issue of curfews, checkpoints and the quest for respect for those in the immediate course of displacement, when many encounter the State in a contentious situation, marred by demands for security and control, on the one hand, and offers of immediate emergency relief, shelter and respect as a human being and citizen on the other. Second, no displacement, as disruptive as it may be, takes place on a clean slate but within specific sociocultural, political and economic parameters and stratifications, with gender being one key denominator. Therefore, we trace and highlight the experiences of female IDPs of displacement, invisibility and mobility, predominantly burdened by further marginalisation and gender-specific vulnerabilities exacerbated by conflict-induced displacement. Both strands allow us to map, indirectly, state-society relations and the long-term impact of such counter-insurgency interventions as part of the glocal 'Wars on Terror' from a decentred, grassroots perspective more often than not rendered marginal, invisible or unconsidered in prevailing public discourses. Out of repeated, cyclic and/or protracted experiences of displacement, flight and migration emerge narratives of marginalisation, exploitation and sociopolitical exclusion. One key question to be asked is, therefore, what are the consequences of such conflict-induced displacement configurations for individual as well as collective social resilience as well as for the capacity to develop and implement (alternative and sustainable) livelihoods in the different spaces which one must negotiate as an individual, family and community member in times of protracted conflict and displacement. In the interviews conducted, a series of understandings, practices and ideas of how to conceptualise and respond to challenges of belonging, resilience and livelihood is displayed.

Notes on the Conflict, Intervention and Displacement Parameters

Brown University's Cost of War project's multi-disciplinary team investigated 'the costs of the post-9/11 wars in Iraq and Afghanistan, and the related violence in Pakistan and Syria'.[4] What is the record of the body count and what are the glocal ramifications? Its co-director argues that the conflicts in Afghanistan and Pakistan 'have become one larger conflict' due to a series of interlinkages such as refugees and IDPs, drone strikes, cross-border military operations and transport paths for military support equipment along with covert or overt US funding for Afghanistan's and Pakistan's war-related spending in terms of equipment, training and operations (Crawford 2015, 1, 12–13).

The Pakistani military operation Zarb-e-Azb is evidence of these interlinked, translocal geopolitical border 'Wars on Terror', carried out where 'most (19 out of 24) of the US drone strikes in 2014′ worldwide occurred (Crawford 2015, 12). As with other military operations, large-scale internal displacement emerged in its wake, further linked to US drone strikes that are 'disruptive to livelihoods' and 'contribut[ing] to problems of displacement, malnutrition and disease' (Crawford 2015, 12f). It is difficult to establish a clear record of the costs of war, given not only problems of who counts what (or not) but moreover problems of assessing indirect costs of war, that is, its negative effects on social and technical infrastructure, on displacement and human security. Tallying the record of 'costs' other than loss of human life or injury as direct outcomes, such as the psycho-social costs of the experience of war, directly or indirectly, of displacement or deprivation due to the conflict and its geopolitics is beyond the scope of this study. Moreover, the question remains as to whether there was ever a 'peacetime baseline' for the Federally Administrated Areas (FATA) to assess the current impact of the 'Wars on Terror' in the region, as there is none for Afghanistan (Crawford 2015, 20). Taking into account the Geneva Declaration Secretariat's suggestion to multiply by four the number of direct deaths to estimate the ratio of indirect deaths, the scale of humanitarian emergencies in Pakistan and Afghanistan is immense and the silences surrounding them the more worrisome, given the approximately 173,000 direct deaths and the estimated 183,614 directly injured in both countries since 2001 (Crawford 2016, 9, 14, 2015, 20).

Zarb-e-Azb is part of a series of over 600 smaller and larger post-2004 military operations in FATA and KPk which have led to repeated conflict-induced, more often than not cyclic or protracted displacement and migration from FATA (Khan 2014).[5] Indicative of state–society relations in transnational conflict configurations and policy-making settings, the experiences and subsequent narratives of those internally displaced (IDPs, or in military speak TDPs, temporarily displaced) about the very acts and phases of displacement, temporary resettlement and repatriation are rendered nearly invisible in Pakistan's hegemonic discourses. This is true for different media formats, in parliamentary and other policy debates at the national and international levels, which are, however, beyond the scope of this article. One reason is that such discourses and narratives are subject to securitisation and surveillance practices by different stakeholders at various levels of the polity and public. In one of Pakistan's leading monthly magazines, *Herald*, Alizeh Kohari (2014) problematises how those displaced are positioned at the fringes – be it in geographic or psychological terms. Specific labels are employed, which lead to the 'othering' of those internally displaced in the subsequent public imagination and thus to de-solidarisation with those at the 'fringes'. This centring objectification is an expression of a (post-)colonial legacy of fossilising such 'body-borders' of a community within the wider project of contested nation-building:

> So little has been known about our 'lawless frontier' – the tribal areas – for so long; [...] the stories that we do hear now paint its residents as either objects of pity or emblems of fear. More than anything else, fear and pity both create a sense of distance – it becomes easy to think of the displaced merely as haulers of ration cradlers, of sick babies or carriers of a 'contagion' called terrorism, either victims or villains in a faraway land. (Kohari 2014, 37–38)

Those labelled are themselves threatened and victimised by militants in ostensible 'safety', in military-controlled camps and at registration points in Hangu, Peshawar or Bannu (in the province of KPk), militants who terrorise further an already uprooted and traumatised population. Nationalists or provincial stakeholders in parts of Sindh, Balochistan and KPk provinces have tried to bar IDPs' access to safety and relief services by staging sit-ins or stopping their vehicles. Their argument was based on a securitised need for 'containment' from terrorism and polio, thus imposing borders on those from the border-lands, this multitude of displaced 'body-borders' on the move (Human Rights Commission of Pakistan 2015, 343–345).

Overshadowing this scenario was a large-scale, months-long *dharna* (sit-in protest) by opposition politicians and their party supporters in Islamabad, protesting the outcome of the 2013 elections and contesting then Prime Minister Nawaz Sharif's electoral victory and government policies. The *dharna* appeared to relegate concerns with the humanitarian emergencies created by Zarb-e-Azb to the fringes of public affairs, as participants of the sit-in danced in floodlighting in a wave of trendy 'protestainment' at the heart of the country's so called 'red zone' (i.e. where major government institutions are located), without any signs of solidarity or concern with the large-scale displacement and emergencies occurring outside the public's spotlight at the same time. In a country prone to conspiracy theories, a sense emerged that the *dharna* politics – and not the politics of the counter-insurgency conflict – appropriated the attention and resources of the civilian governance epicentre.

The following quotes are typical examples of the constrained and complex state–society relations between Pakistani citizens from FATA and their State, their lack of appropriation of public spaces of solidarity and empathy. This is coupled with power asymmetries vis-à-vis the politico-military elite and within different parts of Pakistan, where the province of Punjab is considered a hegemonic centre in terms of political clout, access to resources and governmental development practices.

> How can you tell these people, little children, that they cannot go to Punjab? Which law, constitution or rights dictate that you cannot go there? We are good people, we love Pakistan and we will continue [to love Pakistan]. God forbid anything should happen to Pakistan. We will be the first to stand up. These big people will be the first to leave.[6]

> We think the operation is necessary. They should definitely do it. Because the presence of foreigners in Waziristan is the government's doing, not ours. (…) I did not bring Uzbeks, Tajiks. Today, if I say there are Tajiks and Uzbeks here, tomorrow, my head will be cut off and thrown there. (…) We do not have the strength to fight the state. We cannot throw rocks at them. Because those who came here, we came in peace. We thought our dignity would stay intact. The destruction of our dignity is beyond your imagination. Our dignity is completely destroyed. Do not give me money. Do not give me flour. But at least stop hitting me. (…) No one will save us. No one asks about us. There are people in Sindh and Punjab but there is no one in Waziristan.[7]

Their emergencies remain invisible, their voices silenced, while those at the centre of the geopolitical contestation, those diverse armed actors on either side of the hegemonic core of the 'Wars on Terror' noisily rumble 'in the wings', regardless of the intervention fatigue, if not exhaustion, of the wider international audience and local populations. Who will ever listen to Fazle Basir, an elderly poet, whose last wish is to publish a collection of his poems? How could he imagine doing so, finding the resources while being displaced in Jalozai camp (35 km southeast of KPk's capital Peshawar and approx. 166 km from Pakistan's capital Islamabad), living in a shared tent with other members of his family from Khyber Agency?

> We were in a situation where fathers could not find their sons and sons could not find their fathers. It was night; it was dark; children were crying. Women left behind their clothes and household items. Our hearts ache – our wounds are so deep that even doctors would not be able to heal them. (…) The conditions back home and in this camp have shattered my poetry, and have shattered my thoughts and feelings so that I am not even aware of myself. I am sick and I am feeble. I cannot work and have no source of income.[8]

Displacement further produces distinct gender-specific experiences and subsequently reproduces marginalisations, be it in terms of coercion and violence faced or that most female-headed IDP households are not properly documented, as human rights defenders have criticized (N.N. 2010). Who at the hegemonic centres of the 'opportunistic indulgence in geopolitics of difference, conflict, and war', its public discourses, policy-making and military planning, as this special issue editors Raza and Shapiro argue its rationale, is concerned with looking beyond the exploited and politicised veils, or 'shuttlecock burqas' as they are often labelled demeaningly, of women from FATA? Who is concerned about their experiences of negotiating gendered dimensions of the conflict along with societal normative regimes such as gendered mobility restrictions, which intersect with the need to resist and to transgress borders to earn a livelihood, seek medical care or escape to safety? Illustrative is the case of the 60-year-old housewife displaced from Kurram Agency, whom we interviewed in Islamabad in late 2015, whose name we omit for security reasons. She has lived in protracted displacement in the country's capital since 2012, after having spent some time in Peshawar (the capital of KPk province), which she considered too insecure to remain in.

> The woman who had a shop at her home was brutally killed by the Taliban while travelling through Afghanistan to bring some clothes to sell. The Afghanistan route was not secure, because many people were killed while travelling. We are in such a difficult situation that even food was not available sometimes. Everything was very expensive. Those who wanted to bring some food items through Afghanistan were sometimes killed or kidnapped. Many families are still waiting for their dear ones. Women's lives were very disrupted; many were not allowed to go to the cities as male relatives said 'you are our *izzat* [honour]; it's better to die from illness at home than to be killed at the road[side]'.

Human rights lawyer Shahzad Akbar (2015) problematises in an exemplary way the everyday politics and societal discourses of human suffering produced by the geopolitical and trans-locally fought 'Wars on Terror', connected trans-border military strikes as well as local military operations like the post-2014 operation Zarb-e-Azb. He describes how those living in the designated 'borderlands' are considered peripheral and at the fringes of sociopolitical concerns, how their own bodies and thus the 'border' that positions them become a way of life, an ontology of embodied experiences – body-borders – of invisibility, de-solidarisation, silences and emergencies, whether back at home or in displacement, in public discourse or counter-insurgency policies.

> It appears that we have decided to count only our losses – and when I say 'ours', I mean those of us living in the cities like Islamabad, Peshawar, Rawalpindi, Lahore and Karachi who belong to a certain economic class. When a civilian life is lost in the Tribal Areas – for instance, when civilians or even children get killed in Waziristan – that is not a national concern. No eyebrows are raised, no accountability is sought and any mention of such deaths is brushed aside. This division between 'us' and 'them', constructed through class, privilege, geography, and ideology has brought us to a point where it is not human life as such that matters but which human that matters. That kind of thinking has made it easy for some to choose to respond to terrorism with more violence. (Akbar 2015)

The Politics of Epistemologies (Alternative or Not) and Politically Charged Terminologies

We take our cue from Nayak and Selbin's (2010) critical approach to decentring international relations and conflicts, to mapping and deconstructing the underlying, overpowering hegemonies along with colonial-infused legacies of *othering* in addition to the neo-colonial contentions which emerge out of contested politics surrounding violent conflict. It appears that many depictions of geopolitical incidents like the 'Wars on Terror' are conceptualised, debated and narrated in a chronology of events and incidents centring on the Global Northwest, according to Nayak and Selbin (2010). On the one hand, this creates a subsequent legacy of perceptions of threats and fear through othering, with a unilateral flow of development and demands for mediation, and, on the other hand, a Global South chronology of dependency, experiences of (neo-)colonial dominance, exploitation and othering, thus requiring interventions with an uphill struggle for alternatives which more than often are devoid of a deconstruction of this hegemonic practice of centring in the first place (Nayak and Selbin 2010).

Mapping silences and emergencies is therefore vital in order to understand the working of conflict-oriented hegemonies, often imposed and sustained by stakeholders who have more to gain from conflict and enmity rather than from peace and more egalitarian sociopolitical projects. Such an approach not only allows an understanding of opinion patterns and narratives to be developed, but also enables the mapping of entry points for indispensable non-military, decentred interventions responding to humanitarian silences and emergencies and their impact on highly strained state–society relations in conflict configurations. Having said that, such an approach is a challenging one as it also problematises key concepts and terminologies in discursive use – be it in mainstream media, political or academic discourses. Developing alternative terminologies and concepts would be beyond the scope of this article; however, it is crucial to take cure from Nayak and Selbin on what kind of data and insights discourses on conflicts and state-society relationships are based and shaped. As incomplete as our tentative exploration in this article is by centring on the displaced in a juxtaposition and thus challenge of hegemonic discourses through narratives collected from displaced persons, this hopefully will lead to first steps towards decentring discourses and thus questioning hegemonic frames and taken for granted terminologies in a very much required debate about alternative conceptual frameworks and empirical data informing academic work on international relations and glocal conflicts. This also includes the need for further empirical research to inform theoretical debates on the issues at hand – something most likely difficult to conduct in an environment of curtailed critical social sciences in conflict settings per se and in contemporary Pakistan's censorship practices of state authorities (and security agencies) in particular.

We would like to challenge the very notion of the 'periphery' of this border region and its people (displaced or not) in that regard, because FATA is at the core and at the crossroads of this geopolitical, transnational and translocal contestation. It is deliberately kept at the socioeconomic and political fringes through specific and violent power-cum-surveillance practices and militarised interventions, part of this 'opportunistic indulgence in geopolitics of difference, conflict, and war' as Raza and Shapiro argue in this special issue. We therefore try to take cure from Nayak and Selbin (2010, 125), who critique the centring of peace and security, because it leads to (i) myopic, centred, marginalised and exclusionary narratives and discourses; (ii) a focus on institutionalised or militarised pathways to peace, which propose linear solutions and good-bad dichotomies instead of critically analysing the question of what counts as 'peaceful', 'secure', or, '[w]hose political sensibilities matter in determining when "peace and security" have been achieved?'. Decentring then engages with the contentious cartography of the *glocally* played-out politics of the 'Wars on Terror' in a way of challenging the very notion of centre, rather suggesting that there are 'no centres – but rather people and places and positions', with the story-telling of conflict and peace to be considered as a corpus of multi-level discourses (Nayak and Selbin 2010, 158–159). There are different forms of centring (or not) and reactions thereto such as distortions, dismissals, conspiracies (as theories of those experiencing powerlessness), hegemonies and dependencies. Even purposeful silences and emergencies are important, presuming that 'purposeful silence tells stories about what cannot yet find words', nevertheless challenging our political imaginary, understandings of phenomena, vision (or lack) of coping strategies and alternatives, to discover '"the large lessons" in "small worlds"'

(Nayak and Selbin 2010, 166; Brooks, DeCorse, and Walton 2008). For us, the centre is not the State and its policies as such but its citizens, in this case its affected citizens, that is, the displaced and their multiple voices, experiences and relationships with the State and its policies in this glocal war-cum-displacement cycle(s).

It is beyond the scope of this article to delve into the increasing problematisation of and contestation over terminologies involved, such as 'internally displaced', 'refugee' or 'migrant', whether in academic or public debates the world over, which are understood to fall short in capturing complex realities (e.g. mixed migration or migration-displacement) and/or face being hijacked by politico-ideological projects of ordering.[9] We therefore follow the approach of a 'deliberately broad analytical lens' which defines displacement and anticipatory movement as well as relocation as non-mutually exclusive categories conceptualising conflict-induced flight/'crisis migration' – 'a descriptive term for all those who move, including those who require relocation in the context of humanitarian crises'; that is, being forced to relocate due to unfolding events, anticipated threats to one's safety or due to being directly or indirectly affected, such as by collapsing basic services or loss of employment possibilities due to conflict or palpable threats thereof to one's livelihood (Martin, Weerasinghe, and Taylor 2014, 5).

Following the 1998 Guiding Principles on Internal Displacement and its Article 2, as endorsed by the United Nations' General Assembly during its 2005 World Summit, IDPs are 'persons or groups of persons who have been forced or obliged to flee or to leave their homes or places of habitual residence, in particular as a result of or in order to avoid the effects of armed conflict, situations of generalised violence, violations of human rights or natural or human-made disasters, and who have not crossed an internationally recognised state border' (United Nations Office for the Coordination of Humanitarian Affairs OCHA 2004, 1; see also Cohen 2014).[10] This definition is not devoid of problems, for example, given its state-centric approach in the light of transnational conflict configurations, longstanding local trans-border communities, unmarked border geographies and the everyday mobility of traders, labourers, nomadic and pastoralist communities or simply schoolchildren, thus leading to habitual 'transgressions' in spaces such as FATA, occurring at contested borders such as the Durand Line. The UN's Office for the Coordination of Humanitarian Affairs (OCHA) Pakistan estimated that around 105,000 IDPs have moved either into Khost or Paktika (Afghanistan) to safety or re-entered Pakistan via Kurram Agency (see OCHA 2014, 2014a und, 2014b). IDPs interviewed have repeatedly reported that their direct path to refuge was blocked due to curfews, violent skirmishes, ongoing military operations, lack of affordable means of transport as well as past habitual travel practices. This is especially true in the case of those who initially stayed behind to take care of property when others left, believing that the operation would be short-lived, a mere couple of days. Ultimately, they had to leave due to the heavy bombardment of the area and negotiate their way to safety. A typical example is the case of a 50-year-old government employee from Miran Shah, interviewed in early 2016 in Peshawar, who had to travel via Khost (Afghanistan), mostly walking, and could only get to Bannu after the route was reopened. A 40-year-old government schoolteacher from Palangzai in North Waziristan, displaced in Peshawar with his family when interviewed in early 2016, encountered fierce bombardments on the exit road when deciding to leave. Without maps or navigation tools they had to wander through the border area in search of a safe passage towards Bannu, unware of whether or not they crossed the Durand Line.

> We were going, so we had to change our route and started going in Afghanistan's direction. We had no vehicles, so our feet were the only support we had for movement. We took three days and nights to reach an area called (…), near the Pakistan-Afghanistan border areas while having nothing with us – nothing to eat, drink and no clothes to change. Everything left behind at home. We took another three days to get back to Bannu, again by foot (…).

A further illustration is the case of a 29-year-old student from the University of Peshawar, interviewed in the city in early 2016. He originates from Razmak in North Waziristan, with his family displaced to Bannu. Deciding to return when Zarb-e-Azb was announced, to help his family leave, he was held up at a military entry point. Subsequently, he had to enter Afghanistan, stay one night in Khost in order to be able to re-enter Pakistan, using camels and trucks on his way home, negotiating 'zig-zag roads', slow travel, taking cover from ongoing fighting when in Afghanistan and bringing his family back the same way, albeit at exorbitantly increased transport costs.

> They started launching rockets so we jumped from the truck and started crawling on the road to the trees. It was the most fearful time of my life. We were hiding there for a long time and then resumed our journey when the firing cooled down. My family went through a lot of troubles when they were leaving the region; all the surrounding areas were sealed. The Miran Shah and Mir Ali routes were completely closed, so we only had the direction of Khost and Afghanistan and that was our only link with the rest of the world.

The same is true for what counts as facts and figures, which are either difficult to aggregate or to gain access to, relying more often than not on estimates and/or data provided by one of the parties in the conflict. In addition, international stakeholders, experts and watchdog organisations usually assume a quantitative underrepresentation of the actual phenomenon, given registration processes, access criteria and the resultant challenges.[11] Classifying what counts or who is counted is a way of ordering/controlling in a highly politicised conflict-displacement situation if one wishes to obfuscate the scale as well as dimensions of the humanitarian emergency at hand, by deflating or inflating numbers to manage (inter-) national responses, by refusing registration to certain groups of people to maintain a specific normative regime (e.g. female-headed households) or to block access to media and humanitarian organisations to generate a specific narrative of securitisation and 'contagion' for the projection of 'surgically concise' operations. Military operations in Pakistan (and not only there) remain literal black boxes for the wider public, secured by hegemonic narratives of securitisation and sacrifice and controlled media templates, which then impact on governance practices such as counter-terrorism strategies.[12]

> Claiming there are no IDPs, only persons who will soon go home, the government created a Temporary Dislocated Persons (TDP) Support and Management Secretariat in July 2014. Headed by a general, tasked with overseeing response to North Waziristan's IDPs and bypassing civilian disaster management entities, it has further increased military control of relief, which is being used as a counter-insurgency tool. (International Crisis Group 2015, 22)

Since 2008 a total of 13.7 million Pakistanis have been displaced due to disasters and another five million due to political violence, mostly confined to the spaces of FATA and KPk, while the country has for years ranked in the world's top 10 countries with internal displacement. Some IDPs are trapped in protracted displacement: since 2005 in Balochistan and 2007 in KPk and FATA. For the years 2014–2015 up to 1.5 million conflict-induced IDPs alone were counted in KPk and FATA, while the country has displayed overall high levels of conflict-induced displacement linked to the glocal 'Wars on Terror' since 2004 (with a peak of three million in 2009). However, all these figures are considered to be underestimates for a number of reasons. First, states – and thus potential conflict parties with vested interests in 'ordering' – along with outdated census data or incomplete field data from local authorities/organisations are primarily responsible for statistics. Secondly, unregistered IDPs are excluded (e.g. those in urban displacement such as in Karachi or those fearing official registration points/ camps due to threats from militants). Third, no regular monitoring of displacement over an extended period of time (e.g. in Balochistan) exists. Fourth, only those are counted who have fled from areas classified by the authorities as 'calamity-hit' (i.e. up to half of IDPs in KPk and FATA might not have been included), and, fifth, many women are not counted given a lack of identity documents and *purdah* (seclusion) norms (OCHA 2016).[13] Only those officially numbered through their computerised identity cards (issued by NADRA and authorised by local elders and FATA's political administration) are able to access benefits. But even then not all were acknowledged – or could pay to be, given a mushrooming 'shadow industry (…), providing IDPs with registration slips and identification documents under-the-table and at a premium' (Shuja and

Wazir 2016). Those left out were, among others, those having more than one address or inaccurate family trees, living with someone registered (even if as a married adult) or lacking necessary documentation. Two months into displacement the rejection rate for registration stood at 42.9%. Moreover, faulty records and capacity limitations for verification processes by the authorities concerned meant that 'nearly half of all IDP heads of household were undocumented' (Shuja and Wazir 2016). A further aggravating factor is that IDP populations are counted in household units, assuming a specific average family size – in 2014 counted as 5.2 members and in 2015 as 6.2 members due to new information provided to IDMC, raising the estimate by 200,000 persons (with the same census, government statistics and field data sets provided!) (see Internal Displacement Monitoring Centre 2016; 'Internal Displacement Monitoring Centre 2015, 2015a).

All of these calculations do not factor in the constant mobility and fluid dynamics of displacement in the decades-long 'Wars on Terror'. A significant number of IDP households remain in *cyclic* displacement-cum-migration (moving back and forth or on to other locations, depending the intensity of the conflict and resources available). Others face *split* (protracted) displacement, i.e. with some (mostly male) family members commuting back to protect assets in FATA while ensuring the safety and well-being of their displaced relatives, as our interview findings demonstrate.

Of Checkpoints, Curfews and the Quest for Respect

Let us return to Rancière's idea of inscribing oneself into a symbolic order. Over the past years, those displaced have attempted to appropriate public spaces to protest for their rights-based claims to access basic services and facilities, not to be curtailed in their movements due to camp-based restrictions or military-imposed curfews upon return, to live secure lives or to receive adequate financial support and compensation for damages suffered. And most of all, not to be subjected to 'the colonial-era Frontier Crimes Regulation' as part of a return 'agreement' (Human Rights Commission of Pakistan 2016, 12; Farooq 2013). Linked to the militarisation of counter-terrorism operations and related relief efforts, entire communities are treated with suspicion, as a kind of rights-devoid contagion to be controlled and contained. 'The prioritisation of security was evident in the bans and controls set in place against the IDPs. It was evident when, (…), preferring to hand over significant aspects of administration to the security forces. And, it is evident in the lengthy clearance processes for humanitarian organisations seeking to work with displaced families' (Shuja and Wazir 2016).

En route to safety as well as upon arrival, multiple 'borders' needed to be crossed; body-borders were demarcated by a series of checkpoints and military-controlled registration points. These registration points were 'called by [the] military "strangulation points"', where one had to establish one's identity (or not) through ID cards, names were noted down as well as livestock carried along, the few belongings carried along were checked or those deemed suspicious were detained (Shuja and Wazir 2016). 'They would look through our belongings and then throw them on the ground. They did this with everybody's personal items. They would throw things around and then command us to pick our stuff up', complains one woman IDP from North Waziristan (Shuja and Wazir 2016), her recollections seconded by many we interviewed.

Testimonies of this series of procedures consist of experiences of humiliation, exhaustion and pain owing to long waiting lines without any provisions such as water, food or shelter in the summer heat, in particular for vulnerable groups such as women, children and the elderly. In addition, IDPs frequently reported an abusive demeanour among security forces, resulting in disenchantment with state forces, outright trauma, injury and even deaths. 'At one point in time, I used to lose consciousness; and many times I found myself in hospital without knowing what had happened to me and how it happened', explains a 23-year-old married male student, interviewed in 2016 at Peshawar University. The trauma caused by the loss of his home and belongings, the humiliation and disrespect experienced through being controlled and checked to the last item carried, through witnessing public beatings or persons being killed in public by security forces when queuing for rations or negotiating camp life left him, and many interviewed, with a feeling of powerlessness and of not belonging in this 'traumatic time' of a perceived new Great Game being played out in FATA. 'If someone demolishes your markets, destroys your houses and kicks you out of your area, what could be worse than that? (…) We can't say anything or raise our voice against it, because we get killed then. (…) In Waziristan, only innocent people are dying', he concludes, pointing towards the high levels of psychosomatic stress suffered.

The securitised notion of a 'cordon' was also enforced via polio vaccinations on those having to cross. One could argue that this is a benevolent compulsion to contain a contagion in a world-wide fight to eradicate this disease. Yet from a displaced individual's perspective, as pointed out in the majority of interviews conducted, the glocal 'Wars on Terror' include powerful tales-cum-conspiracy theories enforced by militants, elders and religious clergy that such vaccination drives are a way of tearing the community's social fabric apart. 'We oppose polio [vaccination]. They [non-Muslims] have mixed something in it, which will destroy our children's morality. (…) I don't want to talk about polio. We don't want it', vehemently argued a 55-year-old male IDP who had previously worked abroad and is now displaced to Peshawar, expressing a representative opinion pattern. Given the propaganda by the Taliban that it represents an un-Islamic, harmful drive to control the community's virility and morality as well as the events surrounding the capture of Osama Bin Laden (whose hideout was ultimately identified in a setup vaccination drive), it is considered as an expression of Westoxification, another violent and disrespectful intervention into people's lives and bodies.

Regardless of the surveillance cartography conducted while people were under duress at registration points, it nevertheless allowed some to be able to access state services, to acquire much needed identification documents to be acknowledged as a citizen, becoming part of a formalised state–society contract. However, many IDPs felt that this included too high a sacrifice, with too little public support and solidarity and too great a dark shadow of surveillance and repression hovering above. Or, in the words of one IDP interviewed, of having to pay 'dearly' for the privilege of being 'made a citizen'. Overshadowed by the prism of securitisation and collective responsibility for citizens mapped, this codified relationship took shape in the form of aid distribution cards, later special *Watan* cards and National Identity Cards (NICs) needed to access much needed state support as well as to be able to return. 'We carry these identity cards around us as if they were passports. And this *Watan* card is our visa to return back to the homes we were driven out of', Shuja and Wazir (2016) explains one IDP living in an informal settlement in Bannu, nevertheless deprived of services and infrastructure benefits in everyday life. Moreover, reports surfaced that those returning had to sign an agreement that assigns the task of post-Zarb-e-Azb security to local communities – without providing necessary equipment and training to do so, 'outsourcing' security responsibility and once again withdrawing the state from key responsibilities. At the same time communities are subjected to tight curfews and mobility restrictions, which once again cut many off from the benefits of state services needed to rebuild livelihoods, such as seeking medical care, school education or simple protection from insecurity in the ongoing 'Wars on Terror'.

Seeing beyond the Veil – Gendered Experiences of Displacement, Invisibility and Mobility[14]

As of 2015, women with children in their care represented 75% of IDPs, heading 10–13% of IDP households (International Crisis Group 2015, 21).[15] Apart from this, women have been one of the main targets of the conflict – a conflict with a distinct gender dimension of this politico-ideological contestation with the State and its normative order, embedded within a wider geopolitical contestation and gender-based violence as part of the conflict configuration. 'Militants would threaten us from the mosque speakers, [or] from speakers on their cars when they drove through the village. They would tell us to not leave our houses without a veil, or there would be consequences', explains 70-year-old Gul Badan, displaced from Khyber Agency (N.N. 2013).

Human rights violations and gender-based violence were either direct outcomes of violence, such as the assassination of health worker Suriya Bibi and women's activist Farida Afridi, or attacks/threats against teachers, nurses and policewomen. Indirect consequences due to the militarisation and insecurity created by the conflict and subsequent displacement have led to under-age marriages, trafficking of women, loss of employment opportunities and mobility in public spaces or loss of access to health care and education (International Crisis Group 2015, 20–21).

> Female students suffered more as compared to males as they [men] can go anywhere. Our students were left with incomplete courses when the military operation started, while [women] IDPs faced great difficulties; because of diseases the miscarriage rate increases, deaths of children occurring while moving to safe areas. (female lecturer from North Waziristan, redeployed to Parachinar due to Zarb-e-Azb, interviewed in late 2015)

A female schoolteacher from a village in Lower Kurram, interviewed in late 2015 in Parachinar, spoke of her fear due to the intensity of the conflict, 'of sending our children outside. People in our village, especially women, faced a lot of problems. There was a shortage of food items. It was difficult to go outside the home, such as working in the fields, fetching water. We were imprisoned in our homes'.

Khwendo Kor [Sisters' Home], headed by Maryam Bibi, renowned women's activist from South Waziristan, is one of the few civil society organisations working across FATA and KPk for over two decades, mobilising women for the FATA reform process, providing basic services and working on women's rights for those in displacement or not. In one of its reports already published in 2011 (thus prior to Zarb-e-Azb), the organisation documented 'accounts by displaced women from FATA of sexual and other physical violence by militants and security officials. Armed conflict has contributed to men abusing or murdering women relatives with impunity' (International Crisis Group 2015, 20–21; see also interview with the head of Kwendo Khor, Maryam Bibi, N.N. 2012).

Gender-specific vulnerabilities substantially increase when in displacement, such as risks of trafficking and sexual exploitation, apart from obstacles to access to relief goods and services such as food rations and health care (International Crisis Group 2015, 21). Women were disadvantaged either when not in possession of a national identity card necessary for registering with the government and aid organisations or when not accompanied by a male relative, for instance, when widowed or as a female relative of one of the many working migrants to the United Arab Emirates. Women might not have been aware of the importance of ID cards, having been prevented by militants or male relative members from procuring them. There were no gender-segregated registration points and even women with identity cards faced difficulties. These difficulties range from attempting to access relief goods while not being allowed to queue alongside men at ration distribution points etc., to accessing washrooms/toilets constructed adjacent to men's ones in a culturally-insensitive and thus exclusionary manner or accessing health care given the lack of female nurses and doctors as well as female security forces. Supported by political parties, in-camp held *jirgas* (tribal councils/consensus-based assemblies) decided to disallow and thus bar women from direct access to relief goods, regardless if from a female- or child-headed household or part of a family. There are also reports of women being threatened by officials when attempting to access relief or file complaints (Glatz 2015; Human Rights Commission of Pakistan 2016; Human Rights Commission 2015).[16]

On their way to safe passage, women encountered many a traumatic experience: living and travelling under constant fear of a militant ambush or when fighting was ongoing, leaving homes empty-handed and with open doors, running bare-footed and without *chador* (large veiling cloth wrapped around the head and upper part of the body). Or when no transport was available, when having no food, milk or water to provide for children or when having to give birth by the roadside. Many interviewed described that being displaced meant being without access to basic necessities in unfamiliar, disturbing and highly restrictive circumstances such as in military-controlled camps or in an unchartered urban setting and infrastructure outside one's habitual social network.[17] Typical for many experiences narrated by female IDPs from Kurram and South Waziristan interviewed in late 2015 and early 2016 is the following quote from a 60-year-old woman, displaced repeatedly, the last time in 2007 to Parachinar.

> For the third time we left our homes completely. There was firing of tracers and mortar shells while we were barefoot. Our feet were injured with thorns while running. When I looked behind, it seemed to me as [if] all stars are falling from the sky. (…) The scenes from that night keep playing in my mind. (…) Unlike the first time, we were not welcomed this time. (…), my brother told me 'It is better to leave, because we cannot bear pictures of our women in militants' cell phones'. (…) Most of the village was empty. My brother told me to go empty-handed. It was difficult to leave everything for a third time, so I looked around in the room and hid an iron under my *dupatta* [large scarf/shawl]. I gave it to my relative after reaching Alizai. I was worried about my brother. Our large family was separated from one another. We left our beautiful homes unlocked. I can bear everything, but my brother's death is unbearable [crying]. We faced a lot of problems [crying]. (…) When we came here, we stayed in the *Imam Bargah* of Parachinar for some time. People provided us food, burqas and *dupattas*. Then we entered empty homes which were left by people. We entered empty homes and we had nothing to eat.

Out of the interviews conducted with women IDPs emerge various narratives of suffering, trauma, insecurity and deprivation. These encompass tales of walking bare-footed, without proper *chador* and losing one's children when running to save one's life or of dealing with mental disturbances of children and relatives. How to negotiate conflict-induced insecurities while providing care featured prominently in women's narrations – either as direct experiences or indirectly when helping other IDP women upon their arrival. Such accounts are also replicated by many of the men displaced, concerned with the specific hardships for female relatives. Pashto poetry has always served as poetry of resistance, also in displacement, such as in the words of Muhammad Salem, displaced to Bannu: 'Look at what has happened, o Khattak, our women are bareheaded and barefoot, forced out of their homes; see what has become of us' (Kohari 2014, 40).

More often than not it is an accumulation of stressful incidents and challenges to negotiate while lacking access to adequate support and resources, as in the case of one woman interviewed in late 2015. While being displaced in 2007 to Parachinar, her daughter and sister were injured. After reaching Parachinar and setting up life there, she lost her husband and nephew in a bomb blast, while her son was also seriously injured. Having to negotiate the hardships of displacement as a widow, she struggles to provide care, not only for her traumatised sister-in-law, but also without sufficient familial and government support, as she explained in the following interview quote.

> I had a good life before. After [my] husband's death, I face many problems. It's very difficult to provide food, education and other facilities to my children. My son was in bed for one year. We had to take him monthly to Peshawar for treatment. (…) Even our family did not support us in times of difficulty.

Displacement also tears the social fabric of the community and more often than not shrinks protected spaces of interaction, such as the space and time for women to discuss their problems when habitually fetching water during the evenings. The shrinking of spaces for interaction, for example, in camp-based or urban displacement, thus leads to further isolation of women. In villages they could participate in the economic activities of their family, particularly in growing crops, vegetables on the family landholdings, apart from looking after the livestock, the production of milk, butter, ghee and cheese. These rural spaces are also in stark contrast to towns and cities, the urban displacement, and when the separation from one's extended family support system presents additional challenges to tackle in situations where basic service provisions and infrastructure are lacking.

> It's better to have relatives in other villages, so that they can help you in times of need. My sister provided us blankets, pillows and other utensils. The house in which we were living was in a deserted area, I was afraid of insects. (…) There were

> scorpions, centipedes and other insects in the home. After some time I bought a hen which produced chicks, and after a few months, we had a lot of hens. So these centipedes were eaten by the chicken and we relaxed. There was a large uncultivated piece of land at this house. I asked my sister to give me seeds of red beans and other vegetables. So I spent most of my time in cultivating vegetables and beans. In front of our home, there was an empty house, which was destroyed, so water from different places like the hospital's waste water, the city's *nullah* [here: open sewer] and rain water collected in the basement of the house. We used this water for the laundry, bathing and keeping personal hygiene. For drinking, we fetched water from faraway places, while for other purposes we used water from the basement. (…) For three years we used that water.

They had to negotiate strict normative regimes and gendered restrictions on mobility and access to resources as highlighted above. Such restrictions are not only due to situations of displacement but also arise in the course of a rising insurgency able to control areas of FATA and to impose gender-restrictive, misogynist interpretations. Implications are the destruction of schools for girls; acid attacks on female students; threats or active bans against women engaging in agricultural activities, employment in government and private institutions such as schools, hospitals, vocational training centres or travelling for private or professional reasons. One violent attack can send shock waves and signals through the community, as was the case of the health worker Suriya Bibi from Parachinar, mentioned to us during the course of interviews without daring to disclose details such as her name. The attack led to large-scale disenfranchisement of women from public spaces and salaried work, and from seeking medical care in other cities. As outlined by academic and activist Noreen Naseer after conversations held in 2013 in Parachinar, many women health workers and teachers resigned or went on indefinite leave after Suriya Bibi 'was ambushed on her way back to Peshawar in an ambulance, [when] she was raped and brutally killed by [the] Taliban. This was not reported in newspapers […] nor [was] any security provided by [the] local administration to female staff working in health services' (Naseer 2015, 134).

Veiling is also affected (and thus mobility, among other things) – changing from *chadors* being used in villages to burqas when in displacement, as highlighted by a schoolteacher from Lower Kurram, living as IDP since 2007, interviewed in late 2015. 'We had a good life before. Women were free to go outside for their work and jobs. Our children were playing in the fields. In Parachinar, we are limited to our homes while in the village we had a free life. The *purdah* system is strict here'. Despite the observance of *purdah*, she feels that this is in vain, having being displaced in the first place: 'Women are the honour of men in our society. We lost our honour after leaving our homes'. While this is an outlier opinion documented, many men were distressed about concerns over women's *purdah*, thus privacy, in public spaces and on the move – be it in camps, on the roadside, in houses rented, at registration or aid delivery points. Such violations of gender seclusion were repeatedly recorded in the interviews with male IDPs, which impacts negatively on practices regarded as integral to their specific socio-cultural identity. One negative outcome was not only the isolation of many women once in displacement – except for those girls able to access educational institutions – but also their being barred from accessing basic services and aid delivery while in (most frequently urban) displacement. Displacement could also have been a potential opportunity to link women with governance processes and networks, thus positively impacting on women's well-being as well as state-society relations in an otherwise highly constrained, violent and exclusionary setting of practices back at home.

Any Larger Lessons from 'Smaller' Worlds?

What emerges from the stories shared by those displaced is a perception of 'being between the devil and the deep blue sea', of being caught in the glocal 'Wars on Terror', of being orchestrated in a disempowering and dehumanising way in a revamped conflict configuration of a neo-colonial 'Great Game' which demands an exceedingly high cost of protracted sacrifice from local communities while at the same time silencing them and rendering them invisible.

Another narrative crystallising out of the many testimonies shared are experiences of othering, control and vilification, aided by the highly militarised context in which displacement as well as relief-cum-rehabilitation takes place. This taps into existing colonial legacies of the label of 'tribal communities', leading to de-solidarisation and contagion-based public responses and hence the further securitisation of intervention approaches and the invisibility of local communities' resilience and resistance towards militancy, political violence and displacement. This is linked to the narrative of 'only God is with us rather than anyone in Pakistan' – one of experiencing disrespect, humiliation and sacrifice as citizens of a State in conflict. Of a State that extends its citizenship rights and basic services in asymmetrical ways, if not imposing border regimes and body-borders at its centre as well as its periphery.

While displaced communities have displayed high levels of resilience in rebuilding livelihoods, in resisting political violence and radicalisation, this toll has a negative impact on building the sustainable and constructive state-society relations needed to overcome the conflict in the long term and to allow for healing and dismantling the many borders imposed, which are more than militarised gateways and obstacles to belonging as well as to post-conflict governance.

We can only reiterate that our explorations here are explorations – tentative and incomplete when juxtaposing displaced and their experiences and narratives thereof at the centre of our analysis without dismantling the prevailing hegemonic discourses or replacing the taken for granted terminologies and concepts with alternative ones. But turning the spotlight, allowing for visibility of those largely rendered invisible and pointing towards a number of problems of key terminologies used are for us small but nevertheless important submissions to a very much required debate about alternative conceptual frameworks and empirical data informing academic work on international relations and glocal conflicts.

The last words belong to Fazle Basir, the elderly poet from Khyber Agency, whose last wish is to publish his own poems. At least this one will be seen:

> I live the days and nights in this world. Some in glee, some in gloom.
>
> I'm left alone amid the lashings of anguish. And I had to endure them all alone.
>
> Some in glee, some in gloom.
>
> These are the kinds of days I live in this world. If someone thinks I feint; I swear this is how I live.
>
> These are the kind of days I live in this world. Some in glee, some in gloom.
>
> Don't say it all Basir, cease here. I'll tell you these tales some other day.
>
> These are the kind of days I live in this world.
>
> Such are the days I pass in this world.[18]

Notes

1. Interview conducted in late 2015 with 60-year-old woman, living since 2007 in displacement in Parachinar, Kurram Agency.
2. This represents the case of a large-scale military operation, for example, Zarb-e-Azb, and often repeated / cyclic large-scale displacements of a predominantly Sunni population from FATA, mainly driven by state-imposed, military-controlled mobility corridors to adjacent parts of Khyber Pakhtunkhwa.
3. This represents the case of a protracted context of political violence-cum-ideological-economic conflict and repeated to protracted displacement of a predominantly Shia minority population. Given discussions with interview partners from Kurram Agency, Rahat Batool argues that many see the conflict in this agency as one driven by geopolitical and ideological, as well as economic interests of insurgents given the strategic location and trans-border illicit trade routes of Kurram.
4. Accessed December 5, 2018. http://watson.brown.edu/costsofwar/about.
5. This data was provided by Ehsan Mehmood Khan (2014, 38) in the glossy magazine *Pique* in what appears to be one of the many contracted articles in favour of the military operation and its approach, given the tenor of the photos displayed, demonstrating the military as protector, as well as the data provided, objectifying IDPs as a 'contagion' to be taken care of, to ensure the safe crossing of 'body-borders'. Among the assistance details outlined, vaccination ranks prominently: 'polio vaccinations of 221,000 IDPs' along with details about cattle and poultry vaccinated. Such record taking also featured in the regular OCHA updates on Zarb-e-Azb.

6. Transcription of video interview of M. Ahmad with M. N. Rehman, IDP from North Waziristan, now living in Bannu, as interviewed in July 2014. Accessed December 5, 2018. http://www.tanqeed.org/2014/07/they-are-not-friends-to-the-pashtuns-voices-from-north-waziristan/.
7. Transcription of video interview of M. Ahmad with Nur Gul, IDP from North Waziristan, as interviewed on 24.06.2014. Accessed December 5, 2018. http://www.tanqeed.org/2014/07/i-am-from-waziristan-and-i-am-not-afraid-of-anyone-voices-from-north-waziristan/.
8. Transcribed from the interview conducted with Fazle Basir in the UNHCR Pakistan video 'The Displaced Poet'. Accessed October 5, 2016. unhrcpk.org/gallery/videos.
9. For a debate on terminologies see the long-standing analyses and debates in *Forced Migration Review*, e.g. on the term 'crisis migration' (Fagen 2014; Martin, Weerasinghe, and Taylor 2014; McAdam 2014).
10. Pakistan has signed this document and is also bound by further international humanitarian law.
11. For example, UNHCR and OCHA figures only refer to IDPs registered by the government, which by no means capture the whole scale of the displacement and which is problematised by the IDMC.
12. An example is the case of Cyril Almeida, journalist with Pakistan's leading English-language daily DAWN, who has been barred from leaving the country after writing critically about the Pakistani security agencies' dealing with militant outfits (Boone 2016).
13. At the time of writing, OCHA provided the following data on registered IDPs from FATA: since March 2015 188,963 families returned home (76,190 in 2016 alone) while 114,828 families remain in protracted displacement, amounting to a return ratio of 62% (17% of these returning households were female-headed). Those returnees continue to face a situation in which 72% of houses are fully damaged, thus shelter remains a huge problem in the upcoming winter months. The return ratio varies within FATA, ranging from the lowest with 42% in Orakzai to 88% in Khyber. The situation in the Waziristan agencies is one of continuously high protracted displacement: 44% of IDP families (out of which 7% female-headed) in the North and 54% (out of which 22% female-headed) in the South, equal to 84,521 registered IDP families (out of a total of 114,828) remain displaced from FATA due to military operations (OCHA 2016).
14. In this section, we rely on interviews conducted by Rahat Batool (2016) during her MPhil thesis research on *Women's Everyday Life Experiences of Militancy in FATA: A Case Study of Kurram Agency*, whose transcripts were made available to us. All subsequent steps of interpretation, evaluation and judgement are solely ours, the authors of this article. We would like to thank Rahat Batool for her support by granting us access to the interview data.
15. According to the Internal Displacement Monitoring Centre, the number of women IDPs is underrepresented due to a lack of identity documents, estimating that women represent 23% out of the total IDP population and children 54% (Glatz 2015, 3, 7). In the infographic of the Jinnah Institute disaggregated data for IDPs from North Waziristan / Zarb-e-Azb alone are provided, which slightly differ from the aggregated data from IDMC: 5% of households are headed by women, 0.6% by children while women represent 48.79% of IDPs (Jinnah Institute 2016).
16. In a report by UNHCR's former community development officer in Peshawar during the 2008/9 FATA displacements, Khadka (2010) outlines as one of the challenges for participatory camp management the restrictions faced by displaced women, be it in terms of ensuring the observance of *purdah* combined with related mobility restrictions in the access to washrooms, be it in terms of interacting with female staff members without

permission, be it in terms of women participating in gender-segregated committees formed to deal with issues such as water, education, food or security/protection while aiming to ensure inclusive representation of the whole IDP community.

17. As experienced during the course of the interviews conducted, many women faced multiple displacements and were not used to being given voice to share their worries and feelings or to narrating in a chronological way. A number of them preferred to sit in groups and share their experiences, often with strong emotions displayed, having rather learnt to silence themselves, augmented by the lack of psychosocial care and constrained, secluded living conditions in displacement.
18. Transcribed from the English subtitles of the poem recited in Pashto by Fazle Basir in the UNHCR Pakistan video 'The Displaced Poet'. Accessed October 5, 2016. unhrcpk.org/gallery/videos.

Acknowledgment

We acknowledge support by the Open Access Publication Fund of Humboldt-Universität zu Berlin.

References

Akbar, A. 2015. Selective mourning after Peshawar. *Tanqeed* (March). Accessed December 5, 2018. http://www.tanqeed.org/2015/03/selective-mourning-after-peshawar/.

Batool, R. 2016. *Women's everyday life experiences of militancy in FATA: A case study of Kurram Agency.* MPhil thesis (unpublished), Quaid-i-Azam University.

Boone, J. 2016. Leading Pakistani journalist banned from leaving the country. *Guardian* October 10, 2016. Accessed December 5, 2018. https://www.theguardian.com/world/2016/oct/10/pakistani-journalist-banned-leaving-country-cyril-almeida.

Brooks, J., C. DeCorse, and J. Walton. 2008. *Small worlds: Method, meaning, and narrative in microhistory.* Santa Fe NM: School for Advanced Research Press.

Cohen, R. 2014. Lessons from the development of the guiding principles on internal displacement. *Forced Migration Review* 45 (February):12–14.

Crawford, N. C. 2015. Costs of war. War-related death, injury and displacement in Afghanistan and Pakistan 2011-2014. Cost of War Project Discussion Paper. Providence: Brown University. Accessed December 5, 2018. http://watson.brown.edu/costsofwar/files/cow/imce/papers/2015/War%20Related%20Casualties%20Afghanistan%20and%20Pakistan%202001-2014%20FIN.pdf.

Crawford, N. C. 2016. Update on the human costs of war for Afghanistan and Pakistan, 2001 to mid 2016. Cost of War Discussion Paper. Providence: Brown University. Accessed December 5, 2018. http://watson.brown.edu/costsofwar/files/cow/imce/papers/2016/War%20in%20Afghanistan%20and%20Pakistan%20UPDATE_FINAL_corrected%20date.pdf.

Fagen, P. W. 2014. Flight to the cities. *Forced Migration Review* 45:14–17.

Farooq, U. February 11, 2013. Civilians bear brunt of Pakistan's war in the northwest. *Foreign Policy.* Accessed December 5, 2018. http://foreignpolicy.com/2013/02/11/civilians-bear-brunt-of-pakistans-war-in-the-northwest/.

Glatz, A.-K. 2015. *Pakistan: Solutions to displacement elusive for both new and protracted IDPs.* Geneva: Internal Displacement Monitoring Centre. Accessed October 5, 2016. http://www.internal-displacement.org/south-and-south-east-asia/pakistan/2015/pakistan-solutions-to-displacement-elusive-for-both-new-and-protracted-idps.

Human Rights Commission of Pakistan. 2015. *State of human rights 2014*. Lahore: UB Printers 2015.

Human Rights Commission of Pakistan. 2016. *State of human rights 2015*. Lahore: UB Printers 2016. Accessed December 5, 2018. http://hrcp-web.org/hrcpweb/wp-content/uploads/2016/04/Refugees.pdf.

Internal Displacement Monitoring Centre. 2015a. *Pakistan IDP figures analysis*. Geneva: IDMC. Accessed October 5, 2016. http://www.internal-displacement.org/south-and-south-east-asia/pakistan/figures-analysis/.

Internal Displacement Monitoring Centre. 2015. *Pakistan. Solutions to displacement elusive for both new and protracted IDPs*. Geneva: IDMC. Accessed October 5, 2016. http://www.internal-displacement.org/south-and-south-east-asia/pakistan/2015/pakistan-solutions-to-displacement-elusive-for-both-new-and-protracted-idps.

Internal Displacement Monitoring Centre (IDMC). 2016. *GRID 2016. Global report on internal displacement*. Geneva: IDMC. Accessed October 5, 2016. http://www.internal-displacement.org/assets/publications/2016/2016-global-report-internal-displacement-IDMC.pdf.

International Crisis Group. 2015. *Women, violence and conflict in Pakistan*. Asia Report No. 265, 8 April. Brussels: International Crisis Group. Accessed December 5, 2018. https://d2071andvip0wj.cloudfront.net/265-women-violence-and-conflict-in-pakistan.pdf.

Jinnah Institute. 2016. Rebuilding lives after Zarb-e-Azb. Accessed December 5, 2018. http://jinnah-institute.org/rebuilding-lives-after-zarb-e-azb/.

Khadka, S. B. 2010. Social mobilisation in IDP camps in Pakistan. *Forced Migration Review* 34:65.

Khan, E. M. 2014. Two months into Zarb-e-Azb. *Pique* (August):38.

Kohari, A. 2014. Home truths. How displacement means different things to different people. *Herald* (August):37–38.

Martin, S., S. Weerasinghe, and A. Taylor. 2014. What is crisis migration? *Forced Migration Review* 45:5–9.

McAdam, J. 2014. The concept of crisis migration. *Forced Migration Review* 45:10–11.

N.N. 2010. Most women-headed households not documented during military operations. *The News* December 30, 2010. Accessed December 5, 2018. https://www.thenews.com.pk/archive/print/277231-most-women-headed-households-not-documented-during-military-operations.

N.N. 2012. Women in tribal areas still live in fear. *The Express Tribune* January 30, 2012. Accessed December 5, 2018. http://tribune.com.pk/story/320569/women-in-tribal-areas-still-live-in-fear/.

N.N. 2013. Pakistani families forced to flee 'FATA paradise'. IRIN News June 10, 2013. Accessed December 5, 2018. https://www.irinnews.org/fr/node/253599.

Naseer, N. 2015. Federally Administered Tribal Areas (FATA): Impacts of militarisation and war crimes on tribal women and children. *Pakistan Journal of Criminology* 7 (4):129–39.

Nayak, M., and E. Selbin. 2010. *Decentering international relations*. London: Zed Books.

Rancière, J. 2006. *Disagreement: Politics and philosophy*. Minneapolis/London: University of Minnesota Press.

Shuja, S., and D. Wazir. 2016. Suspect citizens. *Tanqueed* (June). Accessed December 5, 2018. http://www.tanqeed.org/2016/06/suspect-citizens/.

United Nations Office for the Coordination of Humanitarian Affairs (OCHA). 2004. *Guiding principles on internal displacement*. Geneva: United Nations. Accessed December 5, 2018. https://docs.unocha.org/sites/dms/Documents/GuidingPrinciplesDispl.pdf.

United Nations Office for the Coordination of Humanitarian Affairs (OCHA). 2014. Pakistan: North Waziristan Displacements Situation Report No. 10 (as of

2 September 2014). Accessed December 5, 2018. http://reliefweb.int/sites/reliefweb.int/files/resources/OCHA%20Pakistan_NWA%20Displacements_Situation%20Report%20No.10_Final.pdf.

United Nations Office for the Coordination of Humanitarian Affairs (OCHA). 2014a. Pakistan: North Waziristan Displacements Situation Report No. 4 (as of 30 June 2014). Accessed December 5, 2018. http://reliefweb.int/sites/reliefweb.int/files/resources/OCHA%20Pakistan_NWA%20Displacements_Situation%20Report%20No.4.pdf.

United Nations Office for the Coordination of Humanitarian Affairs (OCHA). 2014b. Pakistan: North Waziristan Displacements Situation Report No. 3 (as of 27 June 2014). Accessed December 5, 2018. http://reliefweb.int/sites/reliefweb.int/files/resources/OCHA%20Pakistan_NWA%20Displacements_Situation%20Report%20No.%203_ah.pdf.

United Nations Office for the Coordination of Humanitarian Affairs (OCHA). 2016. FATA return weekly snapshot (from 23 to 29 September 2016). Accessed December 5, 2018. http://reliefweb.int/sites/reliefweb.int/files/resources/weekly_return_snapshot_from_23_to_29_september_2016.pdf.

The Moving Border of the China-Pakistan Economic Corridor

Alvin Cheng-Hin Lim

ABSTRACT

This article will read the China-Pakistan Economic Corridor (CPEC), whose infrastructure and installations are currently being built across Pakistan, as a moving border-making event which inscribes difference within Pakistan. The article will begin with a discussion of borders and border-making. The discussion will then turn to the different registers of difference that will be created in Pakistan through CPEC. The article will conclude with a speculative look at how Pakistan and the wider region may be impacted once the construction of CPEC is complete.

Introduction

Chinese President Xi Jinping's Belt and Road Initiative (BRI) has attracted attention in recent years as it represents a special mode of globalization that is led by the Chinese state (Fallon 2015). This article will focus on one of the showpiece projects of the BRI—the China-Pakistan Economic Corridor (CPEC), whose infrastructure and installations are currently being built across Pakistan. To better understand CPEC, the project will be read as a moving border-making event which inscribes difference within Pakistan. The following registers of difference which are being inscribed within Pakistan by CPEC will be discussed: the installation of technology; changes in the population; changes in financial flows; and the entry and propagation of new media images and their associated ideas and ideologies. As the planners of CPEC expect neighbouring countries to welcome the extension of CPEC's infrastructure into their territories once the project is completed in Pakistan, this moving border of difference-making may expand outwards from Pakistan into the region. This article will conclude with a speculative consideration of how the region may be transformed should this happen.

Color versions of one or more of the figures in the article can be found online at www.tandfonline.com/fgeo.

Borders and Border-Making

While borders are commonly recognized as their material manifestations—'territorial fences . . . border walls, and ports of entry'—each of which is 'composed of a complex mixture of different types of power,' the border broadly understood may be seen as 'a process of social division,' in that it generates 'a division or bifurcation of some sort into the world' (Nail 2016, 1-10). Ulrich Best's Deleuzian reading of the border draws on this general understanding of the border, and identifies it as 'the line where things cease to be and become different.' On this reading, the border has the potential to be 'a line of flight, a line along which deterritorialization takes place.' Such deterritorialization may be understood as the process of the erasure of meanings which had earlier been overcoded onto things by the State, leaving a 'smooth space' upon which new meanings may be inscribed onto things (Best 2003, 184-188). Gilles Deleuze and Félix Guattari themselves have highlighted capitalism as having triumphed over the State with its 'superior deterritorialization,' allowing it to form 'a de facto supranational power untouched by governmental decisions' (Deleuze and Guattari 1987, 453-454). As we shall see, one source of suspicion about CPEC stems from fears of constituencies within Pakistan of its deterritorializing potential—that is, its potential to recode the meanings of things which had originally been overcoded by local communities. On this view of CPEC as a deterritorializing force, its gradual expansion across Pakistan may be seen as a moving border which introduces difference into the territories it expands into (Nail 2016).

The differences that are thereby generated from border-making may be analysed according to the distinct registers of social and economic life that are impacted by the arrival of the border. Arjun Appadurai's famous analysis of the five '-scapes' of globalization gives us a useful framework for studying these different registers of difference, beyond the usual tripartite demarcation of the 'social, economic, and political' (Agnew 2009, 30). Appadurai's 'ethnoscape' focuses on the mobile bodies ('tourists, immigrants, refugees, exiles, guestworkers and other moving groups and persons') who constitute the human capital of global flows; the 'technoscape' focuses on the flows and distribution of technology; the 'finanscape' focuses on global flows of financial capital; the 'mediascape' focuses on the audio-visual content disseminated through global media channels; and the 'ideoscape' focuses on the ideas and ideologies disseminated through the global flows of media content and human bodies (Appadurai 1990, 297–301).

Engseng Ho observes that anthropologists like Appadurai who have theorized the mobility of globalization have 'reintroduced a teleology of progress that had previously been derided and, so it seemed, discarded,' and that when documenting the mobility of non-Western peoples, have placed them 'in Western-pioneered vehicles that are overwhelmingly technological and modern' (Ho 2006, 10). In the case of CPEC, such a teleology of Western technological progress is warranted, insofar as CPEC is part of the Chinese Communist Party's long-term project to help other developing countries achieve economic growth through the implementation of the same model of industrialization and strategic adoption of modern Western technology that had allowed the Chinese economy to rapidly expand from a low level of economic development—'squarely between Mozambique and Burma'—just after the Cultural Revolution to the world's second-largest economy just a few decades later (Brautigam 2009, 46–54). Insofar as Appadurai's '-scapes' enable us to track the microhistories of local communities undergoing globalization—be it Western- or Chinese-led—the application of his schema will also enable us 'to track the origin of the personnel, financing, and technology of the system in order to develop a more holistic image of the forces at play on the global stage' (Valentine 2015, 9).

Using Appadurai's schema, we may hence unpack the differences created by CPEC *qua* border-making event (Figure 1). At the register of the technoscape, CPEC may be understood as the event of installation of the technological infrastructure required for the future industrialization of the underdeveloped regions of Pakistan. At the register of the ethnoscape, CPEC has introduced into Pakistan not just the inbound migration of Chinese management and labour but also, as we shall see, covert inflows of other bodies disguised under the cover of CPEC. At the register of the finanscape, CPEC has opened the Pakistani economy to global flows of Chinese capital and debt. At the registers of the

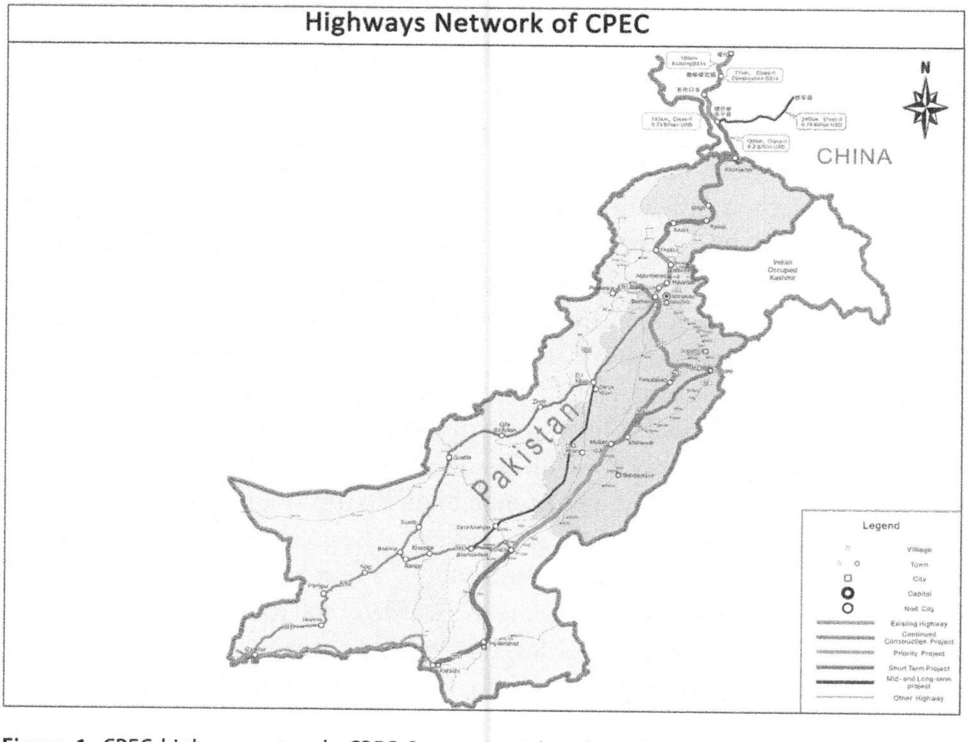

Figure 1. CPEC highway network. CPEC Secretariat, Islamabad, Pakistan.

mediascape and ideoscape, the new communications infrastructure that will be installed under CPEC may be expected to expose communities in Pakistan to new media images and ideas from the outside world, including news and entertainment productions from global media corporations like the Chinese state-owned China Global Television Network. The new communications infrastructure may also be deployed by non-state actors such as separatist and jihadist militant groups to propagate their particular non-state-sanctioned ideoscapes.

Instead of being just 'residual spaces' in given territories, borders are also 'key sites of contestation and negotiation' in these different registers of social and economic life (Korf and Raeymaekers 2013, 5). As we shall see of the violence triggered by the expansion of CPEC, the transgressive and subversive behaviour of populations at the border—including those at CPEC's moving border of difference—demonstrate how 'creating a bounded space is ... a violent act of exclusion and inclusion; maintaining it ... requires constant vigilance and the mobilization of threat; and challenging it necessarily entails a transgression' (Elden 2009, xxx). Such acts of transgression or compliance don't just occur at border crossings, but also when people 'encounter borders in their multiple locations in their daily lives' (Johnson and Jones 2014, 6). Borders, as Étienne Balibar reminds us, 'are no longer entirely situated at the outer limit of territories,' and have instead become diffused throughout the territory, 'dispersed a little everywhere, wherever the movement of information, people, and things is happening and is controlled' (Balibar 2003, 1). Balibar's notion of the diffuse border may be read as an elaboration of the Deleuzian notion of contemporary societies having finely modulated controls like 'a sieve whose mesh will transmute from point to point' (Deleuze 1992, 4). In the case of CPEC, the securitization that will accompany the establishment of its critical infrastructure (Gwadar Port, the oil and gas pipelines, the new network of power stations) and its industrial zones will create precisely this diffusion of the border throughout Pakistani territory, with only screened and approved personnel being allowed to cross into CPEC installations. Such securitization will also shape the technoscape whose growth in Pakistan and the region will accelerate under CPEC. With the rapid development of security technology, the increasingly sophisticated surveillance and securitization measures that may be expected to be installed at CPEC will inflect the Pakistani and regional technoscape with a strong tilt towards the mass deployment of hermetic security technology and controls.

CPEC and the BRI

The origins of CPEC can be traced back to 2012 when Wang Jisi, the Dean of Peking University's School of International Studies, proposed that China pivot its geopolitical strategy westward into the Eurasian landmass. This proposal become state policy in 2013 when Chinese President Xi Jinping officially announced the Silk Road Economic Belt (SREB) and the twenty-first-century Maritime Silk Road (MSR), the dual development plans for large-scale Chinese outward direct investment spanning not just the Eurasian landmass but also the coastal states of the South China Sea and the Indian Ocean (Garlick 2017; Wang 2012; Yun 2013). Together the SREB and MSR comprise the two arms of the BRI. For countries like Pakistan, the BRI offers opportunities to upgrade their transportation, energy, communications, and industrial infrastructure with Chinese financing; for China, the BRI serves as one of the new engines of growth powering its economic transition from double- to single-digit GDP growth. By generating external demand for the export of industrial capital from Chinese state-owned and private enterprises, the BRI facilitates the government's strategy of transitioning China from its 'old normal' manufacturing-based economy to a 'new normal' consumption-based economy, and also facilitates the progress of China's supply-side reform process by helping reduce China's domestic industrial overcapacity ('China to resolutely implement supply-side reform' 2016; Lim 2015a, 2-3; 2015b, 3-5).

In April 2015, President Xi made his inaugural state visit to Pakistan and used the occasion to announce the details of CPEC, which had been launched 2 years earlier by Chinese Premier Li Keqiang during his 2013 state visit to Pakistan. CPEC, which China sees as its flagship BRI project in South Asia, consists of a range of infrastructure investments which at the time of President Xi's visit were worth 46 billion USD. By April 2017, China's planned investments in CPEC had increased to 62 billion USD, and in May 2017, during the inaugural Belt and Road Forum in Beijing, President Xi and Pakistan's then-President Nawaz Sharif signed agreements for additional CPEC projects worth 500 million USD. The large value of China's planned investments in CPEC reflects Pakistan's strategic position in the BRI, as CPEC provides a physical connection between the SREB and the MSR through the port of Gwadar on the Arabian Sea. While corruption and violence in Pakistan had derailed previous Chinese projects in the country, CPEC is expected to be different as the Chinese government is committed to the success of the BRI. A number of 'early harvest' CPEC projects—several highway projects and power plants—are scheduled to be completed by 2018, and their completion is intended to demonstrate to the Pakistani public the commitment to the full completion of CPEC of the Chinese and Pakistani governments (Lim 2017a, 2015c; Siddiqui 2017).

Technoscape

When complete, CPEC's technoscape will consist of an upgraded and expanded highway and railway network, new oil and gas pipelines, new power plants, an upgraded and expanded electrical grid, new and upgraded communications infrastructure—including the installation of a fibre optic cable which will extend from the Chinese border city of Kashgar in the Xinjiang Uygur Autonomous Region to the Pakistani city of Rawalpindi—as well as new industrial zones that will generate the economic activity that will in turn increase usage of the new infrastructure. The CPEC transportation corridor and the oil and gas pipelines will cross the 2,000 miles from Gwadar Port to Kashgar. The CPEC oil pipeline in particular will provide the geographically shortest route for China to receive its oil imports from Africa and the Middle East, and when complete, will transport 1 million barrels of oil per day, with China eventually planning to receive 17% of its oil imports through this pipeline. CPEC's highways and railways will likewise provide logistics companies with an attractive alternative to the increasingly crowded maritime route through the Straits of Malacca, with CPEC's overland route potentially reducing shipping times and costs by half (Lim 2016a; Yousafzai 2016).

The CPEC technoscape will also include a number of new coal-fired and clean-energy power plants—including hydroelectric, wind, and solar—which will help Pakistan double its electricity generation capacity. This is particularly important as one of the major impediments to Pakistan's industrial development has been the country's insufficient supply of electricity. Once the construction of CPEC is complete, the increase in the electrical supply, the accessibility provided by the new transportation infrastructure, and the employment and business opportunities generated by the new industrial zones will together be expected to generate significant amounts of new economic activity that could deliver developmental benefits to the local communities. The tantalizing prospect of the establishment of peace and security in Pakistan and the wider region arising from the acceleration of economic development is a key reason why the U.S. has voiced its support for the CPEC initiative (Garver 2006; Lim 2015c).

Ethnoscape

As the moving border of CPEC gradually expands across Pakistan, the settlement in local communities of the Chinese ethnoscape which has arrived with the establishment of the growing number of CPEC installations will increasingly lead to contact between the migrants and the local communities, and in some cases such contact may lead to violent conflict. The Baloch people of Balochistan province—home of the strategic CPEC installation of Gwadar Port—are a prime example. The conflict of the Baloch with CPEC stems from their perception of the territory of Balochistan as their own, and of the projects initiated on Baloch land by the Pakistani state or foreigners like the Chinese as essentially alien. The Baloch have a long history of the capture and reorganization of their traditional lands by external powers, and

Baloch separatist leaders—functioning as 'ethnopolitical entrepreneurs'—have highlighted to their followers the ethnic differences between the local Baloch and the Chinese ethnoscape that has been brought into Balochistan by CPEC, and have also warned their followers of the threat to Baloch identity and sovereignty posed by these foreigners. The Balochistan Liberation Front, for instance, has denounced CPEC as an 'occupation' of Baloch land, and has warned that 'its fighters would attack anyone working on the project' (Brubaker 2002, 166; Lim 2016b).

The fear of the Baloch of the potential of CPEC's ethnoscape to erase their local identity is succinctly expressed through George Ritzer's conception of globalization as the production of 'nothing,' in that globalization erases the substantial world of locally rooted objects and replaces it with the nothingness of a world of objects that is radically disconnected from the local community (Ritzer 2007). As he explains, while objects in the local world count as 'something,' given that they are 'indigenously conceived, controlled, and comparatively rich in distinctive substantive content,' the products of globalization count as 'nothing' as they are 'centrally conceived, controlled, and comparatively devoid of distinctive substantive content' (Ritzer 2003, 191). The marketplace of objects brought by the Chinese ethnoscape into Balochistan hence threaten to swamp out the smaller number of locally rooted objects which hold substantive meaning for the Baloch.

In addition, the unfamiliarity to the Baloch of the distinctive cultural practices of the Chinese ethnoscape could exacerbate ethnic tensions and further racialize the territorial contestations over the use of Baloch land. Here Slavoj Žižek describes how differences in cultural practices may intensify ethnic tensions:

> We always impute to the 'other' an excessive enjoyment: he wants to steal our enjoyment (by ruining our way of life) and/or he has access to some secret, perverse enjoyment. In short, what really bothers us about the 'other' is the peculiar way he organizes his enjoyment, precisely the surplus, the 'excess' that pertains to this way: the smell of 'their' food, 'their' noisy songs and dances, 'their' strange manners, 'their' attitude to work. (Žižek 1993, 202-203)

Sinophobia among the Baloch could be further intensified with the discovery of the covert infiltration of Chinese Christian missionaries into Baloch lands under the cover of CPEC. Such missionary work was exposed in May 2017 when two Chinese nationals who had set up what was ostensibly a Chinese-language school in Quetta, the capital of Balochistan province, were kidnapped and murdered by Islamic State (IS) militants. The police investigation into their murders soon revealed that the language school had actually been a front for missionary work, and the Pakistani government subsequently repatriated back to China eleven other Christian missionaries who had arrived in the same group as the murder victims (Abdelaty and

Yousufzai 2017; Lau 2017). Covert ethnoscapes such as this transnational flow of missionaries highlight the structural complexity of human migratory flows under CPEC—what appears to be a simple state-led flow of bodies for economic co-operation disguises flows for other purposes, some of which may be at odds with the intentions of the Chinese and Pakistani states. The murders of the two missionaries may also be seen as a preview of future clashes in the expanding CPEC zone between the Chinese ethnoscape and local populations such as the Baloch. Underground church leaders in China have set the target to increase the number of their covert missionaries in foreign countries from the estimated 1,000 at present to 20,000 by 2030, and they fully intend to use the BRI as their gateway into foreign mission fields. As the pastor of an underground church in Shanghai explained: 'We have the Belt and Road policy, so there will be economic entry. Alongside the economic entry will be companies and other groups entering, including missionaries' (Hancock 2017).

Baloch rage against the Pakistani state and CPEC has economic roots in their province's resource curse: while Balochistan has the greatest share in Pakistan of the country's natural wealth, the province remains the poorest in the country. This is due to the history of the external exploitation of Balochistan's natural wealth—a history which involves the Chinese. The profit-sharing arrangement for the Saindak copper mine, for example, grants 50% of its profits to its Chinese owners, 48% to the Pakistani government, and just 2% to the Baloch provincial government. It is through such external exploitation that the Baloch have found themselves excluded from their land's natural bounty. The Baloch separatists hence not only seek autonomy for Balochistan, but also full control over its natural resources (Khan 2009).

The Baloch perception of the unfairness suffered by their people is a related factor that has given rise to their resentment of CPEC and its ethnoscape. The Chinese development of Gwadar Port became the 'main trigger' for the intensification of separatist unrest not just after the arrival of Chinese migrants, but also after it emerged that the Pakistanis who had been hired to work in Gwadar had been recruited primarily from provinces outside Balochistan, while the few Baloch who had found employment there had primarily been employed in the lowest-paid jobs. The Baloch hence quickly perceived Gwadar Port to be not just as an instrument of foreign exploitation by the Chinese and colonization by the Chinese ethnoscape, but also internal colonization by the Pakistani state (Khan 2009, 1078–80).

Finanscape

With CPEC, Pakistan has become an active participant in the Chinese finanscape. The Pakistani government is paying for CPEC projects with loans from Chinese policy banks such as the Export-Import Bank of China, as well as

Chinese international financial institutions such as the Silk Road Fund and the Asian Infrastructure Investment Bank. In the case of the CPEC energy projects, the Chinese lenders providing the estimated 35 billion USD in loans will receive 'uninterrupted payments' from Pakistan through 'revolving funds backed by sovereign guarantees' ('ECC approves plan to set up special funds for CPEC projects' 2016; Dasgupta 2016; Markey and West 2016). To ensure that the cost of constructing CPEC does not overwhelm Pakistani state finances, the projects which will be constructed under the CPEC framework have been divided into three groups: short, medium, and long term; these projects have to be completed by 2020, 2025, and 2030, respectively. Hence, instead of having to pay for all the projects at one go, the Pakistani government will pay for them in manageable groups. In 2017, the Pakistani government budgeted 180 billion rupees (approximately 1.71 billion USD) for CPEC projects, up from the 151 billion rupees allocated in 2015 and 115 billion rupees in 2016 (Rana 2015; Rehman 2016).

While the size of loans for BRI infrastructure projects can be large, from the perspective of the Chinese government they need not be burdensome for the indebted country. As Zhang Ming, China's Vice Foreign Minister, explained at the opening in Kenya of the standard-gauge Nairobi-Mombasa railway line—one of the key MSR projects in Africa: 'When a debt is put in the right project, it is not a burden … It will lead to economic growth of the whole region, which means that the debt will be paid' (Mutambo 2017). Given the huge cost of the CPEC projects, however, there is a risk that they could have a negative impact on the economy if the completed infrastructure turns out to be underutilized. Atif Ansar *et al.* warn that 'unproductive projects carry unintended pernicious macroeconomic consequences.' These negative consequences include 'volatile movements in interest, exchange, and inflation rates; unpredictable movements in asset prices, such as house prices and listed public equities; adverse growth outcomes; rising unemployment from deleveraging; and lack of capital to finance productive investments.' Indeed, China's slate of poorly planned domestic infrastructure investments have led to 'cost overruns and benefit shortfalls,' with the cost overruns contributing to 'approximately one-third of China's US$28.2 trillion debt pile,' and contributing in turn to the Chinese economy's 'increased financial and economic fragility' (Ansar et al. 2016, 382-385).

Sri Lanka's unhappy experience with the Chinese finanscape offers a cautionary tale for the Pakistani government. As of May 2017, the Sri Lankan government owes China 8 billion USD in debt—out of almost 64 billion USD in total debt—and almost 95% of the country's 'government revenues go towards debt repayment.' The Sri Lankan government had spent its 8 billion USD in Chinese loans on major infrastructure projects—Hambantota Port and Mattala Rajapaksa International Airport—which when completed turned out to be very poorly utilized. Violent protests erupted in January 2017 when the Sri Lankan government, in exchange for

1.1 billion USD in Chinese debt relief, granted a Chinese state-owned enterprise an 80% stake in Hambantota Port and a 99-year lease on a neighbouring 15,000-acre special economic zone. Fears of forced evictions from the planned special economic zone and Sinophobic fears that Hambantota would become a 'Chinese colony' fuelled the social unrest, and the dispute has threatened further Chinese investment in the country (Lim 2017b; Limaye 2017).

A separate cautionary tale comes from Venezuela, where the government's 63 billion USD in Chinese debt has exacerbated the country's economic crisis. Preempting the possibility of regime change, China has taken care to warn Venezuela's opposition leaders 'not to default on the existing debts.' Instead of an advanced technoscape, the Venezuelan government's failure to keep up payments to the Chinese contractors constructing its major infrastructure projects such as the Tinaco-Anaco high-speed railway—which would have been 'South America's first'—has instead littered the Venezuelan landscape with the gutted ruins of abandoned construction sites (Balding 2017; Goodman 2016).

Despite these political and economic risks, Pakistan's participation in the Chinese finanscape has improved its position in the global finanscape, thanks to the inflow of 'China-funded loans and investments.' On 31 May 2017, the global investment research agency MSCI officially recognized this by promoting Pakistan from its Frontier Market (FM) to its Emerging Market (EM) Index. Pakistan had been in the MSCI EM Index between 1994 and 2007 but had been downgraded to the FM Index following its poor economic performance during the 2008 global financial crisis. With its return to the MSCI EM Index, financial experts expect Pakistan to receive 'inflows of $300-$500 million into the Pakistani equity market from global players who invest through EM index funds' (Hussain 2017; Malik 2017). As with the early harvest projects in the CPEC technoscape, these global financial inflows may be seen as an early harvest for Pakistan's participation in the Chinese finanscape.

Mediascape and Ideoscape

While the Pakistani state has delivered developmentalist narratives of the benefits of CPEC to the public though its media apparatuses, jihadist groups like the Pakistani Taliban have disseminated anti-CPEC media content through their internet-based mass media networks such as the Global Islamic Media Front, and their channels on smartphone applications such as the Telegram app. These competing mediascapes, and the ideoscapes which are propagated through them, are poised to reach larger populations within Pakistan and the region once Pakistan's communications infrastructure is upgraded and expanded under CPEC (Anzalone 2011; Bodetti 2016).

Just as jihadist militias pose significant threats of violence against the Pakistani people and the Chinese ethnoscape, the jihadist mediascape and ideoscape seek to attract volunteer fighters and raise public support for their stated cause of defending the global *Ummah* (Muslim community) against infidel threats. To attract recruits and to motivate their fighters, the content of the jihadist mediascape includes news and video footage of successful terrorist strikes, including those on CPEC personnel and installations. Of particular concern for CPEC are the jihadis from IS, as the group regards Balochistan as offering 'an opportunity to not only strike at Pakistani interests, but also those of China' (Hussain 2016). One such attack which was publicized on IS' media channels was the aforementioned kidnapping and murder in Quetta of the two Chinese-language teachers-cum-missionaries (Ahrari 2000; Hussain 2016).

Conclusion: CPEC beyond Pakistan

This article has examined how the moving border of CPEC is generating difference across Pakistan. At the level of physical infrastructure, the establishment of CPEC projects across the country is either expanding the technoscape or establishing a proto-technoscape upon which the technoscape may eventually expand into. This repurposing of land by the Pakistani state and Chinese investors has provoked resistance—with occasional violence—at the local level. At the level of the population, a Chinese ethnoscape has arrived with the CPEC projects, transforming the ethnic mix of the local populations and turning the project sites into targets of violence for separatist and jihadist militants. At the level of financial capital, Pakistan has been enfolded into the Chinese finanscape. While this has attracted further inflows of global financial capital, the increased indebtedness also brings with it increased risks for the Pakistani economy. At the levels of the media and ideas, the improvements to Pakistan's communications infrastructure under CPEC will offer the local population not just greater access to audiovisual and ideological content from state-approved global media providers, but also from media providers which are not sanctioned by the state, such as the international jihadist media. As CPEC moves into its middle phase, the intensification of these different registers of difference could potentially trigger greater acts of violence from separatist and jihadist militants, thereby threatening the final completion of CPEC.

In response to the threats posed by the separatist and jihadist militants, the Pakistani government has established 'a 15,000-strong army division' to protect CPEC. Apart from this special army division, the province of Punjab has established a special protection unit for CPEC installations within its territory which 'has more than 6,000 officers and is set to grow to 10,000.' Sindh and Khyber Pakhtunkhwa provinces are also establishing special protection units for their CPEC installations (Jorgic, Hassan and Yousafzai 2017). Over time, these nascent security forces may be expected to form the material basis for the eventual securitization of the diffuse border which CPEC is establishing throughout Pakistan.

In the case that CPEC is successfully completed in Pakistan, it could potentially expand outwards from Pakistan into the wider region, bringing along with its moving border its ethnoscape, technoscape, finanscape, mediascape, and ideoscape. These countries' interest in CPEC stems from its potential to facilitate the economic integration of the region, as well as other economic benefits that the new infrastructure could deliver. The Central Asian countries of Kazakhstan, Tajikistan, Turkmenistan, and Uzbekistan, for example, are interested in the access to the maritime trade of the Arabian Sea and the Indian Ocean that the extension of CPEC's highway and railway networks into their territories will provide. One possible connectivity project is the proposed SREB railway line that would extend the Gwadar-Kashgar railway that will be built under CPEC from Kashgar through Kyrgyzstan to the Uzbek industrial hub of Andijan. Such infrastructure development under the SREB is expected to stimulate regional economic growth by expanding Central Asia's connectivity with the Caspian and Caucasus regions. The optimal forecast for the economic integration that could be catalysed by the expansion of CPEC into Central and South Asia sees the creation of 'a trading bloc of 3 billion people, nearly half of the planet.' Khurram Dastagir, Pakistan's former Commerce Minister, observes that such economic integration would deliver a significant boost to global development, as this potential trading bloc includes 'half of world's extreme poor,' and the increased economic activity arising from trade would create 'opportunities of new and better work for the poor' (Lim 2016a; Norling and Swanström 2007, 365; Shahbazov 2017). However, should CPEC expand beyond Pakistan, terrorism and other transnational problems could become further complexified by the deeper entanglement—facilitated by the increased physical connectivity—of the countries concerned with the anti-state or criminal activities of groups such as IS.

In the longer term, the successful completion of CPEC and its anticipated expansion into Central and South Asia may be seen as a restoration of China's ancient economic and cultural ties with Pakistan and the region, which were historically manifested in the transcontinental trade and missionary networks across the ancient Silk Road (Docherty 2007; Frankopan 2015). In the twentieth century following the post-war period of decolonization, China and Pakistan had famously declared their friendship to be that of 'iron brothers,' and the fruits of their relationship were primarily found in the covert military realm, where the Chinese and Pakistani intelligence services exchanged material and knowledge to facilitate their development of strategic military technologies such as nuclear weapons and ballistic missiles (Afridi and Bajoria 2010; Small 2015a). In the economic realm, prior to the launch of CPEC, the showpiece project of Sino-Pakistani co-operation had been the Karakoram Highway across the Karakoram mountain range, which was successfully completed despite significant economic and security challenges (Small 2015b). However, other economic co-operation projects were failures, with insecurity being a major cause. Pakistan eventually 'developed a reputation as the most dangerous country to be an overseas Chinese, with kidnappings and killings taking place with disturbing regularity' (Small 2015b, 99–102). The establishment of reliable security arrangements for CPEC will hence be critical towards ensuring its successful completion and the future mass utilization of its infrastructure. The spatial distribution of CPEC, covering troubled areas like Balochistan and the Afghan-Pakistani borderlands where the jihadist militant groups are based, poses significant security challenges; but if these are met, the moving border of CPEC promises to bring significant economic and social transformation not just to Pakistan, but also the region.

ORCID

Alvin Cheng-Hin Lim http://orcid.org/0000-0001-9356-2122

References

Abdelaty, A., and G. Yousufzai. 2017. Islamic State says it killed two Chinese teachers kidnapped in Pakistan. *Reuters*. http://www.channelnewsasia.com/news/asiapacific/islamic-state-says-it-killed-two-chinese-teachers-kidnapped-in-pakistan-8930506.

Afridi, J., and J. Bajoria. 2010. China-Pakistan relations. *Council on Foreign Relations*. http://www.cfr.org/china/china-pakistan-relations/p10070.

Agnew, J. 2009. *Globalization and sovereignty*. Lanham, NC: Rowman & Littlefield.

Ahrari, M. E. 2000. China, Pakistan, and the 'Taliban syndrome'. *Asian Survey* 40 (4):658–71. doi:10.2307/3021187.

Ansar, A., B. Flyvbjerg, A. Budzier, and D. Lunn. 2016. Does infrastructure investment lead to economic growth or economic fragility? Evidence from China. *Oxford Review of Economic Policy* 32:360–90. doi:10.1093/oxrep/grw022.

Anzalone, C. 2011. The Pakistani Taliban's media jihad. *Foreign Policy*, June 17. http://foreignpolicy.com/2011/06/17/the-pakistani-talibans-media-jihad/.

Appadurai, A. 1990. Disjuncture and difference in the global cultural economy. *Theory, Culture & Society* 7 (2):295–310. doi:10.1177/026327690007002017.

Balding, C. 2017. Venezuela's road to disaster is littered with Chinese cash. *Foreign Policy*, June 6. http://foreignpolicy.com/2017/06/06/venezuelas-road-to-disaster-is-littered-with-chinese-cash/.

Balibar, E. 2003. *We, the people of Europe? Reflections on transnational citizenship*. J. Swenson (trans.). Princeton, NJ: Princeton University Press.

Best, U. 2003. Gnawing at the edges of the state: Deleuze and Guattari and border studies. In *Routing borders between territories, discourses and practices*, ed. E. Berg and H. Van Houtum, 177–90. Farnham, UK: Ashgate.

Bodetti, A. 2016. The Taliban's latest battlefield: Social media. *The Diplomat*, September 8. http://thediplomat.com/2016/09/the-talibans-latest-battlefield-social-media/.

Brautigam, D. 2009. *The dragon's gift: The real story of China in Africa*. Oxford, UK: Oxford University Press.

Brubaker, R. 2002. Ethnicity without groups. *Archives Européennes De Sociology* 43 (2):163–89. doi:10.1017/S0003975602001066.

China to resolutely implement supply-side reform. 2016. *Xinhua*, July 27. http://www.china.org.cn/business/2016-07/27/content_38965349.htm.

Dasgupta, S. 2016. First financing by China-backed AIIB goes to Silk Road plan in Pakistan. *Times of India*, May 2. http://timesofindia.indiatimes.com/world/china/First-financing-by-China-backed-AIIB-goes-to-Silk-Road-plan-in-Pakistan/articleshow/52082622.cms.

Deleuze, G. 1992. Postscript on the Societies of Control. *October* 59:3-7. Volume 59.

Deleuze, G., and F. Guattari. 1987. *A thousand plateaus: Capitalism and schizophrenia*. B. Massumi (trans.). Minneapolis, MN: University of Minnesota Press.

Docherty, P. 2007. *The Khyber Pass: A history of empire and invasion*. New York, NY: Union Square Press.

ECC approves plan to set up special funds for CPEC projects. 2016. *Dawn*, February 19. http://www.dawn.com/news/1240546.

Elden, S. 2009. *Terror and territory: The spatial extent of sovereignty*. Minneapolis, MN: University of Minnesota Press.

Fallon, T. 2015. The new Silk Road: Xi Jinping's grand strategy for Eurasia. *American Foreign Policy Interests* 37 (3):140–44. doi:10.1080/10803920.2015.1056682.

Frankopan, P. 2015. *The Silk Roads: A new history of the world*. London, UK: Bloomsbury.

Garlick, J. 2017. Can China's Belt and Road Initiative successfully lead to a new Eurasian economic zone? *All China Review*, April 10. http://www.allchinareview.com/can-chinas-belt-and-road-initiative-successfully-lead-to-a-new-eurasian-economic-zone/.

Garver, J. W. 2006. Development of China's overland transportation links with Central, South-West and South Asia. *The China Quarterly* 185:1–22. doi:10.1017/S0305741006000026.

Goodman, J. 2016. Chinese bullet train in Venezuela stalls as alliance derails. *AP*, May 14. https://apnews.com/3367297bb5cc4fc497579164f679ec75/chinese-bullet-train-venezuela-stalls-alliance-derails.

Hancock, T. 2017. China missionaries seek converts along the Belt and Road. *Financial Times*, August 11. https://www.ft.com/content/69a41f7e-6b96-11e7-bfeb-33fe0c5b7eaa.

Ho, E. 2006. *The graves of Tarim: Genealogy and mobility across the Indian Ocean*. Berkeley, CA: University of California Press.

Hussain, D. 2017. MSCI upgrades Pakistan to emerging market index. *Dawn*, May 17. https://www.dawn.com/news/1333640.

Hussain, T. 2016. Karachi to Kashgar: How Islamic State poses a threat to China. *South China Morning Post*, August 13. http://www.scmp.com/week-asia/article/2003041/islamic-states-threat-china.

Johnson, C., and R. Jones. 2014. Where is the border? In *Placing the border in everyday life*, eds. R. Jones and C. Johnson, 1–11. Farnham, UK: Ashgate.

Jorgic, D., S. R. Hassan, and G. Yousafzai. 2017. Pakistan scrambles to protect China's 'Silk Road' pioneers. *Reuters*, June 11. http://www.channelnewsasia.com/news/asiapacific/pakistan-scrambles-to-protect-china-s–silk-road–pioneers-8937202.

Khan, A. 2009. Ethnonationalist insurgency in Balochistan, Pakistan: The militarized state and continuing economic deprivation. *Asian Survey* 49 (6):1071–91. doi:10.1525/as.2009.49.6.1071.

Korf, B., and T. Raeymaekers. 2013. Introduction: Border, frontier and the geography of rule at the margins of the state. In *Violence on the margins: states, conflict, and borderlands*, ed. B. Korf and T. Raeymaekers, 3-28. New York, NY: Palgrave Macmillan.

Lau, M. 2017. The secret lives of Chinese missionaries in northern Iraq. *South China Morning Post*, July 16. http://www.scmp.com/news/china/society/article/2099968/secret-lives-chinese-missionaries-northern-iraq.

Lim, A. C. H. 2015a. Africa and China's 21st Century Maritime Silk Road. *The Asia-Pacific Journal* 13 (11):1–19.

Lim, A. C. H. 2015b. China's 'Belt and Road' and Southeast Asia: Challenges and prospects. *JATI: Journal of Southeast Asian Studies* 20 (1):3–15.

Lim, A. C. H. 2015c. 'Iron brothers': Sino-Pakistani relations and the China-Pakistan Economic Corridor'. *Eurasia Review*, May 7. http://www.eurasiareview.com/07052015-iron-brothers-sino-pakistani-relations-and-the-china-pakistan-economic-corridor-analysis/.

Lim, A. C. H. 2016a. The China-Pakistan Economic Corridor one year on. *Eurasia Review*, May 16. http://www.eurasiareview.com/16052016-the-china-pakistan-economic-corridor-one-year-on-analysis/.

Lim, A. C. H. 2016b. The Quetta Massacre and the China-Pakistan Economic Corridor. *IPP Review*, August 22. http://ippreview.com/index.php/Home/Blog/single/id/220.html.

Lim, A. C. H. 2017a. The China-Pakistan Economic Corridor two years on. *IPP Review*, May 29. http://ippreview.com/index.php/Blog/single/id/449.html.

Lim, A. C. H. 2017b. Protest erupts in Sri Lanka's Hambantota over Chinese megaproject. *IPP Review*, January 13. http://ippreview.com/index.php/Home/Blog/single/id/328.html.

Limaye, Y. 2017. Sri Lanka: A country trapped in debt. *BBC News*, May 26. http://www.bbc.com/news/business-40044113.

Malik, A. R. 2017. Pakistan: The Next Asian Tiger? *The Diplomat*, May 31. http://thediplomat.com/2017/06/pakistan-the-next-asian-tiger/.

Markey, D. S., and J. West. 2016. Behind China's gambit in Pakistan. *Council on Foreign Relations*, May 12. http://www.cfr.org/pakistan/behind-chinas-gambit-pakistan/p37855.

Mutambo, G. 2017. Loans not a burden to Kenya—China. *Daily Nation*, June 2. http://www.nation.co.ke/news/China-defends-Kenya-SGR-debt/1056-3952474-14aagu9/index.html.

Nail, T. 2016. *Theory of the border*. Oxford, UK: Oxford University Press.

Norling, N., and N. Swanström. 2007. The virtues and potential gains of continental trade in Eurasia. *Asian Survey* 47 (3):351–73. doi:10.1525/as.2007.47.3.351.

Rana, S. 2015. Budget 2016: Development budget allocated Rs700b, up 29%. *The Express Tribune*, June 5. https://tribune.com.pk/story/898413/accommodating-the-pm-govt-allocates-rs700-billion-for-development-spending-up-29/.

Rehman, D. 2016. Govt slowing down CPEC? Why the mega project got peanuts in FY 2016/17. *Daily Pakistan*, June 8. https://en.dailypakistan.com.pk/pakistan/govt-trying-to-slow-down-cpec-why-the-mega-projects-got-peanuts-in-fy-201617-federal-budget/.

Ritzer, G. 2003. The globalization of nothing. *SAIS Review* 23 (2):189–200.

Ritzer, G. 2007. *The globalization of nothing 2*. Thousand Oaks, CA: Pine Forge Press.

Shahbazov, F. 2017. Will the China-Pakistan Economic Corridor be a gateway to Central Asia? *The Diplomat*, May 25. http://thediplomat.com/2017/05/will-the-china-pakistan-economic-corridor-be-a-gateway-to-central-asia/.

Siddiqui, S. 2017. CPEC investment pushed from $55b to $62b. *Express Tribune*, April 12. https://tribune.com.pk/story/1381733/cpec-investment-pushed-55b-62b/.

Small, A. 2015a. China-Pakistan: A strategic relationship in the shadows. *YaleGlobal*, April 7. http://yaleglobal.yale.edu/content/china-pakistan-strategic-relations-shadows.

Small, A. 2015b. *The China-Pakistan Axis: Asia's new geopolitics*. London, UK: Hurst & Company.

Valentine, E. H. 2015. Global flows and the globalization of nothing: Synthesizing the incongruous. *Black & Gold* 1 (8):1–15.

Wang, J. S. 2012. 'Xi jin': Zhongguo diyuan zhanlue de zai pingheng' ['Go West': Rebalancing China's geopolitical strategy]. *Huanqiu Shibao*, October 17. http://opinion.huanqiu.com/opinion_world/2012-10/3193760.html.

Yousafzai, F. 2016. China to build mega oil pipeline from Gwadar to Kashgar. *The Nation*, June 13. http://nation.com.pk/national/13-Jun-2016/china-to-build-mega-oil-pipeline-from-gwadar-to-kashgar.

Yun, S. 2013. Westward Ho! As America pivots east, China marches in the other direction. *Foreign Policy*, February 7. http://foreignpolicy.com/2013/02/07/westward-ho-2/.

Žižek, S. 1993. *Tarrying with the negative: Kant, Hegel, and the critique of ideology*. Durham, NC: Duke University Press.

Index